Outside the Paint

In the series ***Asian American History and Culture,***
edited by Sucheng Chan, David Palumbo-Liu, Michael Omi,
K. Scott Wong, and Linda Trinh Võ

Benito M. Vergara, J. *Pinoy Capital: The Filipino Nation in Daly City*

Sucheng Chan and Madeline Y. Hsu, eds., *Chinese Americans and the Politics of Race and Culture*

Jonathan Y. Okamura, *Ethnicity and Inequality in Hawai'i*

K. Scott Wong, *Americans First: Chinese Americans and the Second World War*

Lisa Yun, *The Coolie Speaks: Chinese Indentured Laborers and African Slaves in Cuba*

Estella Habal, *San Francisco's International Hotel: Mobilizing the Filipino American Community in the Anti-Eviction Movement*

Thomas P. Kim, *The Racial Logic of Politics: Asian Americans and Party Competition*

Sucheng Chan, ed., *The Vietnamese American 1.5 Generation: Stories of War, Revolution, Flight, and New Beginnings*

Sucheng Chan, ed., *Chinese American Transnationalism: The Flow of People, Resources, and Ideas between China and America during the Exclusion Era*

Outside the Paint

When Basketball Ruled at the Chinese Playground

Kathleen S. Yep

TEMPLE UNIVERSITY PRESS
Philadelphia

Temple University Press
1601 North Broad Street
Philadelphia PA 19122
www.temple.edu/tempress

Published 2009
Printed in the United States of America

∞ The paper used in this publication meets the requirements of the American National Standard for Information Sciences—Permanence of Paper for Printed Library Materials, ANSI Z39.48-1992

Library of Congress Cataloging-in-Publication Data

Yep, Kathleen S.
Outside the paint : when basketball ruled at the Chinese playground / Kathleen S. Yep.
p. cm. — (Asian American history and culture)
Includes bibliographical references and index.
ISBN 978-1-59213-942-2 (cloth : alk. paper)
1. Basketball—California—San Francisco. 2. Playgrounds—California—San Francisco. 3. Chinese Americans—California—San Francisco. 4. Chinatown (San Francisco, Calif.) 5. Basketball—United States—History. I. Title. II. Title: When basketball ruled at the Chinese playground. III. Series.
GV885.73.S83Y46 2009
796.32309794'61—dc22 2008047857

2 4 6 8 9 7 5 3 1

Dedicated to

Oliver Chang, Thomas J. Kim, and Paul Whang
Chinese Playground leaders

Spike Yep and Terry Yep
my parents

Raymond Young
my husband

Contents

Acknowledgments

In the fifth grade, I became consumed with basketball, convinced that I would grow up to become the first female player in the National Basketball Association. I fueled my dream by playing two-on-two at a local schoolyard with my brother and grandparents. The games combined playfulness and intensity. My brother did not hesitate to swat the basketball away from any opponent, and my grandmother had no qualms about flagrantly fouling. After an afternoon of scrimmages, drills, and shooting contests, we would eventually make our way home. During the meandering walk from the playground to their house, my grandparents shared stories about their basketball days at the only public playground in San Francisco's Chinatown. Thomas Gim Yep, my late grandfather, was night director of the Chinese Playground in the early 1940s. His Angel Island immigration file started me on my doctoral journey; and through researching and writing my thesis, I learned about his adventures at the Chinese Playground–as a player, kite-maker, coach, and *de facto* social worker. Franche Yep, my grandmother, was one of the Mei Wah players, and she taught me the value of story-telling and community. Thank you to both of you.

In addition to thanking my grandparents, I would like to show my appreciation and respect to the basketball players named in *Outside the Paint,* and to their families, who were all collaborators of this work: Albert Lee, Fred Gok, Helen Wong Lum, William Woo and Jennie Wong, Lily "Tiger Lil" Leong, Josephine "Jo" Chan Lee, Paul and Ruth Whang, Alice Leung, Rachel Mark, York Jue, John Henry Wong, Alfred Lee, Richard Tong, Emma Dong, "Smokey Joe" Wong, Winston and Felton Suen, Norma Lee Hom, Jane Chew Wong, Alfred Lee, June Choy Wong, Jeannie Chong Jue, Percy Chu, and Hank Wong. Your openness and generosity were humbling.

Many San Francisco Chinatown community members made *Outside the Paint* possible. I appreciate the guidance I received from Dr. Michael Lee, Ryan Yip, Rick Quan, Gail Whang and Robert Gin. My aunties and uncles not only preserved the sporting history of Chinatown, but also willingly shared the knowledge. I appreciate the support I received from Ray Lee, Beverly Tom, Michael Lee, Nan Lee, Richard Kim, Roger "Butchie" Kim, Bill Kim, Jeannette Kim, Linda Kim Jann, Arliss Jann, Joanda Rowan, and Judy Kim.

I owe thanks to many others who helped me along the way. Numerous scholars offered perceptive insights. My dissertation committee–Michael Omi, Jere Takahashi, Ling-chi Wang, Elaine Kim, and Waldo Martin–offered professional and intellectual guidance. Alice Yang, my advisor during my University of California (UC) presidential postdoctoral fellowship, made important suggestions to develop ideas. And Judy Yung served as an important guide for me. I also appreciate the comments from all the external reviewers who offered their time and expertise to improve *Outside the Paint.*

I had the opportunity to rethink and refine *Outside the Paint* through conference presentations and subsequent conversations. I want to acknowledge the generosity and kindness of C.L. Cole,

Adrian Burgos Jr., Harry Edwards, Samantha King, Mary G. McDonald, Michael Messner, Douglas Hartmann, Jack Tchen, and Henry Yu.

Many librarians and archivists were creative in helping me track down sources. I wish to thank Wei-chi Poon and John D. Berry at UC Berkeley's Ethnic Studies Library, the staff at the San Francisco Historical Photograph Collection in the San Francisco Public Library, and the Bancroft Library staff. Although the focus of *Outside the Paint* was on San Francisco, I conducted research about Chinese American basketball players across the United States, and I received help from the Montebello City Library, the Schlesinger Library at Harvard University, and Karin Samulenas of Philadelphia.

Basketball is fascinating, and many researchers and institutions have done groundbreaking research about the sport. Many provided information about the Harlem Globetrotters and the Native American barnstorming teams. I wish to thank J. Michael Kenyon, Kevin Grace, Ben Green, Governor Vaughn, the Amateur Athletic Union, Terry Bertolino, the Basketball Hall of Fame, and the Association for Professional Basketball Research.

I am grateful for the Ethnic Studies graduate student dissertation group and for the support of Michael Chang, Harvey Dong, Wesley Ueunten, Isabelle Thuy Pelaud, Nerissa Balce, Carolyn Valverde, Mimi Nguyen, Vernadette Vicuna Gonzales, Jeff Ow, Steven Lee, and Minh-ha Pham.

Many friends, family, and colleagues offered their support and intellectual prowess. I thank Nancy Reiko Kato, Michael James, Debbie Lee, Joyce Lu, Ainissa Ramirez, Joanne Doi, Dyana Valentine, Brooke Yoshino, Renée Pacheco, Jodi Kim, Marie Lo, Maikiko James, Evelyn Nakano Glenn, Frances Leung, Christopher Chua, King Edwards, Paul Li, Gwyn Kirk, Margo Okazawa-Rey, Jenni Morozumi, Lisa Hirai Tsuchitani, Jean "Ish" Ishibashi, the Urban Amish, the YANGS, the Hendrikse-Lius, Roy Gesley, Yvonne Allen, Eithne

Luibhied, Jill Esbenshade, Caroline Streeter, Mike Hurt, Karen Liao, Ayize James, Akani James, Stephen Wong, Mana Hayakawa, Chris Robb and the Ketchum YMCA tennis community Alex Juhasz, Carmen and John Fought, Beth Jennings, the Youngs, Erika Young, May Young, the Kona Yeungs, and the Wans.

Since I arrived at Pitzer College of the Claremont Colleges, I have been intellectually nourished by faculty, staff, and students. David Yoo has been generous with his insights and mentorship. The Intercollegiate Department of Asian American Studies faculty writing group provided helpful forums for my research and writing. I benefited from the insights of Linus Yamane, Seung-Hye Suh, Tom Kim, Ming-Yuen Ma, and You-Young Kang. My colleagues—Peter Nardi, Phil Zuckerman, Ann Stromberg, Jose Calderon, Joe Parker, Sharon Goto, Lynne Miyake, Sefa Aina, Gilda Ochoa, and Hung Thai—provided important feedback. I owe thanks to the Pitzer faculty writing group—Carina Lee Johnson, Bill Anthes, and Sumangala Bhattacharya—and mentors from the "women of color faculty group"—Maria Soldatenko, Laura Harris, Dipa Basu, Mita Banerjee, Emily Chao, Ethel Jorge, Kebokile Dengu-Zbogo, and Norma Rodriguez.

Staff members who were invaluable with helping to birth *Outside the Paint* include: Madeline Gosiaco, Sandy Hamilton, Lynda Casey, Summer Espinoza Palacios, Ken Olitt, Anthony Sanchez, Joanne Zhang, and Joan Mason.

I am grateful to the students in the Sport Sociology classes who were brave enough to dissect and discuss drafts of this manuscript. In particular, Cynthia Ting, Vincent Chen, Matty Wise, Natalie Yuen, Yuki Lin, Patrick Miller, James Kato, Mary Rose Go, Emma Duarte, Kevin Shih, Shiyuan Deng, Katie Soe, Liana Cohen, Liz Hatayama, Betty Limon, Glenn Rice, Ansel Schmidt, and Danielle Lefevre offered important perspectives on *Outside the Paint.* And my student research assistants were not only diligent, but also grounding. I am grateful to Erica Alexakis, Sophia Cheng, Cheryl Yin, Genevieve Cheng, Susette Cheng-Grosveld,

Alex Margolin, Alexander Su, and AJ Doty. *Outside the Paint* was made possible by generous financial support. I thank the UC Berkeley Graduate Division for the Berkeley Fellowship, the Soroptomist Founder Region Dissertation Fellowship, the UC President's postdoctoral program, and Pitzer's research and awards grants. I especially want to thank Sheila O'Rourke and Kim Adkinson for their kindness, vision, and guidance with the UC President's postdoctoral program.

I want to acknowledge the creativity and vision of my editor at Temple University, Janet Francendese. With verve and precision, she posed important questions that sharpened the manuscript and allowed the stories to shine. I appreciate her support of the project and how she valued the importance of these voices as much as I did.

My gratitude goes to my uncles and aunties who help shape the 1930s and 1940s Chinatown basketball scene: Olliver Chang, Davisson Lee, Mary Lee Kim, Tommy Kim, Francis Mark, Wahso Chan, Esther Jue, Mae Fung Tom, George Lee, and Susan Lee.

I want to thank Audre Lorde, June Jordan, Merle Woo, Barbara Christian, Chandra Mohanty, Paulo Freire, bell hooks, Maya Angelou, Antonio Gramsci, and Ella Baker. Their words and lives provided guidance and hope.

Finally, I thank the following loved ones for their unwavering kindness and support. My father, Tom "Spike" Yep, crossed many racial barriers in Silicon Valley, and he showed me that it never hurts to ask. My mother, Terry Yep, taught me to value the extraordinary in ordinary voices, and she broke new ground in the 1970s by developing Asian American Studies curriculum. My uncle, Laurence Yep, and my aunt, Joanne Ryder, generously shared their creativity and writing expertise. My uncle Laurence interviewed one of the Hong Wah Kues many years before my research for *Outside the Paint* began and shared his findings with me. He used his research to write a young adult novel entitled *Dragon Road,* which is published by HarperCollins. My siblings have been my teachers throughout my entire life. I cannot imagine my life without Franny Yep, Lisa Yep, and Mike Yep. I am grateful for my in-laws—Simon Labov, Jesse Salinas, and Gloria Alcala—and my eight nieces and nephews—Gabriel, Estéban, Felicia, Cory, Lee, Matthew, Sam, and Jackson.

My life partner, Raymond Young, supported me unconditionally. He kept me writing at the computer when I needed to and pried me loose when I didn't. And somehow he knew the timing for both. His kind heart and generous spirit make me a better person, and his editorial eye made *Outside the Paint* a better book.

Outside the Paint

Introduction

In the 1930s and 1940s, hundreds of Chinese American youth found refuge on a small plot of land in San Francisco's Chinatown. Officially designated the "Chinese Playground" by the city of San Francisco, this public playground was a place where young people made lasting friendships and formed basketball teams that excelled in competitions. Girls' and boys' teams from the Chinese Playground developed their own style of playing, a style that emphasized speed and made stature almost irrelevant. Quick and agile, they were able to score against their generally much taller and much wealthier white opponents and to dominate their divisions in the citywide league. Mike Lee, a member of a Chinese Playground basketball team in the late 1940s, recalls the last moments of the citywide recreational league championship game:

> There were only a few seconds left in the game. We were behind by a point but we had the ball. Our coach, Paul Whang, called a time out. He said, "Ten seconds is a lot

> time. We could skin a cow in that amount of time." (*He smiles.*) We went back on the court. My stomach was in my throat. My teammates got me the ball. I tossed it up. The buzzer rang with the ball in the air. We all stood there watching the ball. Including the refs! (*He laughs.*) When the ball sank in the basket, we jumped and hugged each other. We couldn't believe it. We won. (*He laughs.*) Paul ran out on the court and hugged us. After the game, we went to Paul's house and his wife made a big spaghetti dinner to celebrate. I'll never forget that. (*He smiles.*)[1]

Some fifty years after the victory, Lee's face still lights up as he describes the win. The victory was particularly sweet against the context of his family background. Like many other youth in San Francisco's Chinatown, Mike Lee came from a household struggling to survive. Five Lees squeezed into a single room and somehow managed without a kitchen or bathroom. Wearing donated clothing, the kids resorted to putting folded cardboard in the bottoms of their shoes to cover the holes and get as much wear out of them as possible. For Mike Lee, and presumably for some of his teammates, basketball offered an escape from the daily grind of poverty in an urban ghetto and a place to experience joy and small triumphs. The championship gave recognition to youngsters who were mostly invisible as working-class Chinese Americans in the 1940s.[2]

This book recovers stories like Mike Lee's and those of others who spent countless hours at the Chinese Playground. My purpose is to understand how people with meager resources have used basketball for empowerment. On one level, I am documenting a hidden cultural history. On another, I use the Chinese American experience to examine the varying political functions of sports. I consider the ways in which these youth learned strategies through basketball to deal with the rigid racial, socioeconomic, and gender hierarchies of the 1930s and 1940s. The stories speak to the way individuals carve out space for themselves within the context of poverty, patriarchy, and racial segregation. For the Chinese Americans who made up the Chinese Playground teams, basketball was part of the long-standing and widespread network of organized sports in Asian American communities that had thrived since Chinese began coming to the United States.[3] For more than 150 years, Asian Americans and Pacific Islanders who lived in the mainland United States and in Hawaii had created their own sports teams in rural and urban settings.[4] Until very recently this extensive legacy was known primarily through stories circulated among family and community networks; academics and the mainstream public are only beginning to engage with this history. Scholars of Asian American studies, such as Joel Franks, Samuel Regalado, and Henry Yu, have broken ground with their work on Chinese American sports, Japanese American sports in the internment camps, and Tiger Woods, respectively, each examining social constructions of race in sports.[5] These studies demonstrate that sports have been a significant institution in Asian American history and provide an important lens with which we may examine how Asian Americans have both endured and responded to racial inequalities.

Combining a cultural history with a discussion of racial and gender formation, this book examines the various political functions of basketball in San Francisco's Chinatown from 1930 to 1950. Each chapter features a particular story—a playground, a professional barnstorming men's basketball team, a championship amateur women's team, and brother-and-sister sports icons. And, each story sheds light on the multiple and contradictory uses of sport. For example, mainstream communities viewed basketball as a way to assimilate second-generation Chinese Americans into the American "melting pot," while many second-generation Chinese Americans simultaneously used basketball to build community and assert ethnic pride.

This book attempts to speak to a broad audience. Some readers will be more interested in the stories and the history than in their theoretical implications, but I hope that the political nature of sports and the inventiveness of people facing oppression come to light. The following pages discuss the historical context of Chinese Americans in the 1930s and 1940s and the theoretical framework for the book, before outlining the book's methodology and structure.

Historical Context

In the 1930s and 1940s, restrictions of physical space reflected and reinforced the inferior status of Chinese Americans. Stringent institutional and cultural rules dictated and normalized ideas of where Chinese and Chinese Americans belonged and did not belong in America. Restrictive covenants and real estate practices limited most Chinese Americans to residences within the borders of San Francisco's Chinatown.[6] With 159 persons per acre, San Francisco's Chinatown quickly became the most densely populated area of the city.[7] In 1948, close to twenty thousand Chinese were packed into twenty San Francisco city blocks.[8] Chinatown residents struggled with these forms of spatial discrimination; families of seven to twelve people commonly lived in compact two-bedroom flats.[9] Various social welfare reports documented how these "absolutely unsanitary, unhealthful and inadequate quarters" exacerbated public health concerns such as the spread of tuberculosis and other communicable and deadly diseases.[10]

Such spatial restrictions mirrored and strengthened the social segregation experienced in other areas of life. Overt racial discrimination and violence ruled the day for Chinese Americans and other people of color.[11] Specifically, Chinese and other Asian Pacific Americans confronted ethnic- and race-based laws of discrimination that barred them from entering and leaving the country

(Immigration Exclusion Act of 1924), owning land (Alien Land Law of 1913), and marrying whomever they wished.[12] While the United States grappled with the Great Depression, Chinese Americans faced segregation that relegated them to low-wage factory and service occupations, with 24 percent of all gainful workers in laundry work, 24 percent in domestic service, and 14 percent in the restaurant labor sector in 1930.[13]

In the 1930s and 1940s, popular culture portrayed "Chineseness" in various ways. Movies, radio programs, magazines, comic books, and novels depicted Chinese Americans as static caricatures in dehumanizing ways.[14] Mainstream America (which avidly went to the movies) cast them in a variety of stereotyped roles, including the inscrutably evil villain (for example, in the Fu Manchu series beginning in 1911 and lasting until 1958) and the hypersexual yet sinister "oriental dragon lady" (such as the femme fatale in the popular 1931 Hollywood movie *Daughter of the Dragon)*.[15] Magazines, newspapers, and school textbooks also fostered the notion of Chinese as alien and unassimilable. Surveying prevalent stereotypes of Chinese from the 1910s through the 1940s, sociologist Rose Hum Lee found that elementary school textbooks described Chinese people as savoring the taste of rats and snakes and as lacking souls because they were not Christian.[16] Popular culture depicted Chinese language, religion, and values as foreign and oppositional to mainstream American society.

In the late 1930s and 1940s, the portrayal of Chineseness changed from primarily the threatening foreign invader to include more sympathetic characters. Examples include the listless but benevolent peasant in the popular Hollywood 1937 movie, *The Good Earth* and the asexual, nonthreatening detective Charlie Chan.[17] Although the Chinese exclusion laws were in effect from the mid-1800s to the mid-1900s, various events in the 1930s and 1940s changed mainstream America's perception of the Chinese from the yellow horde to the good ally. For example, the 1931 invasion of Manchuria and Japan, the ensuing Sino-Japanese War (1937–1945), and the World War II alliance of China and the United States made Chineseness more palatable to the American public. In addition, Chinese Americans mobilized to make the public aware of Japanese atrocities and to send aid to China.[18] Mainstream media portrayals shifted from representations of various undifferentiated Asians to ethnic-specific representations of Chinese hyper-Americanness and loyalty. [19] For example, the roles given to Anna May Wong, one of the most visible Chinese American actresses of the time, changed from the generic evil Asian temptress to the loyal Chinese with an identifiable ethnic identity.[20]

In daily life, discrimination kept Chinese Americans separate from mainstream America.[21] For example, during these years Chinese Americans had limited access to public facilities ranging from swimming pools and movie theaters to music clubs.[22] Adherence to these rules of racial separation became embedded in daily life in Chinatown. Thomas J. "Tommy" Kim, a former Chinese Playground staff member, explains: "You *know* there's discrimination. In other words, you know where you don't go. You know there is a dividing line. We realize that. We know how far we can go as far as mingling with others. Because I knew that no way in those times, you are yellow, you are brown. You know your place."[23]

Such segregation governed sports as well. In racially segregated basketball leagues, Chinese American basketball players rarely encountered players of other races and thus reinforced the idea of appropriately separate spaces for different races. Most Chinese Americans played on Chinese-only basketball teams such as the Nam Kus and the Boy Scout Troop Three team and in segregated tournaments such as the Wah Ying League and the Chi-Hi Basketball League.[24] Because Chinese Americans lived and worked in conditions largely shaped by their subordinate social status, they seized every opportunity to break out of those conditions. Young Chinatown athletes with few options for mitigating or resisting their marginalization realized that on the basketball court they could be assertive—even aggressive—visible, and celebrated.[25]

I selected *Outside the Paint* as the book's title in recognition of the ways that these Chinatown athletes used sports as a means of crossing borders set by segregation and rigid social codes. On the basketball court the paint is the area from the free throw line to the closest baseline in front of the basket at each end of the court. "Outside the paint" describes the distinctive way in which Chinatown youth played basketball. Their momentum to score points occurred "outside the paint" because of defensive pressure that caused turnovers. Their games also involved intricate passing, teamwork, quickness, fast breaks, and rapid passes on the perimeter of the basket—in contrast to other teams that slowed the pace by dribbling the ball unhurriedly down the court or playing a zone defense.

The players themselves would not have described the Chinatown style of playing basketball as a collective response to poverty, patriarchy, and racial discrimination. However, they were keenly aware that their game temporarily disrupted dominant beliefs about the inferiority of Chinese American men and women. For example, the first annual National Oriental Basketball Tournament (NOBT) in 1947 was a unique pan-ethnic gathering of Asian American male basketball players from all over the United States.[26] The Japanese, Chinese, and Filipino teams that participated in the tournament came from California, Oregon, Washington, Hawaii, British Columbia, Utah, and Illinois.[27] Drawing crowds as large as two thousand, the NOBT provided a public gathering space for large numbers of Asian Americans after World War II, which was significant given the recent wartime Japanese American internment. Moreover, the NOBT offered Asian American male basketball players the unusual opportunity to compete against a deep pool of opponents at a high level. Calling the NOBT the "little World Series of basketball" and the athletes "hoop warriors" who demonstrated "sparkling cage play," the mainstream took it as a serious sporting event.[28] At the NOBT, Asian American players were recognized and celebrated.

Theoretical Framework

From young girls playing street hockey in the suburbs of Pennsylvania to kids kicking a soccer ball on the beach in Bali, sports are a global phenomenon. Furthermore, they serve as the basis of a transnational business economy that deals in everything from the production of athletic shoes and video games simulating professional basketball players to international sports competitions and Internet magazines about World Cup soccer. This omnipresence is sometimes mistaken for freedom from politics or a symbol of democracy and meritocracy, especially by people in the United States.[29] The mainstream culture in the United States regards sports as the great social leveler and as a means for transmitting quintessentially "American" values like teamwork, competition, and discipline.[30]

Sports sociology scholars, such as Susan Birrell, Pierre Bourdieu, and Richard Gruneau, dispel such popular myths by arguing that athletics reinforce social hierarchies, discrimination, and prejudice.[31] One trend in the literature emerged in the 1970s and looked at racial and gender inequities in sports institutions. This area of scholarship has studied sporting structures, practices, and policies in relation to discrimination.[32] For example, in 2005, George B. Cunningham and Michael Sagas examined the number of racial minorities in intercollegiate coaching positions.[33] Analyzing 191 National Collegiate Athletic Association (NCAA) Division I men's basketball programs, they found that white head coaches were more likely to have white assistant coaches on staff.

A second area of scholarship looked at inequities in sports but instead emphasized the ideological function of sports. This approach explores the use of media images to strengthen popular beliefs that support discrimination and prejudice.[34] Utilizing Michael Omi and Howard Winant's racial formation theory, this research tends to be qualitative and to center on content analysis of discourse or visual images in television, newspaper articles, and magazine advertisements.[35] For example, C. L. Cole and Amy Hribrar analyze how Nike's "just do it" ad campaign reduced feminist empowerment to wearing a product with a Nike logo, thereby narrowing feminism to an individual act of consumerism.[36] This association of a product with gender equality shifts the goal of feminism. Rather than dismantling institutional inequalities like equal pay for equal work, its object is to promote an individual's choice to play sports and purchase a Nike product. These two research approaches to sports discard the somewhat simplistic assimilationist interpretation of the links between sports and power. Instead, they analyze how sports reinforce discrimination and prejudice. For example, Mary G. McDonald examines how dominant norms are supported in media representations such as touting whiteness and heterosexuality in Women's National Basketball Association's advertisements.[37]

A third area of scholarship discusses how sports are contested political terrain.[38] This strand of sport sociology analyzes the multiple and sometimes contradictory uses of sports. Influenced by this third area of scholarship, I attempt to highlight how sports are used to strengthen and, at the same time, challenge inequalities.[39] Although sports perpetuate stereotypes and discrimination, they can help facilitate and give rise to new identity formations and possibly political change.[40] For that reason, an examination of basketball and cultural practices as part of a continuum of empowerment can be enlightening.[41] In the racial climate of the 1930s and 1940s, members of all marginalized racial groups faced overt institutional discrimination and segregation.[42] Yet, people are not merely submissive victims overrun by discrimination.[43] The Chinese American athletes in this book proved to be astonishingly resourceful in developing vibrant cultures and communities through basketball.

My aim in this book is to explore how people living under segregation develop a sense of belonging. My goal is neither to romanticize basketball as overcoming barriers to equality nor to wallow in the basketball players' victimization. Chinese American women and men in the 1930s and 1940s faced racial segregation, patriarchy, and poverty but found ways to create spaces of empowerment. And they did so in unexpected places, such as basketball courts.[44] The Chinese American players in this book were segregated through sports at the same time as they used it to engage with society. In broader terms, these Chinatown basketball players show how solidarity emerges and how sports gain political importance among marginalized peoples. Second, they tell us something about how multiple aspects of identity play a role in empowerment. The players used basketball to assert themselves not only as Chinese Americans but also as working-class men and women.

Methodology

Excavating this history of Chinatown basketball in San Francisco was both challenging and thrilling. Oral histories were central to the project because of the paucity of documentation of the lives of working-class Chinese American women and men born in early part of the twentieth century. To contextualize the interviews, I also examined newspaper articles from the *San Francisco Examiner,* the *San Francisco Call-Bulletin,* the *San Francisco Chronicle,* the *Monitor,* the *Chinese Digest* and the *Chinese Press.* In addition, I looked at government reports, existing oral history collections, and personal documents.[45] Over the past decade, I have interviewed approximately thirty-four former players, coaches, and opponents, using the snowball method of referral and personal contacts.[46] Thirteen of the interviewees were women and twenty-one were men; they ranged in age from sixty to ninety at the time of the interviews; and all respondents were born in the United States and identified English as their primary language.[47] Three central questions framed the interviews: (1) Why did men and women play basketball? (2) What meanings did the mainstream and Chinese communities in America attach to their athletic participation? and (3) How did the players view their basketball playing? The interviews were transcribed word-for-word and included phrasings. For quotations used from the transcripts, I deployed Dennis Tedlock's method of "scoring the text," and I attempt to honor the voices of the narrators as much as possible by including their personal phrasings.[48] Influenced by feminist oral historians Sherna Berger Gluck, Alice Yang, and Daphne Patai, I regard the stories as the anchor of the text; yet, my authority and perspective are present in all stages of the book, whether interviewing the athletes, selecting quotations, or framing the stories.

In the end, I selected five stories on which to focus. By no means is this project a random sampling, nor is it intended to be representative of all sports in San Francisco's Chinatown during this period. Although a wide variety of basketball teams and players in the 1930s and 1940s existed, I selected these five stories because they revealed how second-generation Chinese Americans created a sense of community. The existing literature on second-generation Chinese of the early 1900s emphasizes mostly middle-class, college-educated informants. My research involves people with varied occupations and levels of educational achievement. This is important because it highlights the different socioeconomic positions within Chinatown. In addition, I chose basketball because it reveals—more than any other sport—analytical nuances about socioeconomic class. Urban youth often become engrossed with basketball because it requires a relatively small amount of resources, space, and training compared to sports such as tennis, baseball, and golf.[49] In 1937, Hsien-Ju Shih conducted a survey of Chinese and white public high school students in

San Francisco in order to look at the social and vocational adjustment of second-generation Chinese. Chinese boys and girls in the study overwhelmingly selected basketball as their favorite social activity.[50]

In America, the 1920s ushered in a "golden era of sports."[51] By the late 1930s and early 1940s, organized sports were an established social institution in American society.[52] During this time, amateur, semiprofessional, and professional basketball flourished across the country among all races, ethnicities, and class backgrounds.[53] For example, the Amateur Athletic Union (AAU), was founded in 1888 to provide a national infrastructure for sports in the United States. Since 1926, the AAU sponsored a national women's basketball tournament that drew school, club, and business teams from around the country and attracted thousands of spectators.[54] In addition, the Iowa Girls High School Athletic Union began in 1925 with twenty-five membership schools; by 1950, seven hundred schools were members. One of the marquee events, the girls' state basketball tournament, drew as many as twenty thousand spectators.[55] Moreover, basketball players competed in collegiate competitions such as the National Collegiate Athletic Association (NCAA), industrial leagues, and recreational leagues.[56]

The Chinese American male and female basketball players in this book shared the general enthusiasm for basketball that took hold in the United States during this time. Many Chinese American basketball teams beyond the ones in this book thrived in San Francisco's Chinatown. In the 1930s and 1940s, a constellation of institutions created a vibrant basketball scene in San Francisco's Chinatown, including the Young Men's Christian Association (YMCA) headed by Chingwah Lee and Henry Shue Tom and the Chinatown Young Women's Christian Association (YWCA) led by Caroline Chew. Chinese language schools and Chinese student clubs also supported basketball such as the Hip Wo Academy and the Inter-School Chinese Basketball League. In addition, Chinese associations and faith-based organizations encouraged basketball in Chinatown such as the Cathay Club, the Presbyterian Church of Chinatown, the First Chinese Baptist Mission, and the Chinese Congregational Church. These Chinatown basketball teams played in racially segregated leagues against Chinese American teams from San Francisco and other California cities. Some Chinatown teams competed against non-Chinese teams in city competitions, such as the city-sponsored recreational leagues and the Pacific Association tournament.[57] Several standout Chinatown players, such as Fred Gok and Erline Lowe, broke racial barriers and played on their integrated school basketball teams.[58]

Many fiercely competitive women's and men's basketball teams existed in Chinese American communities across the United States, in Canada, and in China.[59] The *Chinese Digest* reported on Californian Chinese American basketball teams in Watsonville, Salinas, Berkeley, Oakland, Stockton, Monterey, Palo Alto, Bakersfield, Locke, Sacramento, and Vallejo.[60] Basketball also thrived in Santa Barbara, Los Angeles, Boston, New York, Philadelphia, Portland, Seattle, Vancouver and Victoria, Canada, among other locations.[61] While Chinese in the United States and Canada were playing basketball, Chinese men and women in China were also competing in the sport.[62] For example, men played basketball at the first National Games in 1922, and women basketball players participated in the National Games starting in 1930.[63]

I chose San Francisco because it was the home of one of the most established communities of American-born Chinese during this period. Between 1930 and 1940, Chinese in San Francisco made up over one fifth of the total U.S. population of Chinese, with 16,303 Chinese in the city in 1930 and 17,782 in 1940.[64] The 1930s also saw a change in the status of Chinese Americans inside and outside Chinatown. By 1940, American-born Chinese outnumbered Chinese immigrants for the first time.[65] American-born Chinese grappled with racial barriers in housing, employment, and social life in the United States, as well as with concerns over the Sino-Japanese War, especially those with families in China.[66] Researchers have often discussed the assimilation of the second, or American-born, generation during this period; some scholarship emphasizes identifying the stages of Americanization, while other research examines whether sports served as evidence of this inevitable social process. Scholarly depictions at the time framed American-born Chinese as rootless and dispossessed. According to social scientists in the 1930s and 1940s such as Elliot Mears and Edward Strong, the "second-generation problem" consumed American-born Chinese. Their immigrant parents were said to be "clinging to Old World culture. They had Americanized identities, and faced racial prejudice.[67] My research shifts the perspective, looking beyond vertical relations between generations to include horizontal relations within a generation. Furthermore, this book joins a burgeoning field of scholarly literature that focuses on the 1930s and 1940s; instead of lumping these decades together within the Exclusion era (the 1800s to the 1940s), these works explore the varied racial, class, and gender constructions about and within Chinatown during the 1930s and 1940s.[68]

Map of the Book

Each chapter of this book focuses on one of five stories and explores a different aspect of how subordinated people use basketball as a medium to engage with society. In order to show the multiple and contradictory uses of sports, each chapter describes the team or player and then discusses how basketball was used to reinforce inequalities. Each chapter then closes with an analysis of how the players built community and asserted themselves through basketball. The first chapter sets the scene with the founding of the Chinese Playground, which the San Francisco Playground Commission viewed as a means for integrating Chinese American youth into dominant American culture. Exploring how empowerment was created through a sense of place, it shows how Chinatown youth crafted a style of playing basketball that asserted their pride as predominately working-class Chinese American girls and boys. Chapter Two moves from playing basketball to considering the popular representation of Chinese American male athletes. Centering on a men's professional team, the Hong Wah Kues, I examine how people create solidarity through media representations of Chinese American masculinity and community support of ethnic male sports icons. Chapter Three emphasizes the physical act of playing basketball, particularly by working-class Chinese American females. In the early 1930s, the Mei Wahs, an amateur women's team, played under restrictive girls' rules designed to steer young women into dominant norms of white, middle-class, heterosexual femininity. However, these mostly working-class Chinese American women developed an aggressive style of play that created a sense of solidarity. Chapters Four and Five discuss the Wongs, Woo and his sister Helen (later Helen Wong Lum), who dominated the basketball scene in the late 1940s. These Chinese American siblings were noteworthy because they received much media coverage inside and outside Chinatown. Woo Wong, the first Chinese American man to play at the famed Madison Square Garden in the late 1940s, shows how the ethnic male sports icon served as an important vehicle to create ethnic visibility in mainstream communities. The chapter on Helen Wong Lum explores how female athletes used sports to gain economic mobility even as newspaper coverage of their athletic exploits trivialized them. Although basketball can provide lifelong enjoyment to anyone, segregated communities attach specific meanings to the sport. Playing basketball in the 1930s and 1940s was a way to experience solidarity, temporarily unfettered by poverty, gender discrimination, and racial segregation. These are the stories of their "hoop dreams."

1 / The Chinese Playground

Sandwiched between buildings in the congested ghetto, the only public playground in San Francisco's Chinatown became a source of community pride. An English-language newspaper, the *Chinese Digest*, praised the success of Chinese Playground teams in an integrated citywide basketball league:

> Under [Oliver Chang's] guidance, the Chinese Playground has made a name for itself in the annals of the city recreation leagues. The teams he enters in the city-wide competitions usually bring home the bacon; 1936 was no exception as it found five basketball teams carrying off top honors in their respective classes, while 1937 discovered three championship quintets from Chinatown.[1]

Opening in 1927, the Playground, as the neighborhood called it, became a second home for many working-class youth in the 1930s and 1940s. Young Chinese working-class women and men representing the Playground won basketball championships and thus made a place for themselves in a world that otherwise disregarded them. These young players developed a degree of empowerment by mastering a style of playing basketball and claiming a place as their own. The Playground was meant to be a site where young people could be socialized into becoming "moral" or "good" U.S. citizens, but in spite of the efforts to assimilate them, Chinese American youth used the Playground to assert their power and pride.

From 1920 to 1940, the Chinese population in San Francisco doubled, growing from 7,744 to 17,782.[2] In the same period, the U.S. population of American-born Chinese children quadrupled.[3] In San Francisco in 1940, approximately 12 percent of community residents were between the ages of ten and nineteen.[4] During the interwar years, Chinatown had no public recreational facility for its growing number of American-born children; overcrowded and still growing, Chinatown badly needed a place for its young people to play. By the 1930s and into the 1940s, policy makers and community newspapers turned their attention to the needs of youth in the entire city.[5] According to the San Francisco Recreation Department, Chinatown had a greater "number of children than any other single block in the entire city."[6] Municipal, state, and federal authorities made "play in safety" a vital concern during this period, and this catchphrase appeared often in public forums and weekly newspaper columns.[7]

Along with safety, juvenile disorderliness, especially among working-class and minority youth, claimed the attention of social reformers and policy makers across the United States. The "American Play Movement" advocated for playgrounds as a socialization mechanism for urban youth. From the late 1800s to the early part of the twentieth century, a politically diverse coalition of organizations mobilized to address social and economic problems facing working-class and minority youth. This coalition included progressive educators, social settlement workers, child psychologists, and philanthropists. Participants included Joseph Lee, a Boston philanthropist and founder of the Massachusetts Civic League, and Jane Addams, the founder of Hull House, a settlement house in a working-class neighborhood of Chicago. The coalition mobilized to move children's play from the streets to supervised playgrounds owned and operated by city governments.[8]

In 1906, Henry S. Curtis, a child psychologist, initiated the formation of the national Playground Association of America (PAA). The organization conducted research studies on urban youth, lobbied city governments, and fostered the rapid expansion of public playgrounds in the United States.[9] In its advocacy efforts, the PAA argued that the lack of organized play spaces and facilities in urban areas amplified the social and physical dangers confronting urban youth. Without supervised play—and safe places to engage in it—adolescents were free to roam the streets, and thus were more likely to be exposed to physical and moral hazards. In 1917, Curtis wrote a comprehensive needs assessment entitled "The Play Movement and Its Significance," in which he outlined the various pitfalls of using city streets as playgrounds: "It is not the play but the idleness of the street that is morally dangerous. It is then that the children watch the drunken people, listen to the leader of the gang, hear the shady story, smoke cigarettes, and acquire those vicious habits, knowledge, and vocabulary."[10]

The PAA pushed for organized children's recreation and emphasized concepts of morality and citizenry. Luther H. Gulick, the first president of the PAA, was associated with the New York public schools and the Young Men's Christian Association.[11] In his 1920 book *A Philosophy of Play*, Gulick argued that team sports like basketball taught youth the value of teamwork, as well as positively directed them away from focusing purely on individual gain. This development of community-minded morals on the court would then translate into good citizenry in an American democracy, he noted. Thus, according to Gulick and others in the PAA, supervised team sports and the public playground were a means of training youth to become productive members of the workforce and, ultimately, of America.[12] This advocacy and research specifically spoke to assimilating immigrant and second-generation youth into "American" values.[13]

The PAA's promotion of supervised team play and moral growth in urban areas was a response to the effects of industrialization and mass immigration in the late 1880s and early 1900s. Many recent immigrants and children of immigrants were segregated in crowded working-class urban centers, such as Boston, New York, Chicago, Philadelphia, and San Francisco. In 1908, Otto Mallory, the director of the PAA Philadelphia affiliate, wrote how a play event mollifies the deleterious effects of industrialization and encourages a unified national spirit among ethnically diverse youth:

> German and Italian, Slav and Hebrew played side by side. The day was a prophetic glimpse of the social spirit which will one day permeate the commingled nationalities which in the modern industrial city now crowd and jostle each other. Field Day and playgrounds are weighty units in the mass into which a solid republic is being welded, hammered into one rich alloy from many diverse races and nationalities.[14]

In other words, assimilation of all ethnicities was not only possible, but inevitable. However, this portrayal of national unity through play blurred the distinctions between race and ethnicity and overlooked long-standing systemic discrimination, such as the 1882 Chinese Exclusion Act that was in effect until the mid 1900s and the Jim Crow laws that institutionalized the racial segregation of African Americans in the South.

The Chinatown community also was concerned about increasing juvenile delinquency.[15] An English-language newspaper, the

Chinese Press, regularly reported on "Chinatown hoodlums in street brawls" and expressed apprehension that unruly youth would scare off tourists.[16] Lim P. Lee, a prominent civic leader in Chinatown, wrote: "Juvenile delinquency is a social pathology, and it is . . . growing in our community. It will take the combined efforts of . . . home, school, church, community, public and private agencies to attack the problem."[17] Law enforcement, Chinese parents, and the Chinatown elite agreed that structured and supervised recreation would "build character" in the younger generation and serve as "one of the best correctives" for "dead-end kids."[18] And so, Chinatown leaders avidly lobbied for recreational resources for decades.[19] By early 1925, the San Francisco Playground Commission (SFPC), an appointed municipal entity overseeing all playgrounds, was actively developing plans for a playground in Chinatown. The project stalled in late 1925 and it seemed it was about to wither away. However, San Francisco mayor (and later California governor) James Rolph, Jr. made a personal appeal to the Playground Commission and the logjam ended.[20]

In early 1927, the Chinese Playground opened to the public. One of twenty-six public recreational playgrounds in San Francisco when it opened, the Playground occupied 0.51 acres and became one of the most used of such spaces in the city.[21] During fiscal year 1938–1939, it logged almost a quarter of a million visits.[22] The SFPC supported the PAA's idea of the playground as an assimilation tool, describing playgrounds as a "moral force."[23] The city government allowed the Chinese Playground to flourish precisely because it believed that basketball taught Chinese American kids to perform and embody "American" themes of democracy, discipline, and hard work.[24] In the words of one city employee, the Chinese Playground completed the "fine work of Americanization."[25]

On Sacramento Street between Stockton Street and Grant Avenue, the Playground enjoyed a central location within Chinatown's

Figure 1.1 Overview of Chinese Playground showing top two levels.
(San Francisco History Center, San Francisco Public Library.)

borders. The Playground was surrounded by churches, the Young Men's Christian Association (YMCA), residential apartments, and a garment factory. Enclosed by a chain-link fence and open for all to see from the street, the Playground's three different levels of play facilities generated great interest and provided seemingly endless entertainment for onlookers (see Figure 1.1).[26] Chinatown's senior citizens often sat on the benches in the Playground and sunned themselves while watching the kids at play. People walking by on busy Sacramento Street might also stop and look at the kids through the fence.[27]

Despite the wide variety of organizations serving youth in the neighborhood, many young girls and boys found themselves drawn to the Playground. Richard "Goonie" Tong, a regular at the Playground and its eventual night director, remembers: "(The Playground) was a place that you naturally gravitate to. You're out on a Sunday afternoon and you don't have much to do. You walk around—pretty soon you wind up at the Playground—and you might sit around a table tennis game. You might sit around the swings. But pretty soon other kids would come—it was a social place."[28]

Smokey Joe Wong, a member of a boys' club at the Chinese Playground, recalls: "I used to go to Commodore Stockton Elementary School. . . . Every time we'd get through [with] school, we'd come right down to the Playground at 3:30 P.M. and fight for the tennis court and the paddle court."[29] Ruth Whang, wife of longtime Playground staff member Paul Whang, affirms: "The kids practically LIVED at the Playground."[30]

The Playground hummed with activities. The younger children were busily digging in the sandbox behind the clubhouse or happily hanging from the monkey bars in front of the building.[31] The older kids mostly played more organized games, like volleyball, tether ball, and basketball. Under the direction of male and female staff members of different racial backgrounds, the Playground also offered storytelling hour, harmonica bands, checkers tournaments, model airplane construction, and kite making. In addition, there were organized girls' and boys' clubs such as the Thunderbirds, the Blue Stars, and the Square Fellows (see Figure 1.2). June Choy Wong remembers: "We'd play until we had to go home at 10 o'clock."[32] Yearly basketball tournaments and the annual national Chinese tennis championships drew large crowds (see Figure 1.3). The Playground was known for many sports and a wide range of activities, including tennis lessons by Paul Whang, Fred Mar, Tommy Kim, and Mary Lee, and the construction of prize-winning kites under the instruction of Olliver Chang, Wasso Chan, and Gim Yep.

For many hard-working parents, the Playground was an unofficial social welfare center where they could literally drop off their kids on their way to work.[33] Whereas other organizations required resources and/or invitations to join, the Playground was free and public, requiring no membership fee or declaration of

Figure 1.2 Volleyball tournament at the Chinese Playground.
(Chinese Playground Anniversary Celebration collection.)

religious affiliation.[34] The Playground hosted many of the poorer kids from the neighborhood.[35] Some of the families owned and worked in small businesses, and others were the piecework laborers, cooks, or servers in these businesses. Felton Suen, a member of a Chinese Playground basketball team and club in the early 1940s, reflects: "We didn't have no place to go. That's why we all always went to the Playground."[36] Similarly, Tong says: "If it weren't for the Playground . . . we would be relegated to nothing"[37] As one of the few physical spaces they could call their own, the Playground was the foundation for their sense of belonging.

Young people savored their time at the Playground because they felt recognized.[38] They might be conspicuous yet anonymous

Figure 1.3 The Square Fellows, a championship basketball team from the Chinese Playground. Front row (sitting, left to right) Winston Suen, Smokey Joe Wong, unidentified, Felton Suen. Circa early 1940. *(Author's private collection.)*

at school, at work, and sometimes even at home, but the children were acknowledged by the Playground staff. Tong recalls:

> I started hanging out at the Chinese Playground around age seven. . . . I remember the open gates. . . . You walk in, there's ALWAYS activities around. I remember seeing people making kites on weekends and things like that. . . . And the directors were really friendly with the kids. . . . You walk in, the [Playground] directors ask you: "What's your name?" And everybody starts talking to you and calling you by name.[39]

Whether young people were in elementary or high school, the staff acknowledged all those who entered the gates of the Playground and made them feel welcome.[40] Many Chinatown youth thought of the Playground as a second home, and the staff became their surrogate parents.

Most of the staff members were in their early twenties and came from a variety of racial and ethnic backgrounds, including African American, Chinese American, Irish American, and Korean American. This mixture of races was unusual in the 1930s and 1940s. Social conventions dictated that men of color did not work side-by-side on equal footing with white women, that Chinese Americans did not have many opportunities to work for the city, and that Chinese American women did not rise to leadership positions. Thus, the Playground was an exceptional place where men and women of various races and ethnicities forged ties with each other and with hundreds of youth. In addition to being the first Playground director, Oliver Chang became the first Chinese to be hired by the Recreation Department, and he opened the door for others.[41]

The Chinese Playground regularly supported girls' and boys' basketball teams, with boys' teams competing in six weight classes from the 90s up to the 145s.[42] They entered the citywide recreational league that included Caucasian, Japanese, and later African American teams.[43] "Bring[ing] home the bacon" in all the weight divisions, the Chinese Playground basketball teams repeatedly won championships in their divisions. For example, all five boys' Playground teams won their division in the 1936 playground tournament.[44] In addition to representing the Playground in city league play, Chinese American girls also competed in an intramural basketball league at the Playground starting in 1937. Organized by Playground staff members Polly McGuire and Mary Lee, this league included several age divisions and drew more than eight teams from within Chinatown.[45]

The teams were successful in their divisions because they developed a distinct style of playing basketball that maximized their strengths. Chinatown youth initiated point scoring outside "the paint"—the area from the free throw line to the closest baseline in front of the basket at each end of the court. They created turnovers with pressure defense outside the paint and with in-your-face defense. In other words, Playground ball relied on creating turnovers while on defense, transitioning the turnovers into fast breaks, and putting rapid points on the scoreboard while their opponents were still running down the court. Winston Suen, a member of a Playground basketball team, reflects on how their style of game suited their bodies: "We're so small . . . we run, we're speed."[46] On offense, Playground teams quickly moved the ball down the floor and around the paint with maneuvers like backdoor cuts and give-and-go—a move in which a player passes the ball to a teammate, cuts toward the basket, immediately receives the ball back, and tosses a quick shot near the basket. Give-and-go capitalizes on speed and circumvents height differences, giving the advantage to shorter and faster players. This style of playing basketball emphasized quick movement of the ball by passing and then finding the most open player who could make a swift shot.[47]

The Chinese Playground girls and boys were not only fast; they were also tough. On defense, they would stifle their opponents using one-on-one or a zone defense that would collapse and trap opponents. Opponents would often find several Playground players swarming around them. Terry Lee describes the Playground girls' style of play:

> We were like mosquitoes. . . . [My sister Beverly Lee Tom] used to smother her opponents. She was much shorter. But she was relentless. She would grab on to the ball and not let go. *(She laughs.)* They would try to pry the ball loose or swing her around because they were so much taller. But then, she would tie them up. So, it was jump ball. People

> use to laugh because she would be in this jump ball situation and she was *so much shorter. (She laughs.)* But, we were faster. So it didn't matter. Even if the [taller opponent] won the jump ball, the Chinese team would be quicker and could get the ball.[48]

Beverly Lee, a basketball player at the Playground in the late 1940s, remembers: "I would be all over and then try to grab on to the ball. They would just fling me around. But I would hold on until the whistle blew. Then, I kind of walked into the jump ball with this smile."[49]

The Playground girls developed a particular style of playing because the girls' rules restricted them to only one or two dribbles (depending on the era) before they were required to pass. Instead of dribbling close to their bodies, the teams strategically created a combination dribble-pass in which they would hurl the ball ahead of them and catch it as if they were passing to themselves. They used their speed to move the ball around quickly and to utilize the dribble to their advantage. Terry Lee reflects: "Usually, the white girls would play it straight. So they would use the dribble dainty like. They would barely *move*! We would throw the ball way in front of us and then run and catch it. . . . [W]e would be dribbling *way ahead* of us. Now the guys could dribble as much as they wanted. We had to be strategic."[50]

The Playground style of playing basketball contrasted with the slower pace that was characteristic of non-Playground teams in the recreational league.[51] While Playground teams pushed the ball down the court fast on offense, opponents walked as they dribbled the ball down the court and relied on rebounding for points or possession of the ball. This slower style of play tended to burn the clock and was focused on preventing the opposing team from scoring rather than on scoring more baskets for one's own team.

Basketball also offered these Chinese youth a structure in which they could exercise spontaneity as well as agility. Free from the constraints of the crowded physical spaces in their homes and at work, they moved in tandem and collaboratively with their teammates. They came to know and rely on the power of their own bodies and to savor the freedom of movement. On the court, they relished the autonomy of choosing when, how, and where they moved. Playing a "speed" game required synchronicity among team members, a keen awareness of the ball, and a sense of how plays unfolded on the court. In this basketball "zone," they focused on the present moment and flowed with each other. They communicated verbally and nonverbally and achieved a deep level of connectedness that few experienced elsewhere in their lives. Chinese Playground teammates created a somewhat autonomous space that they could all claim together, apart from the hardships in other facets of their lives.[52]

Playground basketball, like any other set of athletic skills, had to be learned and cultivated. To join a Playground basketball team, boys and girls had to prove their mettle and earn the respect of experienced players. Joining a Playground club and team at the age of eleven, William Woo Wong, for example, had to catch up to boys who had been playing for several years. He reflects on how Playground players pushed each other to be better:

> Those were tough games [at the Playground], and I really mean tough, because . . . both sides are cement wall, so in order to really play, you really have to take your lumps, because everybody knows your moves. . . . If you . . . drive [to the basket], . . . you better be ready to get wrapped around the pole or hit the walls. They'll test you, and once they hit you, they going to see if you going to come again, or not. . . . You have to give it back, otherwise you'll never survive play in Chinatown.[53]

While mainstream society may have viewed basketball and playgrounds as a means of Americanizing immigrants and regulating youth, the Playground staff and youth focused on developing their prowess as Chinese American teams. On the court, they could challenge socially determined limits to their achievement and stake a place in the world as Chinese Americans and as mostly working-class youth. Playing outside the paint led many young Chinese American teams to championships and widespread public recognition beyond Chinatown. The championships helped them cross racial and gender borders even as they played on segregated teams. They not only traversed Chinatown's boundaries by traveling to other parts of San Francisco for games but also disrupted conventional ideas of the racial order through their wins on the court.

The Chinese Playground basketball teams dominated in the recreational league; their many championships fostered a sense of self-respect, visibility, and collective empowerment among the players and their communities.[54] In the late 1920s and early 1930s, the season's championship team had its name engraved onto the sturdy Sigmund Stern trophy and had the honor of caring for the trophy until the next championship season. When the Playground won for several consecutive years, its name covered most of the trophy starting from the late 1920s. Consequently, the Recreation Department retired the prize, leaving it in the Playground's possession.[55] The 1928–1929 San Francisco Playground Commission annual report featured a photograph of a Playground team that covered half of the page (see Figure 1.4). Depicting the Chinese Playground boys' team standing above a younger white boys' team that was seated on the ground, this photograph and its caption—"the winners" in neutral language—do not refer to ethnicity.[56] In the context of the 1920s, this was a striking departure from the prevalent narrative of white supremacy, and the young Chinese men seemed to be experiencing temporary

Figure 1.4 Photograph of Chinese Playground team from 1928-1929 Playground Commission Annual Report.

recognition by dominant society. This acknowledgment happened during several moments: when they won the championship, when the photograph was taken, and when it was circulated and viewed in an official document.

Playground teams crossed Chinatown borders to go to areas normally off-limits to Chinese American people, such as Presidio Heights and Pacific Heights. In these games, they encountered people of other racial and socioeconomic groups who normally did not associate with them either socially or in school.[57] Such encounters heightened their sense of being marginalized. Rather than seeing barriers dropping, they felt that the mainstream believed that Chinese Playground boys and girls did not belong outside of Chinatown. As a result, their delight was enhanced when they beat non-Chinese teams outside of Chinatown.

The success of the Playground teams has special significance when the socioeconomic status of the players is compared to that of the teams representing playgrounds in wealthy San Francisco neighborhoods. Playground sponsorship of the many winning teams over many years was accomplished on a meager budget.[58] Whereas other schools and playgrounds sported satin uniforms with matching shorts and warm-ups, sports socks, and basketball shoes, the Playground players competed in their street clothes. The different amount of resources was laced with meaning. Mike Lee, a member of one of Paul Whang's championship teams in the late 1940s, reflects on how the opposing teams' clothing affected him: "It was scary to walk on the court. [The opponents] had these fancy uniforms [and] all of these coaches."[59]

In the end, however, the outcome of the game subverted popular ideas about who belonged: the Playground clinched the 1949 title with a score of 14 to 13. The coach of the team, Paul Whang, explains: "[The] Playground [had] no funds.... We had to play in our street clothes. Jeans. And all these clubs had their uniforms. But we won. *(He laughs.)* The uniform don't make the team. *(He chuckles.)* It's the players.... They're fast. They're good shooters."[60] Whang's comments may be interpreted as supporting the idea of sports as the great socioeconomic or racial equalizer: the all-American myth of the scrappy working-class kids succeeding by virtue of hard work and grit. But Whang's manner of speaking conveys the idea that basketball was thick with political meaning. Basketball could not erase inequality, but it could become a vehicle for challenging racial and class hierarchies. The meaning was not simply a team winning a championship. A Chinese American team of mostly working-class kids defeated a more privileged team by making their racial attributes an advantage and their economic deficits irrelevant. Their victories on the court strengthened them for other confrontations at school, at work, or on the street.

Many of the athletes at the Playground describe the common theme of finding a sense of self-respect through basketball and the Playground. A talented Playground regular, Norma Lee Hom, reflects: "You get camaraderie [at the Playground], and then you get self-recognition. . . . I think it builds character. . . . Well, I knew that I'm Chinese, but I wasn't going to let anybody push me down as a Chinese."[61] Playground basketball helped many young people draw strength from their ethnicity despite the rampant discrimination they experienced elsewhere. Jennie Chong Jue, a member of a Playground girls' team, comments on the race and ethnic consciousness she developed at the Playground: "You are who you are. There were things that you experienced that you never forget. How they look at you, how they treat you. You have to take pride in who you are."[62] Chong Jue reconciles an awareness of herself as a member of a racially marginalized group with a sense of self-respect. She recognizes that institutional barriers are beyond her control, but she has gained the fortitude to stand up for herself in the face of such barriers and in personal confrontations. The Playground players did not view basketball as a route to entering mainstream society, and they were not necessarily attempting to Americanize themselves. Instead, they played to prove their humanity as working-class Chinese Americans.

In addition to ethnic pride, the Playground was one of the few spaces where girls could strengthen their athletic skills. Within Chinatown, a wide range of social services and youth activities were available to young women, including fashion shows, charity fundraising groups, beauty pageants, organizations dedicated to public service, and college leadership groups.[63] Yet, working-class young women chose the Playground to find community as athletic women. With laughter in her eyes, Ruth Whang underscores how some of the girls at the Playground were "little fighter[s] and toughies."[64] A self-described "toughie," Norma Lee Hom explains her female peers in Chinatown: "Well, there's two groups. One group that was crazy about boys, and then the other group was more interested in just being, you know, doing activities and stuff, so there is a split."[65]

Being a tomboy in the 1930s and 1940s meant occupying a place in society that was deemed inappropriate for girls.[66] At a time when mainstream movies, radio, and magazines presented Asian and Asian American women as hypersexualized, the toughies rejected stereotypical gender and ethnic roles.

With strong female coaches for their Playground teams, the girls who were (or became) toughies found that basketball allowed them to exercise a different kind of freedom of movement. Coaches like Mary Lee and Helen Wong Lum created a space in which this movement and strength was witnessed.[67] Jane Chew Wong, a member of a Playground basketball team, explains:

> Participation in those groups [Blue Stars and Chinese Playground programs] helped to build our sense of self-esteem, assertiveness, poise; developed our decision making capabilities . . . I believe [basketball] helped us grow into mature women unfearful of our future; helped make us active, prepared, involved and freethinking women.[68]

Outside of school, some of the players had jobs as cooks, maids, and seamstresses and worked in relative obscurity. At the Playground, they created their own definition of Chinese American femininity as publicly authoritative and physically strong. On the court, they not only occupied a visible space but also used the space with authority.

The relationships cultivated at the Playground endured over the young peoples' lifetimes.[69] Before heading out to fight in World War II, some youth returned to the Playground to consult with old mentors.[70] As adults, former Playground youth bowl together in a weekly league, while others gather for weekly lunches in Chinatown.[71] In the late 1980s, former Playground youth streamed into a ceremony to honor the first Playground director, Oliver Chang; and in the early 1990s, they packed the funeral home to pay tribute to former Playground coach Tommy Kim (see Figures 1.5 and 1.6).[72] The working-class youth at the Playground highlight how a sense of place can be created through the collec-

Figure 1.5 Playground staff members (L to R) Richard "Goonie" Tong, Paul Whang, and Tommy Kim. *(Ruth Whang Collection.)*

Figure 1.6 Oliver Chang, the first Chinese Playground director, helped pipeline Asian Americans into San Francisco city jobs, 1957. *(San Francisco history Center, San Francisco Public Library.)*

tive use of athletic bodies. Against the backdrop of crowded housing conditions and race- and class-based restrictions in work, school, and play, the Playground offered the kids freedom and opportunity to express themselves. For some, carving out a place meant creating a brand of basketball that expressed pride as working-class Chinese Americans. The ways in which Chinese American basketball players redefined what it meant to be Chinese American men and women are the subject of the next two chapters.

2 / The Hong Wah Kues Discover America

In 1939, six American-born Chinese men from San Francisco formed the Hong Wah Kues, the first and only Chinese American professional basketball team. For two seasons, the Hong Wah Kues traveled around the United States and Canada on a barnstorming circuit. During the era of the Great Depression and the Chinese Exclusion Laws, basketball provided these mostly working-class men the opportunity to leave the confines of segregated Chinatown and see some of the world. The Hong Wah Kues received a great deal of media attention as well as the enthusiastic support of Chinese American communities in cities on the basketball tour.[1] This chapter examines how U.S. and Canadian newspapers depicted the team and how community support of ethnic sports icons created solidarity among the players and the ethnic group. It begins with a description of the team and its marketing strategies, and it closes with a discussion of the experiences of the Hong Wah Kues and the community's response to the team.

During the Great Depression, Americans were avid fans of sports, movies, and radio. Sports were a relatively inexpensive form of entertainment; and ticket prices for basketball games ranged from twenty-five to seventy-five cents.[2] In the late 1930s, professional basketball teams traveled around the United States and Canada, playing games in different small towns each night. Representing different ethnic backgrounds, men's and women's barnstorming basketball teams at the time included the New York Renaissance, the Toledo Brown Bombers, Olson's Terrible Swedes, the South Philadelphia Hebrew Association, the All-American Redheads, and the Chicago Romas.[3] James W. Porter, a white San Francisco accountant, devised a team with a unique profile: the first Chinese American professional basketball team.[4] One day in 1939, posters appeared around San Francisco's Chinatown announcing openings on a traveling Chinese American basketball team. Young men in their late teens to mid-twenties showed up at the Chinese Playground for tryouts. No one knew what to expect, but most of the players knew each other from the Chinatown leagues.[5] After a series of drills and scrimmages, only six players made the team: Fred Ming Gok, Fred Hong Wong, Albert "Sonny" Lee, George Lee, Robert Doggie Lum, and Chauncey Yip. In the second season, during the winter of 1940, Albert Lee, George Lee, and Robert Doggie Lum returned, and Faye Lee, Arnold Lim, and Douglas Quan signed on to join them. The six players of the first season ranged in height from five feet three inches to five feet eleven inches. All had already earned honors and recognition on school basketball teams and Chinese club teams.[6] Most were in their early twenties and were single, working-class, second-generation Chinese Americans. While some came from wealthier backgrounds and attended college, others were sons of cooks and garment workers (see Figure 2.1).[7]

In 1939, a barnstorming basketball team offered these men an adventure unprecedented for American-born Chinese. Chauncey Yip reflects on his motive for joining: "We didn't have anything else to do. You know, you couldn't go any[where]—we didn't go anyplace, we just stayed in Chinatown."[8] Most of the

Figure 2.1 Promotional team photo. Standing (L to R): George Lee, Fred Gok, Albert Lee, Frank Cullerton. Kneeling (L to R): Chauncey Yip, Fred Hong Wong, and Bobby Lum. *(Mary Lee Collection.)*

players faced a limited future after high school: a mundane job at a restaurant, a grocery store, or a laundry.[9] The chance to travel around the country playing basketball and to get paid for it was a rare opportunity—a chance to live, for some time at least, outside of segregated Chinatown. However, adventure and opportunity came at a price. With some eighty games in a hundred days, the barnstorming tour was brutal.[10] The season ran from November to March, with games every night and two games on Sundays.[11] Generally, the Kues would drive into a city in the morning and play a game at night. Sometimes the team would drive for hours, get out of the car, and play. To limit expenses, the Kues had only one substitute player, and even injured players rarely had a chance to rest.[12]

The Kues launched their first season in Chicago, traveled to South Dakota and Canada; played through the Pacific Northwest, and returned to California.[13] The season had a bumpy beginning. According to Albert Lee: "[Our] first game [was] in Chicago.... We lost the first seven games because we're new... we didn't even get organized yet.... We just started and then, later on we get better... we play every night... and our shooting gets sharper... and then we start winning."[14] The players soon adjusted to their traveling schedule and came together as a team, eventually winning 70 percent of their games that year. Considering their grueling schedule, this was quite a triumph.

The Kues played against white local teams and other barnstorming teams. The local teams consisted of college players and local high school stars. The Kues did well against these local teams. Against other barnstorming teams such as the unbeatable Harlem Globetrotters, the Dominoes (who represented Canada in the Olympic Games), and the Bearded Aces, the Kues usually competed admirably.[15] While most of the publicity for the Kues emphasized their novelty, the team also garnered respect for their basketball skills.[16] The *Helena Daily Independent* described the Kues' athletic abilities as a mixture of "showmanship, cleverness, and genuine basketball ability."[17]

The Kues compensated for their four- to twelve-inch height disadvantage with accurate shooting, speed, and agile passing. In 1938, the professional league stopped requiring a jump ball after each basket—a rule change that favored the Kues' style of playing, which emphasized speed and in-your-face defense.[18] They were fast, and they were physical. This way of playing also required the players to be in perfect harmony with each other. Given their close proximity during the tour, achieving this synchronicity was not difficult. Playing against a different team and in a strange venue every night, they won because they knew one another's style of play and shared a sort of collective intuition for improvising on the court. In one game against the Phantom Bismarks, a team of former all-American college players, the Kues "led till the end." According to the local press:

> The Hong Wah Kues, most of them former San Francisco high school stars, were ball-handling fools. Time and again they drove beneath and around their larger foes for close-in shots at the basket. Their floor play was smooth and they were hitting the basket with amazing consistency at times. Especially surprising was their under-the-basket play, where they ignored their great height handicap to tip in rebounds and take the ball off their own basket time and again. . . . On defense the little Orientals cheerfully made themselves pesky nuisances. They got in the way of the Phantom's (sic) fast break and made them miss a much larger proportion of their shots than has any other club the Phantoms have played this year.[19]

The mainstream newspapers regularly made references to the Kues' masculinity and race. These same papers, however, also praised the players for their basketball expertise. Despite their impulses to belittle the Kues as "little Orientals" and "pesky nuisances," reporters could not deny the Kues' quick ball-handling skills and ability to smother other teams with their expert defense.

The Kues' tour games drew from one hundred to five hundred spectators, with a few exceptions: approximately seven hundred people in Vancouver and about two thousand in Minneapolis.[20] They played in relatively small facilities like high school gymnasiums and even smaller multipurpose community centers.[21] To increase attendance, some of the games doubled as fundraisers for local organizations and charities.[22] Life on the road was far from glamorous for most traveling teams in the 1930s. Each Kues player received $135 a month but had to pay for housing, food, and canvas basketball shoes. The manager provided only a car, gas, a ball, and uniforms.[23] The team owner selected the uniforms, which were black jerseys with the team's name emblazoned in gold lettering and black wool socks.[24] Fred Gok recalls:

> We only just got one [uniform]. After you play, you go to a hotel and you rinse it out and put it over the steam radiator and let it dry overnight. Then when you leave the next day, you put it on and play . . . or sometimes. . . . We drive to another city (after the game); you come and put it back on the radiator to let it dry more. (*He chuckles.*)[25]

Abe Saperstein, who booked the Kues and also owned the Harlem Globetrotters franchise, arranged for the Globetrotters to travel in a private bus, but the Kues drove a new 1939 Plymouth sedan and loaded their luggage on the roof rack.[26] Most of the money from ticket sales went to the team owner and managers, with the two competing teams splitting the ticket revenue after each game.[27]

The Hong Wah Kues' marketing highlights the racially charged nature of publicity and newspaper reporting during the late 1930s. The players did not have much say in the enterprise. Porter chose the name Hong Wah Kues, which translates into "overseas Chinese." The team's publicity purported that the name translated into "brave Chinese warriors."[28] In 1939, Porter arranged for the players to take promotional photos at the famous May Studio on Clay Street in San Francisco. Dressed in their black uniforms with gold lettering, striped knee-high wool socks, and black kneepads, they posed for individual shots.[29] These shots served as the team's press packages and often appeared in local newspapers during the tour.[30] In Gok's photo, he is standing with one hand up and appears to be palming the basketball in the other. Gok is the first to laugh about the photo: "They wanted me to palm the ball. But, my hands were too small. So they did this trick. They tied this black string so I could hold it. If you look, you can't see the string. (*He chuckles.*)"[31]

Porter decided that the Kues' promotional hook was their "Chineseness," or what mainstream American imagined "Chineseness" to be.[32] The promotional machine created a racial spectacle of masculinity. For example, to heighten the foreignness of the team, the press releases and posters used the players' Chinese names exclusively, even though the players, their friends, and the English-language Chinese American press referred to the team members by their English names.[33] The posters consistently rendered the players' names in an "Asian"-style font. On one poster, a dragon prominently occupies the center. Another poster includes a cartoon of a Chinese man with a queue wearing a basketball uniform (see Figure 2.2).[34] Another image in the cartoon shows a different Chinese man with a queue shooting a basketball. The text beneath the image reads: "He knows his queue."

Whether Porter intended it or not, the name of the team invited a racial play on the words *kue* and *queue*. The queue was a long braid of hair at the back of the head with a half-moon shape shaved into the hair in front above the forehead.[35] From the 1644 to 1911, the rulers of the Qing dynasty ordered Chinese men to wear their hair in a queue as a sign of submission. With the overthrow of the empire in 1911, men in China cut their queues off as a symbol of liberation.[36] By 1939, the queue was a rare sight in Chinese America. To most mainstream Americans, however, the Chinese man was a static image who still wore this symbol of strangeness and subordination.

Another character in the same cartoon offensively mimics Chinese language in broken English with a racialized pun: "A basket for washee a basket for the ball." This phrase reflects and reinforces stereotypes of Chinese as laundrymen who are unable to speak anything other than the pidgin language of fortune cookies and of popular book and movie characters like Charlie Chan.[37] The phrase also makes a joke of Chinese masculinity by underscoring the subservient and emasculating connotations of laundry work. Blind to the economic, racial, and political conditions

Figure 2.2 Cartoon from advertising poster. (*Mary Lee Collection.*)

that restricted many Chinese men to jobs in laundries, and disregarding the physical strength and endurance such work actually required, team managers promoted the Kues as a novelty and undermined them as athletes. Finally, such stereotypes ignore the history of Asian and Asian American male laborers, who had performed such feats as blasting through mountains to build the transcontinental railroads, ripping through sugar cane fields in

Hawaii, and converting swampland into fertile farmland in northern California.[38]

In the 1930s, despite decades of athleticism in football, baseball, basketball, and track in Chinese American communities across the United States, society still framed Chinese men as an oddity in mainstream professional basketball. Positioning the Kues as ineffectual, pidgin-talking laundrymen created a stronger image of the prowess and superiority of the white men's home team. Porter also directed the Hong Wah Kues to speak only Cantonese on the court. Although this might have been a strategy to keep the opposing team in the dark, Gok says: "They told us to talk Chinese only on the court, so we make the spectators laugh."[39] All the players were American-born and bilingual, and most identified English as their primary language. Since many of the towns on their tour had never seen any Chinese Americans—let alone heard Chinese spoken—live Chinese bodies added to the mystique and exoticism of the event. One newspaper wrote: "They're fast, they're colorful, they run and shoot and gargle Chinese at the same time."[40] Another article refers to the "the sing-song Chinese instructions which the players shout at each other."[41] With Porter's marketing gimmicks, the players had no choice but to embody these constructions of Chineseness.

Porter also expected the Kues to throw in a few tricks to make things lively. Albert Lee remembers: "When I had two foul shots, I shoot the first one in, then the second one, I bounced it off the floor and then it goes in . . . and they got a shock outta that. (*He laughs.*)"[42] Newspaper articles advertised the "dazzling ball-handling" and "crowd-pleasing stunts."[43] The Kues once broke the Bearded Aces' twenty-eight-game winning streak with a last-second shot from half court.[44] With quick ball handling and a keen ability to read the court, the five-foot-three-inch Robert Lum was the team's star player. According to Lum's teammates, he could put on an astounding ball-handling display and "dribble under [his much taller] opponents."[45] Albert Lee recalls: "We didn't have too much [that was] special, only Robert Lum, he's the dribbler. He dribbles around these big guys, they can't catch him, you know, and the crowd eats it up."[46] In 1940, the *Victoria Daily Times* also recognized Lum's basketball abilities: "[T]he little chap proved one of the smartest dribblers and ball manipulators seen here this season, and his clowning in the bucket and weaving offensive had the spectators in continual laughter."[47] Impressed with Lum's skills, Abe Saperstein invited him to tour with the Globetrotters. Although Lum declined the offer, he was a continual favorite of basketball fans.[48]

The local newspapers also played up race and gender when "reporting" on the Kues. Some used terms now regarded as racial slurs, as in "the Chinks flashed a snappy and deceptive passing attack," reflecting the normality of using racial expressions to identify Chinese Americans (and other minorities) in the late 1930s.[49] Some newspapers highlighted the Kues' Chineseness and foreignness by using phrases such as "the boys from the land of Chop Suey," denying any distinction between Asians and Asian Americans and portraying all Chinese culture as static, inscrutably different, and oppositional to American culture.[50] For example, one cartoon included a drawing of a crated box labeled "a cargo from the Orient" that the viewer is supposed to assume contains the Kues. Despite the fact that all the players were American-born, the illustration depicts the Kues as coming from the strange and mysterious "Orient." Just like the marketing of chop suey, fortune cookies, and egg foo yong, the marketing of the team offered a supposedly authentic Chinese product that actually originated in the United States.

The newspapers also invoked "yellow peril" rhetoric when referring to the Kues. Framing them in terms of racial war, the media often declared that the visiting Kues were going to "invade" and "attack" whatever small town they were in.[51] Although sports journalists also used the term *invade* to describe the activities of non-Asian teams, they had a tendency to elaborate on the war metaphor when discussing the Kues. They attached sports rhetoric to the historical precedent of viewing Asians and Asian Americans as foreign intruders. The headlines read "Chinese Invading Friday," "Yellow Peril Attacks Missoula Tonight," "War with Chinese Tossers Tonight at School Court," and "Warfare with the Chinese Bursts into Shooting Action Tonight on the High School Court."

One poster from Grangeville, Idaho, featured bold capital letters: "WAR! GRANGEVILLE TO BE ATTACKED" (see Figure 2.3). The poster's text explicitly calls for the local white town members to organize and support the home team against the "Chinese invaders." The home team usually consisted of local white athletes who were former college players, coaches, and referees. The desire for the home team to crush the "yellow invaders" on the court reinforced the desire to preserve a homogenous white America as a superior institution. White male players represented the prototypical American citizen, while the Kues symbolized the perpetual trespasser. The athletes thus engaged not just in a game of basketball, but also in a figurative racial war in which white men played the role of heroes and saviors.

Although the Kues were cast as the invaders, the tone was playful and did not portray the Kues as innately barbaric. By the late 1930s, the United States viewed China more sympathetically as a result of widespread news coverage of Japanese brutality against the Chinese in the invasion of Manchuria in 1931 and the Sino-Japanese War starting in 1937. Awareness of these conflicts shifted depictions of all Asians as evil invader to ethnic-specific portrayals such as sinister Japanese and foreign but human Chinese.[52] In this context, the Kues' "invasion" provided racial hype, but the threat was still contained to the safety of the basketball court.

While the portrayal of the Kues relied on "yellow peril" tropes of danger and invasion, basketball introduced a non-threatening form of Chineseness to the general American public

Figure 2.3. Advertising poster featuring yellow peril language. (*Mary Lee Collection.*)

and provided a venue to extol the virtues of American democracy. The Kues played during Adolf Hitler's consolidation of Nazi Germany and on the eve the Second World War. Exotic and supposedly foreign, the team became accustomed to its role in promoting assimilation, Americanization, and the melting pot ideology.[53] Basketball became a metaphor for the success of American ideals of democracy and meritocracy; the fact that the Kues could play an American game and compete against white teams offered proof that America accepted different racial groups, in contrast the Nazi's philosophy of Aryan racial purity. Even if the team owner required the Kues to speak only Cantonese, they still served as physical evidence that Americans value all races and creeds. The entertaining—even amusing—exhibition served to check the racial threat the Kues posed to whiteness.

The acceptance of Chinese Americans both on the basketball court and in American society at large was conditional; the exclusion laws in place since the late 1800s still virtually eliminated immigration from China in the late 1930s. Miscegenation laws prevented Chinese from marrying white Americans, and extralegal practices barred them from white neighborhoods, workplaces, schools, and businesses. The Kues traveled to cities that had rarely, if ever, seen any Chinese, whether immigrant or American-born.[54] Gok recalls:

> When we go over there, they never seen Chinese . . . and then we go to the restaurant to eat . . . they go the window and they can see the people inside. All the kids, especially the kids, they all watch, see how you eat, and all that stuff. You know, they think we're from Mars, or something.[55]

Audience members often rooted for the team using racial slurs, such as "Go Chinky!" Gok and Lee reflected that such language was a sign of the times.[56] In addition, the players had to contend with stares, taunts, and being turned away from some restaurants and hotels:[57] "Well, we can't afford to go to fancy hotel anyway, so we don't go, when we go there they probably won't accept us," Gok remembers.[58]

Their experiences on tour reminded the Kues not only of the historical mistreatment of the Chinese, but also of its endurance. The Kues played in Kellogg, Idaho, a town whose racially exclusive tradition was rooted in the anti-Chinese exclusion era of the 1800s. According to legend, outraged white miners and prospectors had violently expelled "Chinese cheap labor" from town, and the "Chinese fled with their pigtails fanning the breeze." After the game, the local newspaper noted that the "Hong Wah Kues broke tradition" and "hundred of miners and merchants turned out to see . . . one of the gol-darndest basketball games ever played."[59] This article expresses a sense of pride in the town's racial advances, indicating how "miners and merchants turn[ed] out to see the fun" of the Kues' beating the local teams. Yet, it also makes light of the institutional and mass violence affecting Chinese people in the 1800s and ignores the barriers facing Chinese Americans in the late 1930s, such as antimiscegenation and immigration laws. Some sixty years after the town physically excluded Chinese the townspeople still viewed Chinese American men like the Kues as a "pigtailed yellow horde."[60] The Kues' win was acceptable because the game was "only" entertainment; the players remained on the basketball court and were not going to stay in the town or compete for jobs.

The Kues were not the only barnstorming team that used race as a marketing hook. Abe Saperstein, a Jewish man from Chicago, owned the Harlem Globetrotters franchise starting in 1927 and booked the tours for the Kues as well.[61] Saperstein often scheduled doubleheaders with the Kues and the Globetrotters because two theme teams increased the game's marketability.[62] The Harlem Globetrotters, with former college players such as Ted Strong, Inman Jackson, and Sonny Boswell, won the 1940 World Professional Tournament championship.[63] Like the Kues, the Globetrotters had dual audiences: African American communities and mainstream viewers. When the Globetrotters started out in the late 1920s, they usually pulverized the competition, winning 93 percent of their 1,999 games in their first twelve seasons.[64] During their 1939–1940 season, the Globetrotters lost only 3 of their 161 contests.[65] While they were successful as an athletic team, they were less so as a business. The late 1930s was a time of state-sanctioned violence and discrimination against African Americans in housing, workplaces, media depictions, the courts, and on the streets.[66] In the racial context of Jim Crow segregation and lynchings, Saperstein worried that lopsided losses angered white fans of local teams, and he ordered the Globetrotters to use comedy routines to keep the scores close:

> To make money in this business, you've got to give the cash customers one of two things: A good contest or a good show. A good contest is hard to get every night. . . . Crowds won't come out to see us lick these teams by scores like 60–20, as we can without trying. . . . The only answer is a blend of basketball and entertainment.[67]

Once the score favored the Globetrotters by a specified point spread, the players were supposed to throw in a few passing tricks or dribbling displays or a comic routine to lessen the potential for racial backlash.[68] By the mid-1930s, the Globetrotters primarily were known for their "fun and foolery" and "clowning antics" rather than their dominance on the court.[69]

The depiction of the Harlem Globetrotters as clowns resonated with the mainstream image of the Sambo figure, a fictional character that emerged out of the antebellum South and became an enduring cultural icon, symbolic of the compliant and loyal slave who was "affable, indolent, (and) childlike."[70] As a character who was "inevitably a clown and congenitally docile," Sambo served the interests of white supremacy.[71] Like the images of the Kues,

Sambo served to mollify growing white fears of changes in the dominant racial order from the mid-1800s through the 1930s.[72]

The professional basketball circuit also included two Native American male teams. The United States Natives, marketed as an "all Indian team," was sponsored by the Great Depression-era Civilian Conservation Corps—Indian Division. The Sioux Travelers-Warriors came out of South Dakota and featured National Catholic Tourney and South Dakota all-state players such as Chub Bear and Suitcase Little. One season, players Spec Blacksmith and Calvin "Thriller" Valandra netted more than three thousand points and two thousand points, respectively.

The professional Native American players came from a rich basketball tradition.[73] For example, the Interior Department sponsored a recreational league that featured players from the Sioux, Choctaw, Comanche, Chickasaw, Winnebago, and Oneida tribes. Native American students in boarding schools also competed in basketball. From 1879 until the 1930s, Indian children had been removed from the reservations and placed in boarding schools, in line with the philosophy of "Kill the Indian and save the man."[74] Such schools used corporeal punishment, banned Indian languages, and taught American sports to assimilate Indian children into mainstream American culture. The Indian Industrial School in Carlisle, Pennsylvania, the first off-reservation boarding school for Native children, sent girls' and boys' teams to compete in basketball events, as the Tri-State Indian School basketball tournament.[75]

Much like the publicity for the Kues and the Globetrotters, the advertisements for the Native American teams combined respect for their basketball talent with racialized depictions of the players. The publicity linked Native American players' basketball talents to the stereotype of the Indian male warrior, resonating with the fairly static popular culture representations of Indians since nineteenth-century Wild West shows, dime novels, and movies. The 1939 Spencer Bennet film *Across the Plains* and John Ford's

1939 *Stage Coach* featured stereotypical Indian chief characters; and, in some ways, the barnstorming teams merely provided the space for these flat movie caricatures of the Native male warrior to exist in person. For example, one advertisement for the Sioux Travelers-Warriors reads: "Indians on the war path—but this time on the basketball court instead of the wide open spaces. . . . These outstanding attractions by descendants of the great chief Sitting Bull will be through your territory."[76] Another section of the same ad declares: "World famous Indian Basketball Clubs from the Reservations of South Dakota, after every club's scalp. They challenge one and all."[77] Similarly, the promotional materials describe one of the players in this racialized way: "SUITCASE LITTLE—Has played several seasons with the Indians and is a real honest to gosh full-blooded Sioux and will entertain his audience at half time with tribal song. Little is one of the greater showmen in basketball and seeing Jack alone is well worth the price of admittance." Another advertisement announces a racial head-to-head combat between an "All Chinese Basketball Team" and an "All Indian Team" (the United States Natives).[78] In this matchup, mainstream spectators paid to see two marginalized racial groups duking it out on the court. Focusing on different racialized notions of masculinity, the ads emphasize the "Indians on the Warpath" playing hoops against the scampering "little laundrymen" with queues flying.[79] The advertisements also featured masculine themes of war, with the basketball court as a metaphor for the frontier where the foreign threat confronted the noble warriors.[80]

In addition to the Kues, the Harlem Globetrotters, and the Native American teams, the barnstorming basketball spectacle included one white team from a residential religious community from Michigan. From the 1900s to the 1950s, this community sponsored barnstorming baseball and basketball teams called the House of David Bearded Aces.[81] As Christian Israelites, male followers refrained from shaving or cutting their hair, and the Bearded Aces basketball team, like their barnstorming peers, offered an exotic spectacle. Their novelty lay in "thick, bushy beards" and long hair that extended past their shoulders—in some cases to their waists.[82] Promotion machines capitalized on the Bearded Aces' hair and their basketball gimmicks: "trick shots" and "fancy plays," such as the "behind-the-back toss, a fake throw to one of the others, or a roll of the ball down their arms."[83]

Despite their unconventional appearance, the Aces garnered more respect from mainstream media than the Kues did. The media perceived the former all-American college basketball players on the Aces as talented athletes first, and as an oddity second.[84] By contrast, the media portrayed the Kues as peculiar creatures who surprised the audience with their ability to play basketball. One cartoon used in an advertising poster for the Aces shows a swooning voluptuous white female with her palms raised in a submissive position asking the viewer, "Isn't his beard gorgeous?" Although the poster acknowledges the beard as odd in the sense that it is particular to the Aces, it is an object of desire. The Chinese queue, however, was used in the Kues' advertising to highlight their foreignness; it was never depicted as inciting sexual desire in a woman of any race.

Although the Kues were cast as foreigners in mainstream newspapers, the players, whose families had limited resources, saw their tour primarily as a unique opportunity to see different parts of the United States. Previously restricted to the crowded living conditions of San Francisco's Chinatown, these young men suddenly found themselves driving through the expansive spaces of the West and Midwest. As small-town, white America gazed at them on the court, they gazed back at America. Various documents and mementos in their scrapbooks illustrate the Kues' enjoyment of the role of tourists. A majority of the photographs from their barnstorming tour show various state signs (see Figure 2.4). Fred Gok, who was interested in photography, bought a small Brownie camera for $5. He recounts: "[It was] just [like] a trip, like when you go on a vacation, that stuff. When we went from

Figure 2.4 Hong Wah Kues in front of state sign during the first season tour. (L to R) Albert Lee, George Lee, Bobby Lum, Fred Gok, Fred Hong Wong, Chauncey Yip. (*Forrest Gok Collection.*)

here to Arizona, there's a sign that say Welcome to Arizona, so everybody get off and stand and around the sign and I took the picture. When we go to Oklahoma, same things, that's what I did."[85] Just like vacationers, the team members sent postcards and photos home detailing their adventures on the road and put stickers from their travels on their luggage.[86]

On the tour, they saw snow for the first time. In addition to learning to wear boots, they also had to learn how to drive in the snow.[87] For some of the Kues, driving at all was new. Lee remembers: "Those guys didn't want me to get behind the wheel. (*He laughs.*) They didn't trust me. (*He laughs.*)"[88] They had two car accidents—one each season.[89] Lee describes one of them: "We played in Great Fall, Montana, but our car slip off the highway, turn over, turn over, and back upright, and I was the only one hurt. I injured my back. Bruise I guess. I had a night off. . . . You know, we had luggage on top of the car, everything flew off, but the car turn over and completely standing up here. 360 degrees."[90] Since they had only one benchwarmer, this injury meant that the remaining five players had to play the entire game.

Although the Kues were definitely not traveling in luxury, the tour temporarily improved their standard of living. In 1939 and 1940, the country was still reeling from the Great Depression, Chinese immigrants still could not become naturalized citizens, and most Asians were still doing laundry, restaurant, and garment work. Very few members of the Kues—or of their social circle, for that matter—owned cars. As team members, they not only had access to a brand new car, but they also were able to stay in places with hot showers. Many of the players grew up without running water, much less hot water, and lived with more than five people in one-bedroom apartments.[91] The team mostly stayed at the local YMCA for a dollar a night, with two players sharing a room.[92] Bunking with a single roommate and eating in a diner seemed lavish compared to home. Although their salaries did not make them rich by any standard, the tour freed them from the economic struggles common in Chinatown.

The players were also forming their own perspectives and opinions on America's racial hierarchies. Their insights expanded their knowledge of themselves as Chinese Americans and their understanding of race in America. The Kues learned how whites viewed different minority racial groups as well as where Chinese Americans fit in this landscape. For example, Albert Lee recounts one incident in one South Dakota town near an Indian reservation: "So we go in the . . . place to get a beer, and he says . . . 'Sorry, we don't serve you.' We say, 'Why?' 'We don't serve Indians.' They never see a Chinese before! Yeah, so we finally we told 'em, 'We're Chinese from San Francisco!' So it was all right. When we told them we were Chinese, we had beer."[93] This incident should not suggest that the Chinese were accepted in America, or even in this South Dakota town. As visitors who had no part in the historical polarization between Native Americans and whites, they could be served without disrupting the town's racial status quo.

Chinese American, African American, and Native American professional basketball teams all faced different modes of oppression and arrived at different understandings of each others' struggles. On the tour, the Kues spent social time with the Globetrotters and some local black communities. Perhaps out of respect for the Kues' basketball skills, or because they felt camaraderie with them as fellow male players of color, the Globetrotters did not "pick on [them] like they pick on other teams." George Lee recalls playing the Globetrotters about ten times a season.[94] Gok reflects: "They make fools of the other teams, but they don't do that to us. They give us respect."[95] The Kues also became aware that, although they did experience racial discrimination, they also enjoyed privileges unavailable to African Americans at the time. Gok remembers the racist business practices that African Americans had to encounter:

> We played the Harlem Globetrotters and they're all black guys, and then, well, they wouldn't be accepted. And then where we stay in a Chinatown or near a Chinatown, we'd stay in the same hotel, because it's cheap and they accept them . . . and they accept us. And then [the Harlem Globetrotters would] eat at the Chinese restaurant because they know they won't be . . . not accepted, so that's how it was then.[96]

This reflection does not suggest that all Chinese Americans embraced all African Americans or that all African Americans welcomed all Chinese Americans. It does, however, illustrate connections among some Chinese Americans and African Americans.

The Kues understood that promoters, the media, and audiences regarded them as a spectacle, and they found ways to assert themselves. For example, the Kues spun the requirement that they only speak Cantonese on the court to their advantage: "They would eat it up, see; so they don't know what you're talkin' about, and you get back, you know, you can swear and they won't know what you're talking about . . . you say 'you watch that guy in back of you, he's an "A,'" you know an a--hole, in Chinese *(He chuckles.)* . . . You get back at them."[97] They also sought out and connected with Chinese Americans living in the communities they visited. Barred from some hotels and restaurants, the players found eating Chinese food with other Chinese Americans to be a familiar and pleasant respite from uncomfortable race dynamics. Gok remembers that "a lotta time we go to some town, we look for Chinese restaurant; yeah, and then we go in there then we eat up all the rice; they sometime have to cook another batch, you know, yeah—'cause we missed the rice."[98]

Even though the tour was aimed primarily at white audiences, many Chinese Americans came out to see the Kues. If the team members liked a place, they would stay the night and have dinner with the locals. In smaller communities, Chinese Americans expressed their appreciation to the traveling players. For example, a local Chinese American family in Amarillo, Texas made won ton soup for them, and the Seattle Chinese community introduced the Kues to Christmas caroling.[99] The players saved business cards and menus from Chinese restaurants that were friendly to the team.[100] Gok reflects on being a local celebrity: "And then you'd be surprised how many restaurants we went to . . . and they read the papers . . . and then they usually give us a free dinner . . . welcoming us. That's pretty good. It's surprising. Usually, who cares, you know what I mean? . . . All we did was play basketball. You know, nothing fancy."[101] While dismissing what the Kues' did as insignificant, Gok expresses amazement and delight with the way local Chinese American communities treated them.

Although the newspapers trivialized the Kues, the players enjoyed a kind of celebrity status in the satellite Chinese communities that were supportive and somewhat adoring of them. Through their travels, the Kues experienced what it was like to be racial heroes and desirable Chinese American men in a public and wide-scale setting. One article describes how the Kues were "delayed an hour or two signing autographs in locker room."[102] Gok remembers: "You know, you got your picture in the window every town that we played in. [The posters] go on the store windows, you know, telling people to go see the game, advertising . . . and that's all we did, play ball, and then all these people treat us to dinner, gave us a banquet, that was big stuff."[103]

The Kues served as icons of racial pride to various Chinese communities across the United States and Canada. Some Chinese community members viewed the tour as an opportunity for racial uplift, as did Chauncey Yip's father, who arranged a publicity meeting with the Chinese consul in Chicago as part of the kickoff to the first season.[104] The newspaper quoted the consul as saying that he "was proud of these Chinese boys" who were "traveling around the country to give the Chinese people some prestige."[105] A San Francisco English-language newspaper, the *Chinese Digest*, noted their athletic accomplishments and their role as ethnic ambassadors:

> The Nam Wah basketball team, playing under the name of Hong Wah Kues, is now on a six-month tour of the Mid-West and the Northwest. They are spreading plenty of good will for us Chinese wherever they play by their fine sportsmanship, clean behavior, and excellent ball playing. Kellogg, one of the little mining- towns in Idaho, prohibits Chinese in that section . . . an old ordinance set up in the early mining days because of Chinese labor troubles. Nam Wah appeared there recently, thus shattering a sixty-year-old tradition; and what's more—the packed house enthusiastically applauded them when they out-shot and out-sped a taller hometown team to win 35–24.[106]

The largest number of Chinese spectators happened in British Columbia. Over three hundred Vancouver Chinese came to the game, and approximately two hundred attended a postgame banquet for the team.[107] The wedding-banquet-style celebration—sponsored by the equivalent of the Chinatown business elite—allowed the Kues to transcend their working-class status temporarily.[108] At a cost of $2.50 per couple, guests drank liquor out of teacups, a common subterfuge in the Prohibition era.[109] A hostess escorted each player, and a dance band provided the evening's music.[110] One black-and-white photo shows more than forty-five partygoers dressed in formal wear, party hats, and streamers. The handwritten caption reads "Friends across the border=Canada." Over the years, the players kept in contact with several people from that banquet, exchanging correspondence and visits.[111]

In many respects, the Kues countered the media portrayal of Chinese American men at the time. Popular culture had ridiculed, neutered, and diminished the Chinese American man by depicting him as the coolie, the laundryman, the houseboy, or as Fu Manchu. Similarly, sports coverage trivialized the Kues' athletic talent in racial and gender terms (for example, "little laundrymen"). Yet in the Chinese communities, the Kues were the equivalent of matinee idols. Photographs in the players' scrapbooks show all the Chinese American women they befriended on the tour. One menu from the Broad Water Inn restaurant in Helena, Montana, has autographs of various women. One memento from the Vancouver banquet is a cloth napkin with several messages and a lipstick kiss. In black felt pen, Kay Chong wrote: "It's swelling (sic) knowing you. Hope the music will be better when we dance again. Lots of Luck to you!" Almost seventy years later, Gok does not hide his amusement when asked for more detail about the napkin: "A little romance for the romantic," he says, chuckling.[112]

With America's involvement in World War II, the Kues' days were numbered. Many of the players joined the military, and most also wanted to find a stable way of making a living in order to get married.[113] They knew that opportunities for Chinese American hoopsters were slim; none went on to become wealthy basketball celebrities. Robert Lum and Albert Lee did later play for the multiracial San Francisco All-Nations team, which periodically toured with the Globetrotters.[114] Although these tours were thrilling, when the season ended, the young men had to return home to their jobs as ticket takers and waiters. As Kues, however, they temporarily sidestepped many racial barriers, saw the country, challenged popular images of Chinese American men, and gained insight into race relations in America.

More than seventy years after their tour together, only Chauncey Yip and Albert Lee from the first team are still living. In the late 1990s, the Kues began to receive media coverage and community awards. In 1996, for example, sports broadcaster Rick Quan produced an Emmy award-winning piece on the Kues, and in 2000, the Organization of Chinese Americans, a national civil rights organization, honored the Kues with a Chinese American Pioneer Award at its national convention.[115] The Kues challenged racist stereotypes by presenting an empowered version of Chinese American masculinity. They did so at a time when mainstream media depicted Chinese American men in distorted ways and when overt racial segregation was the rule. The Kues used everything available to them—their own inner resources and Chinese American community support—to make history.

3 / The Mei Wahs Knew How to Use Their Elbows and Push

In the early 1930s, a group of mostly working-class, Chinese American women regularly climbed a chain-link fence to squeeze in a game of basketball during early San Franciscan mornings. Franche Lee, one of the players, recalls: "People worked after school. So, the only time we could play was in the morning before school . . . The (Chinese) Playground was our space. Somehow we hopped over the fence in order to play–poking our fingers in the fence to help us climb over. Those games were fun."[1] Unwelcome on their school teams and with few options to play in Chinatown, these Chinese American women formed their own basketball team, the Mei Wahs.[2] Through the Mei Wahs' story, this chapter explores the female athletic body as a means of strengthening popular ideas of women as subordinate.[3] It also examines how these mostly working-class Chinese American women used their athletic bodies to create community.[4] The chapter begins with a description of the team; then it analyzes the separate basketball rules for girls and how they strengthen patriarchy. Lastly, the chapter discusses the Mei Wah's style of play and how they utilized basketball to counter anti-Chinese sentiments and challenge gender norms within Chinatown (see Figure 3.1).[5]

Mary Lee, her three sisters, and a group of friends defied popular conventions inside and outside Chinatown and reveled in playing basketball in the early 1930s.[6] The Mei Wahs learned to play basketball by practicing at a local schoolyard with Chinatown boys in their social circle. One of the players recalls: "We spent most of our time scrimmaging with the boys. (*She laughs.*) Those games got pretty interesting. Somehow, the boys always ended up on the ground! (*She laughs.*)"[7] In addition to the pickup scrimmages against boys, the team formally competed against Chinese American women basketball teams from other cities, a Japanese American team from San Francisco, and

Figure 3.1. The Mei Wahs. Standing (L to R): Josephine Chan Lee, unidentified, unidentified , Rachel Lee, Franche Lee, Mae Fung. Kneeling (L to R): Mary Lee, Camille Wong, Nellie Wong, Ella Mark Chan, Mabel Choy Lee, Susan Lee. *(Author's private collection.)*

white women in a citywide league. Mei Wahs, depending on the Chinese characters, translates into "American Chinese" or "beautiful flower."

Although the team formed because of friendships, the focus of the Mei Wahs was playing sports. Alice Chin Leung remembers: "We mostly spent our time outside—playing basketball, softball, running, hiking."[8] The four Lee sisters—Mary, Franche, Rachel, and Susie—anchored the team. The other Mei Wahs were Josephine Chan, Mae Fung, Janet Hoo, Annabelle Lee, Lily "Tiger Lil" Leong, Peony Wong, and Esther Yee Jue. Occasionally, Alice Chew, Alice Chin Leung, Erline Lowe, Waite Ng, Etna Su Hu, Emma Wong, Lillian Wong, and Norma Wong played on the Mei Wahs as well.[9] Polly McGuire, a white Irishwoman and Playground staff member, also competed for the Mei Wahs. Later, a younger group of girls joined: Mabel Choy Lee, Gloria Lai, Ella Mark Chan, Rose Pan, Camille Wong, and Nellie Wong. Coached by Mary Lee, they were the Mei Wah juniors.[10]

Most of the Mei Wah players were multisport athletes, competing in tennis, track, and softball as well as basketball. For example, Mary Lee won numerous Chinatown tennis tournaments, and her sister, Franche Lee, dominated in Chinatown track competitions. Mei Wah sharpshooter Erline Lowe was described by an English-language newspaper, the *Chinese Digest*, as "Chinatown's foremost all-around girl athlete."[11] The Mei Wahs' brand of basketball involved speed, under bucket shots, and physical aggression. On offense, the team passed the ball quickly and cut into the lane for layups. On defense, the Mei Wahs caused turnovers by suffocating their opponents. Rachel Lee sums up their style of play: "[The white girls] were taller than us. *(She laughs.)* But we were quicker."[12] Franche Lee describes her elder sister's way of playing defense: "Mary was peppy. *(She chuckles.)* She was like a small mosquito or fly—she was everywhere. Five feet and ninety nine pounds. *(She laughs.)* She had to guard some pretty big girls. But she was very effective . . . *(She smiles.)* She did all the dirty work. *(She laughs.)*"[13]

The San Francisco Mei Wahs won the San Francisco playground league championship in their division twice.[14] Other than one Japanese American team, most of their opponents in the league were white. Reflecting the racial tenor of the time and the informal race-based structure of the city league, the members of the Mei Wahs did not feel encouraged to play on integrated teams with other racial groups. Each team was comprised of players from a single racial group. These league games usually started at 8:00 P.M. on weeknights and weekends at Girls High and the French Court. Most players were too poor to have access to cars, and transportation to games outside of Chinatown proved tricky. One of the players would borrow her family's laundry delivery truck, and the others would "rush to finish their housework" at their after-school jobs, "pile into the truck," and drive to the game across town.[15]

As well as playing in the city recreational league and the casual pickup games against the boys, the Mei Wahs competed against Chinese American women's teams from other cities. In contrast to the extensive tournaments and leagues for boys within San Francisco's Chinese American community, there were only sporadic games against other Chinese American girls. Other than one tournament in Los Angeles, the Mei Wahs' archrivals were mostly the Oakland Chinese American women's team, the Wa Kus. These two groups competed regularly in basketball, track, and softball.

The Mei Wahs did not play against other Chinese American women's teams from San Francisco until 1937, when a Mei Wahs player, Mary Lee, organized the first Chinatown girls basketball league. Sponsored by the Chinese Playground, the league included eight teams from different Chinese language schools, such as the Chung Wah School, the Chinese Baptist School, and the Hip Wo School; from other Chinatown organizations, such as St. Mary's Catholic Mission and the Girls Reserve; and the Playground's Mei Wah Juniors. With more than two hundred spectators watching the

1938 championship game, Chinatown women's basketball flourished in the late 1930s.[16]

The Mei Wahs were part of a broader women's basketball scene throughout the 1930s.[17] Women played in Amateur Athletic Union basketball competitions, in industrial leagues such as the Telephone Girls in the San Francisco-based Pacific Association League, and on professional teams such as the Ozark Hillbillies and Helen Stephens' Olympic Co-Eds. They also participated on company-sponsored teams such as the Philadelphia Tribunes (the eleven-time Women's Colored Basketball World Champions), on college teams such as Tuskegee University, and on club teams such as the African American Germantown Hornets and the Los Angeles-based Japanese American Women's Athletic Union.[18]

Although the Mei Wahs relished in playing full-court scrimmages with boys, they were subject to the stringent rules for girl's basketball. Just two years after James Naismith invented basketball in 1891, the Spalding Athletic Library published an official rulebook defining these special basketball rules for girls, and the rules remained in place in various forms for more than seventy years.[19] According to the rules, twelve players competed at once with six players from each team. Basketball players were not allowed to run up and down the court from one basket to another. Instead, the rules designated three spaces and two players from each team had to stay in one of three designated spaces during the game. In one area near a basket, two players from each team played forwards and guards respectively. In the middle space, two players from each team served as centers. In the third space near the other basket, two players from each team played. If the guards or defensive players stole the ball near the basket at one end of the court, they could not dribble the ball to the other basket. Instead, they had to pass the ball to their centers or players in the middle space and the centers passed the ball to their players on offense in the next space. Since players had to stay in their specified areas, women were restricted to areas only twenty-eight feet long. By contrast, basketball rules granted men a fifty-by-eighty-four-foot playing area.[20]

The regulations also dictated how girls could move within the confined space.[21] In the early 1930s, games were thirty minutes long.[22] Players could dribble only once and had to pass the ball twice before taking a shot.[23] The flow of the game was truncated because after each basket there was either a jump ball or a player threw the ball in from the center court.[24] The women's rules barred them from using two arms to guard a player who was near a wall or corner. Whereas no rules limited physical proximity among male basketball players, the rules also prohibited double-teaming an offensive player and blocking the shooter.[25] The 1935 *Team Sports for Women* guidebook advises women athletes to limit physical exertion as a strategy for "more effective" play.[26] It also suggests how women may play defense without draining themselves: "Sometimes it is possible to confuse a forward by following her closely every second, but this is most wearing. It is better to judge her pace and know where she is every moment and then wait and dash when needed."[27] A basketball game that involved active guarding was inappropriate and too "strenuous" for girls. This same book instructed female hoopsters to use "simple plays" and very few of them.[28]

Scholars Susan Cahn and Mary Jo Festle contend that the rules minimized female bodily contact in order to protect women's "dainty" constitutions. According to a male doctor in 1931: "[Females in a] combative game like basketball develop ugly muscles and scowling faces and the competitive spirit. As an inevitable consequence your girls who are trained in Physical Education today may find it more difficult to attract the most worthy fathers for their children."[29] The "competitive spirit" was deemed masculine and therefore undesirable in a woman. A female physical educator from 1924 stated that the "essential feature" of girls' rules was to "discourage personal contact, interference and tussling" because "allowing the female player more contact would foster aggressive qualities which seldom add to her charm or usefulness."[30] To be "useful" as wives serving their men and children was women's only biologically destined function in society. These separate rules restricting movement and physical contact trained the female body to act and move in accordance with social norms of male power and privilege. Playing under these rules gave female basketball players a feel for the game of patriarchy. In other words, the restricted basketball games almost required women to embody and enact female subordination.[31]

The notions that women were delicate and that strenuous activity endangered their reproductive health was the foundation for the "cult of domesticity" that emerged in England in the eighteenth century and spread to the United States in the nineteenth century. In this cult of domesticity, "true" women were biologically driven to be submissive and self-sacrificing; nature dictated that they devote themselves to the private sphere of the home and the care of husband and children. Their participation in the political arena and public life was deemed unnatural. From the late 1800s to the early 1920s, the notion of the "new woman" disrupted the cult of domesticity, and this new woman began to play a more public role as a suffragette, trade unionist, social worker in a settlement house, actress, or athlete. However, even as these modern women occupied more visible spaces, they continued to grapple with significant obstacles and conventional ideas of femininity.[32]

The popular wisdom of the 1930s held that the girl's basketball rules safeguarded womanhood and that women were naturally compliant, noncompetitive, pleasant, and gracious.[33] Medical authority supported socially constructed notions of femininity in biological terms, reinforcing traditional Western heterosexual gender roles.[34] Analyzing popular literature from 1919 to 1930, Helen Lenskyj found many warnings of the detrimental impact of sports on women. According to popular media depictions, women gained "physical toughness and independence" by playing sports. This caused a threat to women's "special place in society" as caretakers and mothers.[35] For many, basketball posed an alarming menace to women's alleged "natural[ly] feminine health and attractiveness."[36]

While 1930s U.S. basketball reinforced unequal gender relations, women basketball players in China competed in the National Games starting in China's republican period (1912–1949) and continuing after the Communist takeover in 1949, according to anthropologist Susan Brownell. Chinese popular ideology lauded women's physical strength as part of building a strong nation. A large number of Chinese women engaged in agricultural labor and urban menial labor in the 1930s, and most female Chinese athletes came from laboring backgrounds.[37] Women's basketball in the United States strengthened popular patriarchal ideals about the biological differences between women and men, but women's basketball in China testified to women's ability to "hold up half the sky." Perhaps, the Chinese popular ideology of praising women's athleticism as a form of nationalism carried over to some of the immigrants who supported the Mei Wahs.

Even within this context of restrictions, the Mei Wahs found room to maneuver.[38] Neither passive victims nor agents of social change, they played basketball as a form of empowerment and redefined femininity in part through their style of play. Playing "man-to-man" defense instead of zone defense, they developed a strategy around the rules by creating a quick passing offense with give-and-go.[39] Franche Lee explains their strategy: "[With the women's rules], it was hard to pass .... It was especially hard playing against taller people. You just had to try to pivot. Do one pivot and get away, then pass quickly. If we could pass fast, then we could usually sink the under bucket shots. ... We had to sorta try and outspeed them."[40]

Lily "Tiger Lil" Leong recalls her team's physicality with delight and amusement: "When we played, we didn't fool around. We had fun, but, let's just say our opponents didn't have any easy time with our elbows."[41] Rachel Lee describes the ways her teammates strategically used their bodies: "We always won. We knew how to win. Jo used her elbows. Esther used her feet."[42] Another Mei Wah player, Josephine "Jo" Chan explains: "As I always say, Mary and Rachel, they play dirty. They know how to use their elbows and push."[43] Chan displayed a clear sense of satisfaction that her teammates knew how to work their elbows. Even while playing within the girls' rules, the Mei Wahs were tough—using their elbows, tripping players, and posting up.

The basketball manuals would most likely have characterized the Mei Wahs' style of playing as "wearing," but the Mei Wahs prided themselves on their quick passing and aggressive intensity. Their creation and execution of this distinctive style of play also expressed their response to the limited opportunities for working-class Chinese American women. Most had no chance of attending college or accessing higher paying jobs. Success in a game—even during a single play—symbolized a temporary triumph over whites and the barriers facing Chinese American women inside and outside of Chinatown. Rather than viewing toughness and heartiness with disdain, many of the Mei Wahs revered these characteristics. To them, women realized themselves as women through their strength, stamina, and toughness. These working-class Chinese American women found gratification using their physical power, agility, and endurance.

In the racial environment of the early 1930s, most Chinese stayed in Chinatown. On the whole, white and Chinese young women in the early 1930s did not mix at school, at work, socially, or after the games. The league games required the Mei Wahs to travel to areas in San Francisco that were otherwise taboo. When the Mei Wahs ventured out, they went in large groups, seeking what Josephine Chan called "safety in numbers."[44] The basketball court was not exempt from the expression of racial hostility. When the Mei Wahs played basketball against white women outside of Chinatown, racial tensions flared. Chinese American players, who experienced racial taunts and remarks at school and on the street, heard them on the court as well. Franche Lee remembers: "Sometimes they were pretty (*She pauses.*) rude. You know, comments would go back and forth on the court."[45]

The Mei Wahs' physical style of basketball expressed their frustration with the gender restrictions and the racial discrimination they faced on and off the court. Josephine Chan was one of the first Chinese girls to attend the predominately white Lowell High School. Chan remembers how white girls would do things to "drive her out" of school, such as placing thumbtacks on her chair before she sat down in class. Chan explains how she dealt with the racial tension: "It's not *my* fault if [the white girls were] too *dumb*—didn't stop before they *slammed (She slams one hand into the other.)* into the wall!" *(She shrugs shoulders.)*"[46] On the court, Chan was free to trip and push the same white girls who harassed her at school. Franche Lee relates a story that demonstrates the physical level of their game and the use of their bodies to challenge racial dynamics:

> Mae [Fung] was a very petite girl. And one time *(She chuckles.)* this white girl did not like how Mae was guarding her. You know, very clingy-like. *(She raises arms to demonstrate.)* So, the girl *slapped* Mae. *(She pauses.)* And Mae looked at her and *slapped* her back. . . . *(She laughs.)* It was *so* funny! She slapped Mae again and Mae slapped her *back*. Back and forth. Back and forth. Slap. *(She pauses.)* Slap. *(She pauses.)* Slap. *(She pauses.)* Slap. *(She laughs uproariously.)*[47]

Both players in this incident countered the dominant view of women as delicate and noncompetitive; a white woman behaved as though she was entitled to physically assault her Chinese American opponent, and Fung responded in kind. Some sixty years later, her teammates recall the incident with approval and amusement. Fung's actions did not strike a blow that would alter gender, class, or racial roles in society, but she seized the opportunity to show her opponents, her teammates, and spectators that Chinese American women would not tolerate physical abuse. Using her body, Fung asserted her strength and dignity as a working-class Chinese American. The Mei Wahs could not respond to overt incidents of racism in school, in the workplace, or on the street because they needed their jobs and there was too much potential for backlash at school or on the street. On the basketball court, however, they could give back as much attitude as they got. While they knew their games were not going to change the world, get them better jobs, or lead to better housing for their families, they could at least respond to racial hostility and white female privilege.

The Mei Wahs reflected a demographic shift in San Francisco's Chinatown. Previously, Chinatown consisted of mostly males and immigrants. In the 1930s, second-generation Chinese American women were a unique demographic group. Race-based immigration laws had delayed the appearance of this second generation until the 1920s and 1930s.[48] Laws such as the 1875 Page Law had barred Chinese women without marketable skills and without male chaperones from entering the United States, and the 1882 Chinese Exclusion Act barred Chinese laborers of both genders. However, one class that was exempt from the Exclusion Act created the opening for Chinese women and children to immigrate to the United States. "Paper sons and daughters" were Chinese born in China who claimed to be children of American citizens and therefore eligible to enter the United States.[49] As a result of the arrival of "paper children" and the high birth rate among immigrant Chinese women, the number of American-born Chinese in the United States quadrupled between 1900 and the 1940s. In 1940, second-generation Chinese American women represented 72 percent of the Chinese female population in the United States.[50] The increasing number of American-born Chinese women shifted the gender balance in Chinatown from predominately male to more equally female. Consequently, this changed how femininities were practiced within Chinatown.

Within this cohort of Chinese American women, groups of Chinese American women crafted various types of femininity besides playing basketball. Middle-class and college-educated women tended to follow a public-service-oriented model of femininity. Some women participated in organizations like the Square and Circle Club and focused on such activities as fundraising for charities, beauty contests, and public leadership.[51] Members of this generation also belonged to groups that organized fashion shows and dances to raise money for Chinese refugees displaced by Japan's 1931 invasion of Manchuria. For other women, Christianity provided an avenue to developing leadership and organizational skills, and they took part in groups such as the Lake Tahoe Chinese Young People's Christian Conference.[52] The influence of Chinese nationalism moved some young women to provide aid to Chinese during the Sino-Japanese War through organizations such as the Women's Patriotic Club and the New Life Association.[53] A few American-born Chinese women staked out new territory by performing in nightclubs such as the Chinese Village, Twin Dragon, Forbidden City, and Shanghai Low's. Through song and dance, they both perpetuated and challenged notions of Chinese American women as exotic.[54] Working-class women organized with their coworkers at markets, laundries, garment factories, and other workplaces.[55]

Against this backdrop of diverse expressions of Chinese American femininity, the Mei Wahs disrupted traditional Western and Chinese gender roles in the community via the athletic body. Franche Lee reflects: "I suppose we would have been considered Chinese American hippies of that time. There were not any actually hippies in the 1930s. *(She chuckles.)* But we were sort of different [from other Chinese American teenagers]. We were always outside, running around, hiking, playing basketball. *(She laughs.)*"[56] Inside Chinatown in the early 1930s, women did not usually play full-court basketball against boys or wear shorts that revealed their knees in public. The Mei Wahs' brand of femininity disrupted not only the sexist ideals of the dominant culture, but also the patriarchal traditions of Chinese femininity. Inside the Chinese American community, the Mei Wah athletes were pioneering an aspect of Chinese American women's identity that involved the sporting body and that was absent among other Chinese women of their generation.[57] Faced with limited resources, their sporting bodies became a main asset for the Mei Wahs. Their bodies furnished a way to develop and articulate a sense of self-respect as a member of a group marginalized by both the mainstream and the Chinese communities.[58]

Within the adult immigrant population, reactions to the Mei Wahs varied. Some immigrant parents supported their participation in sports; others focused exclusively on basic economic survival and expressed no opinion.[59] Some saw their athleticism as improper and indicative of the American-born generation's adopting "loose Caucasian American values."[60] One basketball player remembers: "One girl on our team sprained her ankle playing basketball. Her parents were NOT happy. They said girls should not be running around. And, with boys. They wanted her to go to college and to get married. So, she had to stop playing on the team. But, when she could get away with it, she scrimmaged with us."[61] Other immigrant parents especially objected to the physical contact between the genders during pickup scrimmages at the local schoolyard.[62]

As mostly working-class women, the Mei Wah's socioeconomic status influenced their love of basketball and style of femininity. Many of the players were second-generation, poor, and came from large families. Most of their parents labored in garment factories, grocery stores, and restaurants.[63] During this time, many Chinese American women occupied lower segments of the labor market. The only work Chinese American women in San Francisco could find in the 1930s was manual or unskilled work such as factory or domestic labor.[64] While attending high school and playing basketball, the Mei Wahs worked at the jobs available to them, such as peeling shrimp for ten cents a pound at a factory or folding towels at a laundry. Earning five dollars a week, Franche Lee and her sisters cleaned houses after school and on the weekends.[65] Only one of the players attended college. Most of the Mei Wahs labored in other unskilled jobs with long hours and draining conditions.[66] Therefore, the popular notion of women as "feeble" did not match their reality, thereby providing an opening for creating their own definition of femininity.

The separate girls' basketball rules were justified by alleged concern about women's weak constitutions. The 1933 president of the American Physical Education Association, Agnes Wayman, described the need to shelter the delicate female from stress:

> External stimuli such as cheering audiences, bands, lights, etc., cause a great response in girls and are apt to upset the endocrine balance. Under emotional stress a girl may easily overdo. There is widespread agreement that girls should not be exposed to extremes of fatigue or strain either emotional or physical.[67]

This supposed apprehension over the adverse effects of stress on women was inconsistent with the reality of working-class women, like the Mei Wahs. No similar anxiety was expressed about women who worked ten-hour days sewing in the garment factory or cleaned homes after going to school. Neither was there worry over the strain on a woman forced to live in a two-bedroom apartment in Chinatown with fifteen other people, with only a faucet in the kitchen and no bathroom.[68] Moreover, no alarms sounded about the emotional strain of racial violence, social segregation, and limited educational opportunities. The socioeconomic status of the Mei Wahs—shaped by their race and gender—enabled them to recognize that the "protected" status of women did not apply to them. Drawing from the physical demands of their work lives, they were aware of the strength of their bodies. They constructed what Cindy Himes Gissendanner called an "active ideal of femininity" that stemmed from the economic necessity of working hard, freeing themselves somewhat from the dominant patriarchal ideology that constrained many white and middle-class women.[69] Racism restricted Chinese American women but also reduced their exposure to mainstream male domination.[70] Their position of marginality as Chinese American women both limited them and provided some space to maneuver outside the confines of what was expected of women.[71] Posing as a delicate middle-class woman was not an option for women who worked six days a week while attending school and helping raise their siblings.

Many in the Chinese American community both acknowledged and respected this active femininity. An English-language paper, the *Chinese Digest*, included a regular sports page called the "Sporting News." Founded in 1935 by second-generation Chinese Americans Thomas W. Chinn and Chingwah Lee, the *Chinese Digest* recognized the Mei Wahs' athletic accomplishments.[72] For example, in addition to playing in the citywide basketball league, the Mei Wahs competed against Chinese women from other cities in basketball, track, and softball. The September 1936 issue of the *Chinese Digest* featured the Mei Wahs in a front cover photo and story:

> The Mei Wah Girls' Club of San Francisco is exceedingly popular in the world of athletics. . . . Last winter they won the city of San Francisco Recreation League basketball title (the only Chinese team entered) and last Sunday

> competing against other Chinese girls' clubs, their track team won 49 out of a possible 50 points.[73]

This text indicates not only racial pride, but also recognition of the Mei Wahs' talent as athletic women.[74] Unlike the mainstream press, the *Chinese Digest* did not infantilize women athletes and did not pathologize their physical prowess. Instead, this newspaper praised the Mei Wahs' athleticism for being "as good as any boy's."[75]

The Mei Wahs inspired young people in Chinatown. Smokey Joe Wong, a generation younger than the Mei Wahs, recalls: "Franche [Lee] *was* an athlete. She was fast, see? And, I got to see [the Mei Wahs]. And they were something."[76] Alfred Lee, a regular at the Chinese Playground and the only child of a widow, has this to say:

> Franche [Lee], to me, was the greatest. I mean . . . people in your generation, you watch. . . . Jackie Kersey Joyner and all the others. . . . But to me [Franche] was the fastest. . . . No one could touch her. She was like Flo-Jo. . . . In my childhood. . . . These are my idols, you know. . . . They were doing things that we dreamed about doing.[77]

John Henry Wong, a member of a Chinese Playground team, remembers how one Mei Wah player mentored him: "Mary [Lee] adopted me. She was always playing basketball and tennis. And, she encouraged me to play. My parents were too busy."[78] All three explain how important it had been for younger second-generation members to watch the Mei Wahs, who were positive role models of how to be Chinese American.

During our interviews, the former Mei Wahs began to enjoy reminiscing about long-gone friends and family, and the stories began to roll off of their tongues. Their sense of delight over playing basketball together infused their recollections. The Mei

Wahs pioneered new roles for women in times of hardship and reclaimed the bodies that toiled in white-owned factories and middle-class homes. They used their bodies to speak to the indignities and barriers they encountered as mostly working-class Chinese American women.[79] Although the Mei Wahs did not have the resources to fight for wide-scale political and economic social change, they challenged social inequality on an individual level and created spaces of empowerment on the basketball court.

4 / "Mr. Chinese Cager" Plays Madison Square Garden

Sponsored by the *San Francisco Examiner,* the Pacific Association (PA) tournament in the late 1940s was one of the most illustrious basketball tournaments in San Francisco. In the same period, William Woo Wong was a legendary basketball player in Chinatown and gained wider fame when the *Examiner* heralded him as the "star of the 1947–1948 Examiner-PA basketball tournament." Breaking the tournament record by scoring thirty-seven points in one game, Wong was acknowledged as "one of the greatest box office players in San Francisco history."[1] In the 1948 PA tournament, Wong's sharp shooting and skillful ball-handling were leading his team to a first round win. In the second half of the game, Wong scrambled for the ball at full speed and collided heads with an opponent, losing a tooth and gushing blood from his mouth. Fighting throbbing pain, Wong later rejoined the team and scored the winning basket to catapult his underdog team into the second round of the tournament.[2]

A child of a garment worker and a store clerk, Wong grew up to shatter basketball records against white and Chinese opponents. Wong's story is unusual because he found success in both the Chinese and the white sporting communities and garnered much coverage in the mainstream press. While his athletic achievements are significant, his experience also highlights the political functions of ethnic male sports figures. The mainstream and ethnic-based media depictions of Wong offered divergent meanings of what Chinese American masculinity symbolized in the late 1940s.

Born in San Francisco in 1927 on the eve of the Great Depression, Woo Wong was the third of seven children.[3] His immigrant parents juggled several low-paying, manual labor jobs to support their large family. Wong remembers his parents' struggle:

> I came from a poor family . . . my parents came over from China. They barely spoke any English. So . . . it's hard . . . [for them to] find employment. . . . My dad's always out looking for work. . . . And it seemed like he's never around a lot of times. . . . My mom was the one that used to pick us up at school . . . when we were smaller, she'll go down to the shrimp factory, work, and then when it's time for lunch, she'll pick us up, cook for us. . . . She'll carry her shrimp on her back. . . . About twenty-five pounds . . . and she lugged it back . . . they would peel it for ten cents a pound.[4]

The Wongs lived in housing conditions characteristic of poor working families in San Francisco's Chinatown in the 1940s. Sharing an apartment with another family, they crammed nine people into three rooms without facilities to cook or bathe. The eighteen tenants on their floor shared a community toilet, and the family paid to take showers at the YMCA across the street.[5] Wong's three sisters slept in the living room; he and his three brothers shared another room, with his younger brother in a crib and the three older boys sharing a bed made of boards placed over two wooden horses.[6]

With a father who took an authoritarian approach to parenting, home life was not always a happy place. His father enforced discipline by whipping Wong's legs with a belt. Without much money or much space at home, Wong made the Chinese Playground his refuge, as did many working-class Chinatown youths. Wong would climb the gate at seven in the morning and practice basketball before school.[7] He devoted hours to practicing and used anything available to improve his skills: "Before I had a basketball, in my little bedroom *(He chuckles.)* you know how in the old houses, you use to have those molding on top? Well, I use to just have a tennis ball. My parents were never home anyways. So I just use the tennis ball and try to hit that molding. *(He laughs.)*"[8]

The Wongs struggled to provide food, shelter, and clothes for the family, so sports equipment was hard to come by. Wong treasured the few pieces he had. He recalls a beloved gift from a distant relative:

> I had this uncle from New York. He had never seen [us] before. He wanted to buy each of us a present, and he asked what we wanted. I told him to get me a basketball, and that's what I got. *(He chuckles.)* and I treated it like a baby. I use to put Vaseline [on it] so it would last a little bit longer on the ball. . . . I didn't know any better. *(He chuckles.)* All it did was pick up the dirt and lint.[9]

Eventually, basketball became an escape from life's hardships as well as a source of personal pride: "I would always be the last one to be picked. *(He laughs.)* The other people tell me, yell at me, not to shoot, because I can't shoot. Which was true. *(He laughs.)* I just hated for people to tell me that you can't do it. So, that's a lot of motivation. *(He chuckles.)*"[10]

Although he had few resources and limited opportunities for a prosperous future, Wong could always just walk across the street and play basketball. Honing his game at the Chinese Playground, Wong went on to score significant marks in high school competitions, amateur teams, and college play. He led the Saint Mary's 120 team to a championship in the Catholic Youth Organization league (CYO); in one game, Wong set a new record by posting forty-three points in a single game.[11] In high school league play, he was the only Chinese American chosen for the 1945 city all-star team.

In addition to playing high school basketball, Wong competed with an elite team out of San Francisco's Chinatown called the San Francisco Chinese, which later became known as the San Francisco Saints.[12] Most of the players on the Saints were high school graduates and working full-time; the original Saints included Wong's two brothers, George "Wee" and Hank, along with Percy Chu, Hank Hong, Al Jeung, Charles Lum, Peter Lum, Peter Lung, Ulysses Moy, Ed Shem, and Benton Wong.[13] One newspaper wrote:

> Diminutive Willie Wong, 20, who stands all of five by five and no more, led the classy Frisco Chinese to the title in the first all-Oriental national basketball tournament during Christmas holidays in Seattle. Mr. Wong, who surely is Mr. Chinese Cager, put on a remarkable basketball-shooting skill in his three-day stand. Offensively—65 points in three games—we never have seen anyone who behaved so point-conscious as he.[14]

The Saints played not only other Chinese and Japanese American teams, but also white opponents such as Armed Services teams in San Francisco.[15]

In 1948, a young Pete Newell recruited Wong to play for University of San Francisco (USF). Considered "one of the greatest

Figure 4.1 Posed photo of some of the San Francisco Saints. Kneeling in the front row from the far right to the middle are the three Wong brothers: Hank, William Woo, and George Wee.
(Jennie Wong Collection.)

basketball coaches of all time," Newell led the university to a National Invitational Tournament championship in 1949 and later led the University of California Berkeley to a National Collegiate Athletic Association title in 1959. In 1960, Newell coached the U.S. Olympic team, with players like John Havlicek, Oscar Robertson, and Jerry West, to a gold medal in Rome.[16] After one of several games in which Newell watched Wong play with the Saints, Newell waited outside to invite him to play for USF: "Pete Newell scouted me out. (*He chuckles.*) I was amazed at the opportunity. How could I turn down the chance to play at the college level?"[17]

Like all freshmen, Wong was ineligible for the varsity team. On the freshmen team during his first year at USF, he averaged thirteen points per game.[18] He acknowledges that the transition from playground ball to collegiate basketball required some adjustment: "Well, I had to learn . . . because now instead of playing freelance, I'm playing structured, disciplined and they play real controlled ball. It's a little different. *(He chuckles.)*"[19] Despite the modifications he had to make, Wong mastered this new style of play. With a 70 percent shooting percentage, Wong's shooting and dribbling were "major factor[s]" for the USF freshman team.[20] In the last twenty-five seconds of one game, for example, he scored a "dramatic clutch shot," a swisher from twenty feet, to clinch his team's entrance into the playoffs. According to the *San Francisco Examiner,* "the big crowd gave Willie (Woo) an ovation and his teammates, some of them a foot and a half taller, hugged the little guy all over the court."[21]

In the 1949–1950 season, during his second year, Wong advanced to the varsity squad and made the varsity's elite traveling team. In the spring of 1949, the season before Wong made the varsity team, USF defied the odds and took the NIT national championship.[22] In the 1940s, the NIT was the foremost post-season college basketball event.[23] Working against a bias favoring basketball teams from the Midwest and the East Coast, USF had been the only team west of the Rockies to receive an invitation to this prestigious tournament. Don Lofgran, Joe McNamee, Frank Kuzara, and Rene Herrerias had led the team to the championship. Naming USF the "outsiders" and the "Cinderella" team, journalists splashed USF's 1949 national championship across the front page of all the San Francisco newspapers.[24] Thousands of fans braved torrential rains to greet the team at the airport upon their return, and thousands of others participated in a rally at Kezar pavilion.[25] Most of the players from the championship team had returned the following year, leaving only a few open spots.

Joining the reigning NIT championship team, Wong received national attention at the elite college basketball level. Leaving for New York to defend the title, the USF team had "two rousing sendoffs" with mass rallies at the college and the airport.[26] For the

1950 season, the varsity team drew record crowds of six thousand to twelve thousand people. The players traveled to games across the United States by train and airplane and stayed in hotels such as the Paramount in New York.[27]

During Wong's varsity season, he played "anywhere from two to eight minutes" in games.[28] Out of twenty-six games, he played in fourteen, scoring a total of thirteen points while fouling four times. In that season, he made 35 percent of his field goals and 60 percent of his free throws.[29] In this era, the NIT was held at the famed Madison Square Garden, considered one of the leading athletic venues of the time. A long way from the Chinese Playground, Wong practiced at the Garden and experienced games from the bench in front of "sellout mobs of more than 18,000" fans.[30] As the first Chinese to play at the famed Garden, Wong recalls: "Oh, it's different [walking in to Madison Square Garden]. . . . I've never seen so many people. *(He chuckles.)* And not only that, it was cold. . . . I remember sitting and boy was I freezing. *(He chuckles.)*"[31]

While Wong marveled over the grand scale of the Garden, spectators gathered to stare at him during practice sessions. A teammate of Woo Wong's at USF, Cap Lavin, recalls how Wong attracted attention at the Garden:

> He'd be warming up . . . we'd shoot maybe ten shots and then throw it back to a teammate. He would never miss. *(He laughs.)* And pretty soon you'd have a whole section of Madison Square Garden almost like counting the shots. In other words, he drew the attention of a large segment of the audience at Madison Square Garden. . . . He looked elegant and exquisite. . . . He was in his groove.[32]

Coaches, competitors, teammates, and journalists recognized Wong's talent as a shooter, playmaker, ball handler, and defender. They also acknowledged his work ethic and drive to compete in the sport.[33] Known for his shooting, Wong posted high scoring percentages. When competing against white opponents in the Catholic Youth Organization tournaments, Wong regularly sank over thirty points in a game.[34] In 1949, Pete Newell described Wong's shooting:

> In my born days I never saw a man with a keener eye. . . . Wong throws a "very dead ball," that is, he hits the rim without a spin. A dead ball propelled from the palm of the hand . . . stands a better chance of dropping through the net than one with a contrary gyration. . . . Wong won't shoot unless he figures he has a better-than-even chance of tanking the ball. In his freshman year he held off too much. He certainly isn't a hog. His trouble is he doesn't shoot often enough.[35]

In 2005, Newell still affirms his prior evaluation of Wong's shooting capabilities: "He was a remarkable shooter. You could put a mask on him and he could put the ball in anywhere. He could really play. . . . He could hit the open outside shot. He was effective . . . Especially against the zone defense."[36] Wong was also highly skilled at ball handling and passing. Newell called Wong "one of the finest passers and floor men ever to step up into college competition."[37] These skills translated into the ability to play an up-tempo game. With strength, quickness, and ball-handling skills, Wong and his teammate Cap Lavin were put into the game to stall and hold the lead until the end. Since there was no thirty-second clock at that time, they could move the ball as long as they wanted. This required a great deal of improvisation and ball-handling skills.[38] Wong was also a defensive force. Lavin, reflects on Wong's physical style of guarding the basket:

> He was strong and could rebound the ball. There you have to block out the person behind you . . . keep them on your

> hip, you might say, put a body on them. He could do that very well, in spite of being five foot five or five foot six at the most. He could block out and was strong enough to go up and get the ball—wasn't afraid to mix it up. He could guard you and stick with you like fly paper. *(He laughs.)*[39]

Wong's versatility as a player included his ability to shoot, make plays on offense, and shut down an opponent through defense. Consequently, Wong developed a refined overall game. Newell commented, "Because [Woo] wasn't as big as most players, he had to learn more about the game."[40] Wong reflects on his use of strategy and instinct:

> I think basketball is *(He pauses.)* here again people may not agree with me, but I think it's mental too. . . . In other words, I think it's who's smarter. . . . You gotta be thinking as far as a guy could be bigger, but if you box him out and . . . get position on him. . . . So, a lot of times . . . I'm underneath the backboard . . . rebounding.[41]

Recognized for his athletic talent, Wong regularly graced the mainstream newspapers. The popular media consistently cast him as a positive example of the success of the liberal American racial project by presenting his Chinese American masculinity as comical and nonthreatening.[42] Although Chinese Americans were relatively invisible to the broader white community in the 1940s, Wong had some visibility in the mainstream press. This regional and national media attention included photographs, articles, and newspaper columns. In Northern California, all four of the daily San Francisco newspapers featured Wong. For example, sports journalist Bob Brachman of the *San Francisco Examiner* regularly highlighted Wong. Brachman, who wrote for the *Examiner's* sports department from 1936 to 1977, was considered a "leader in college sports reporting" and worked tirelessly for USF to receive recognition in the national basketball community.[43] Brachman supported Wong even before he joined the USF freshman team and the USF varsity team. For example, during the 1948 season, Brachman showcased Wong in at least six photographs and six headlines, devoting 80 percent of the text to praising Wong.[44] Helen Wong jokes: "Bob Brachman *(chuckles)* . . . used to write about my brother a lot. People [in Chinatown] use to kid that he was my brother's godfather, because he wrote so much [about Woo]."[45]

Wong received not just regional media attention, but also national exposure. As the defending champion, the USF team was of interest to the national basketball community. Newspapers often mentioned or interviewed Wong when USF played at places like Owensboro, Kentucky; Raleigh, North Carolina; and Buffalo, New York.[46] Wong reflects:

> They've never seen any Asians back then. . . . Everywhere I go. I don't know why they wanted to interview me. I mean we've got an all-American. We've got all these better players. They want to talk to me and so I was sort of a novelty to them or something. I go and this writer took me out to lunch and asked me these *(He chuckles.)* questions . . . like how did I enjoy my first plane ride and stuff. . . . I guess being an Asian is a little bit different especially back then.[47]

Mainstream media coverage of Wong bridged the 1940s when China was our World War II ally and the 1950s when Chinese communists were viewed as enemies. The wartime alliance and Madame Chiang Kai Shek's 1943 diplomatic tour of the United States fostered positive public opinion towards China. The goodwill ended with the 1949 communist revolution in China and the beginning of the cold war. In this context, the newspaper coverage of Woo in the late 1940s promoted America's successful racial experiment through novelty poses.

Newspaper photographs of the USF team were generally candid action shots or shots of all players posed in positions of authority.[48] By contrast, the photos of Woo usually showed him in a comical pose. They used novelty in a racialized version of the "Mutt and Jeff" style that once attracted newspapers photographers.[49] Beginning in the early 1900s and lasting until the early 1980s, the syndicated comic strip "Mutt and Jeff" featured the antics of two white working-class men whose clowning around was amplified by their height differences.[50] One newspaper photo shows Wong, perched on the shoulders of his USF teammates, putting the ball in the basket.[51] Newell remembers:

> The hardest time in New York that year was trying to help them get all the different pictures they wanted. . . . My star player, Dan Lofgren was six-six, and thin. He was a good basketball player. They wanted to take these publicity shots. Lofgran lifted Woo into the air. So Woo could dunk. He took three or five shots. Lofgran said "my arm is tired. . . . It was three P.M. and we were going to play later that night. And I said, "well do it with your left arm. Not your shooting arm." . . . I was afraid Willie might fall and get hurt.[52]

Another image depicts two teammates guarding Wong. The caption reads: "High-Low—Low man between the two USF totem poles is Willie Woo Woo Wong, 5 foot 4 inch . . . sophomore forward, being guarded by Don Lofgran 6 feet 6 and Joe McNamee 6 feet 5½."[53] A photo with the headline "Protect Woo-Woo" shows Lofgran and McNamee locking arms in front of Wong who crouches down in the back with a basketball.[54] Here, the motif of protection is used in two ways: (1) to praise Wong as valuable and worthy of protection and (2) to show that he needs protection, which implies that he is somehow weaker than the other players. Lofgran and McNamee stand tall in the foreground of the photo and peer out as if they are sentry guards for Wong. Their linked arms connote a form of solidarity among the white players while Wong stoops low beneath them. The caption also highlights the two interpretations of protection: "There are 18 feet, 4 inches of cagers in this group but Wee Willie Wong (Center) of USF makes up but a small part of the altitude total. The 5 feet, 4-inch sharpshooter is dwarfed by teammates Don Lofgran, left and Joe McNamee, both 6 feet 6 inches."[55] Although the text touts Wong as a "sharpshooter," it focuses on and racializes his height by employing a diminishing pun on his name—"Wee Willie Wong"—and by referencing his "smaller" contribution to the "altitude total" of the three depicted players.

The USF photos promoted American democracy by showing Chinese American Wong with his white male teammates. The postwar media depiction of Wong tried to make Chineseness comprehensible to mainstream Americans. Basketball demonstrated the "success" of liberalism, integration, and the grand vision of the American melting pot. In this moment, Wong symbolized the existence of racial harmony in the United States, where Chinese American men play basketball with white men. Through the sports pages, Chinese and Chinese Americans were no longer the predator, the heathen, and the immoral enemy of the 1920s, but rather the wartime ally of the 1940s and evidence of America's "successful" diversity project.

However, in this effort to show harmonious cross-racial interactions, the newspapers also inserted hierarchies between men of different races. What makes the USF photos "amusing" and "newsworthy" to some is the circus-like nature of the "dwarfed" Chinese American man competing in the white male domain of elite collegiate sports. Viewers could interpret these photographs as just fun. However, Wong's placement in the center of the photos makes his racial and height difference the clear focus. The racialized novelty in the photo resonated with the way mainstream media had portrayed Asian men since the 1880s. In this way, this advertisement for the game at Madison Square Garden also advertises the proper positioning of dominant masculinity as white and subordinated masculinity as Chinese.[56]

Although the mainstream newspapers showed Woo as an ethnic novelty, different portions of the Chinese community promoted Wong's sporting achievements for community uplift.[57] Wong had a presence in both regional and national Asian American communities. Chinese Americans across the country supported Wong when he played for USF. An article covering USF's game at Madison Square Garden describes the Chinese American pilgrimage to see Wong play:

> In this Big Town, Wong also has the distinction of being the first Chinese-American cager of varsity caliber ever to appear in Madison Square Garden. In a final game before coming East, Wong scored the last points to break the San Francisco team scoring record with his 80th digit. As in San Francisco, hundreds of Chinese-American sports fans in Gotham welcomed Wong at the Garden.[58]

Lavin, Wong's USF teammate and roommate, recalls how various communities across the United States honored Wong:

> Whatever city we went to—Philadelphia, New York, Buffalo, Chicago—of course, [the local Chinese American community gave] banquets for him all the time. . . . The mayor and all of them would give a banquet for him, and I'd come and I'd kid him. . . . At least between fifty and 100 [people attended]. It amazed me because . . . every town we went to, there'd be that kind of a turnout. So I guess the word was out. There were people ahead [planning this]—the mayor would be at them and they'd toast Willie and everything.[59]

Wong also enjoyed community support from across the country at the National Oriental Basketball Championship (NOBT). Led by Wong, the Saints won this competition two years in a row, and Wong was named most outstanding player in consecutive years.[60] The tournament's formal awards ceremony and dance at the Palladium Ballroom temporarily elevated Wong's socioeconomic status from working-class son of a grocery clerk and seamstress to a celebrated figure at an Asian American community event.[61]

In San Francisco, the Chinatown elite capitalized on the mainstream status of Wong and reinterpreted it for non-Chinese and Chinese audiences. They promoted him as a hero within their own narratives of what Chinese American masculinity represented in America. Beginning in 1901, the prestigious San Francisco Examiner-PA tournament brought together high school and former all-American college players.[62] With Wong's success, the Chinatown Chamber of Commerce convinced the tournament to designate the quarterfinal game as "Willie Wong night":

> The greatest LITTLE cager in Pacific Coast history, possibly in national annals, will get a reward tomorrow night at The Examiner-PA championships in Kezar Pavilion. A group of prominent San Francisco Chinese, recognizing Willie "Woo-Woo" Wong as a brilliant athlete and real ambassador of good will, have requested tomorrow night be designated as "Willie Wong Night," which tournament officials endorsed wholeheartedly.[63]

Like the popular press, the prominent San Francisco Chinese had a stake in Wong's image. Casting Wong as an ambassador of Chinese America, the Chinatown Chamber of Commerce utilized his fame in white communities as a form of ethnic and economic diplomacy. The Chinatown elite played up Wong's success in non-Chinese contexts to foster their own ethnic pride as well as to increase the exposure of Chinatown businesses. Charlie Low, the owner of the Chinatown nightclub Forbidden City, was known for promoting and selling orientalism to non-Chinese and made a presentation to Wong before the start of the feature game.[64] Dressed in a flashy double-breasted white suit, Low spoke into a microphone and made some remarks about a bashful Wong. As if he were conducting an elaborate wedding toast, Low ceremoniously presented Wong with a wristwatch and presented his teammates with matching sweaters. Before the game, in a festive occasion full of fanfare, the Saint Mary's Girls Drum Corps—a nationally renowned Chinatown performance group—electrified the crowd. Wearing Chinese headdresses and costumes, the fifty-plus performers played percussion while marching in various patterns and formations. This celebration had two distinct but related aims: to honor Wong and his accomplishments, and to exhibit a simultaneously exotic yet Americanized form of Chinese masculinity and femininity to the broader mainstream community. Both goals served to benefit Chinatown commerce and the community in some way.

Relations among China, Japan, and the United States were also influencing Chinese Americans at the time of Willie Wong night. Mao Zedong's 1949 communist revolution was on the verge of maturation as the U.S. government continued to expand the military industrial complex to fight communism at home and abroad. In this climate of fighting the "Red Menace," Chinese Americans were the focus of government surveillance, and some were eager to prove their loyalty to the United States—a desire amplified by the legacy of Japanese American imprisonment just a few years before during World War II.[65] English-language newspapers from San Francisco's Chinese American community featured front-page articles discussing these very issues. One series of columns featured the headline "I am an American." While mainstream newspapers used Wong to show proof of the success of America's "liberal" race experiment, some Chinese Americans also deployed Wong to demonstrate their Americanness and mollify suspicions of their having any communist leanings. For some Chinese and Chinese Americans, Willie Wong night demonstrated a sort of hyper-Americanness that they also wanted to achieve.[66]

As the Chinatown elite capitalized on the Americanized image of Wong, many working-class Chinatown residents saw Wong as asserting ethnic pride. When he played in San Francisco, the Chinese American community headed out in droves. Willie Wong night at the PA tournament recorded "one of the largest crowds in tournament history." The sold-out audience included over two hundred Asian spectators.[67] Although the Saints lost the game, the meaning of Wong to the Chinese community seemed to override any investment in winning or losing: "Disappointed as it was by the defeat of the underdog Chinese, the throng, composed mostly of Willie's followers from Chinatown, roared approval for fully five minutes after the action had been completed."[68] The festive atmosphere cultivated by the Chinese American community contrasted with the carnival treatment of Wong as a curiosity sideshow. Here praise, appreciation, and ethnic pride surrounded Wong.

Many of his peers treated Wong as a role model and followed his press coverage, saving newspaper clippings. They also saw him as a successful straight male athlete and a "catch" for a straight woman. Some forty years after he played for the San Francisco Chinese and USF, a female fan gave Wong's sister some pages from her old scrapbook. As a star-struck teenager, she had clipped photos of Wong from the *San Francisco Chronicle* and even had a small lock of his hair taped to one page. Another use of Wong's image to circulate ethnic and gender pride was a glossy handout with Wong's photo from USF on it (see Figure 4.2). Printed by Father Forrester of St. Mary's Mission in Chinatown, the leaflet is similar to a basketball trading card. The text in English and Chinese says "William 'Woo Woo' Wong of St. Mary's

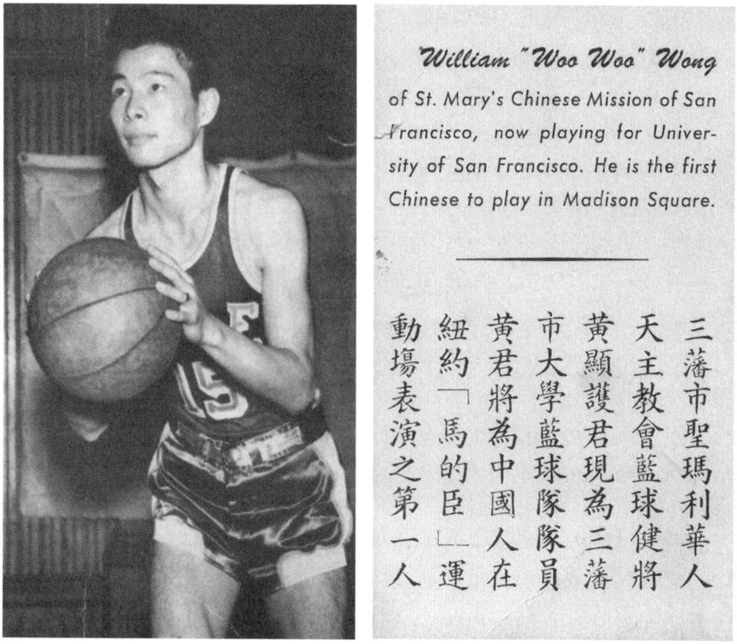

Figure 4.2 Bi-lingual Woo Wong trading card printed in blue ink on glossy paper. (*Jennie Wong Collection.*)

Chinese Mission of San Francisco, now playing for University of San Francisco. He is the first Chinese to play in Madison Square."[69] Although Forrester's motives for printing this advertisement are unknown, it solidified Wong as a sports figure among both English- and Chinese-speaking residents in Chinatown. The close-up image of Wong shooting a basket dramatically differs from the coverage at USF that replicates other trivializing depictions of Chinese American men in popular culture.

With his physical talent and success against much taller white men, Wong countered distorted media images of the Asian man as an effeminate and docile laundryman. Akin to what Joe Louis' career meant to the African American community, but on a smaller, more localized scale, Wong's success in basketball was a shared honor with the Chinese community. Louis, the "Brown Bomber," was the world heavyweight boxing champion from 1938 to 1942 and 1946 to 1948. In 1938, he knocked out self-proclaimed Nazi Max Schmeling in the first minutes of the first round to retain the world heavyweight title. While Louis was a symbol of American democracy's triumph over Nazism on the eve of World War II, his win also represented the success of a black man against a white man.[70] Likewise, Wong's success in basketball against whites proved that Chinese Americans were worthy of America and capable of victory in the hyper-masculine arena of basketball.[71] To Wong's Chinese American fans, he was a representative of the American dream, a symbol of Chinese talent and potential, and an example of the Chinese American male struggle against racial and gender barriers.

Wong broke ground in the field of athletics at a time of racial segregation, stratification, and discrimination. His story also provides insight into the interplay among the mainstream press, the Chinese American press, and Chinese American communities. Mainstream photos and newspaper articles used him to teach American melting pot discourse both by praising his ability to play sports in the United States and by framing him as a racial novelty. From the Chinese American community's perspective, the sporting icon was an accessible ideological tool to prove their ability to be American citizens. While mainstream America could interpret the Chinese American community's touting of a Chinese American male athlete as a sign of successful assimilation, the Chinese Americans could reposition the same body for both similar and different purposes. Under the cover of sports, the Chinese American community reinterpreted the popular depictions of Wong through their own media coverage and trading cards to serve their needs for racial pride, community uplift, an economic boost, and proof of Americanness in the context of red baiting. Wong's story illuminates the relationship between mainstream and community portrayals; it shows that popular media coverage cannot be cast as universally problematic and community depictions as singularly liberatory. The reframing within the community was not necessarily explicitly oppositional to mainstream depictions. Some images resonated with mainstream narratives of diversity and white male privilege. Others provided an alternative understanding of Chinese American masculinity.

Newell left USF after Wong's second year, and the new coach did not envision Wong as part of the USF team. Although Wong stopped competing on the elite college level, he continued to play basketball competitively. In 1948, China's Olympic team asked him to play, but a question of losing his U.S. citizenship thwarted the plans.[72] In the early 1950s, he continued to play for the San Francisco Saints off and on and competed in the Japanese American league tournaments.[73] He competed on a multiracial team in the semi-professional National Industrial Basketball League.[74] Playing for the Atlas-Pacific Engineers and with former all-American college players, Wong participated in the prestigious Amateur Athletic Union (AAU) national tournament.[75] He continued to play basketball into his forties and even participated in old-timer's leagues in San Francisco's Chinatown and in Newark in his sixties.

After Wong's passing, the Chinese Playground was renamed the Willie Woo Woo Playground and USF inducted Wong into its Athletic Hall of Fame.[76] When asked about his fame and athletic talent, Wong said: "I'm just a hamburger. . . . I happened to be at the right place at the right time."[77] In contrast to Wong's self-deprecating tone, a former USF teammate sums up Wong's basketball talent: "Some people would never be very good at [an] improvisational game . . . to have it in the degree that [Woo] had it . . . it is relatively rare and has to be a gift."[78]

5 / Helen Wong and the "Muscle Molls"

If you speak about Chinese American athletes with anyone who grew up in San Francisco's Chinatown in the 1940s, Helen Wong's name inevitably comes up. Wong was arguably one of the greatest athletes to come out of Chinatown before the 1960s. Regularly scoring over half of her basketball team's points, she led her integrated team to two championships in the predominately white Catholic Youth Organization (CYO) league. In tennis, Wong pulled down eleven national Chinese tennis tournament championships and competed as the Northern California representative in the prestigious junior Davis Cup competitions. Focusing on Helen Wong, this chapter explores how sports simultaneously strengthened subordinate roles for women after World War II and created socioeconomic mobility for working-class female athletes.

Born in 1931 in San Francisco, Wong was the daughter of immigrants who worked in a store and a garment factory. "My mother was very hardworking, she had multiple jobs—taking care of us, sewing, peeling shrimp, housecleaning. She was kind and gentle and nice. . . . My father was a clan elder. He was good at taking care of the village members who were here but he was very, very strict."[1] Her family of nine crowded into a small apartment above the Salvation Army on 12 Waverly Place. Without much money or much space at home, Helen Wong made the Playground a second home. "I grew up right in Chinatown. Across the street from the Chinese Playground . . . We played everything under the sun there—from jacks, to paddle ball . . . marbles, horseshoes . . . We didn't have money . . . So, we spent all of our time there."[2] Learning to play basketball at the Playground, Wong was the only one of the three girls in the family to play the sport. Her brothers Woo, George "Wee," and Hank competed for the San Francisco Saints and coached their sister. "My brothers were talented basketball players. They each had different personalities and they each had their own specialty in basketball. So it was good combination. Even though, it could get interesting at times. (*She chuckles.*) You know, coached by three of your brothers. (*She laughs.*)"[3] Woo Wong, the famed USF basketball player, reflects: "My sister was a natural athlete." Hank Wong explains: "[My sister] had a good sense of the court. She knew how to move and had a good eye."[4] Known as a sharpshooter, Helen Wong won many shooting contests, such as at the 1949 *San Francisco Examiner* basketball camp:

> We now know why the kids out in Chinatown were telling us, "Wait until you see Willie "Woo Woo" Wong's sister, Helen." . . . Shooting from all angles . . . , the young Chinese miss proceeded to mesh seventeen out of eighteen attempts. All were one-handed shots. Then, without stopping, she moved to the free throw line where she banged through twenty in a row, touching the rim only once! . . . After Helen had run her string of free tosses to thirty-two for a grand total of 40 out of 51 shots and received a thundering

> ovation from the hundreds of pop-eyed kids, (one coach) shook his head again and declared, "I still can't believe it." . . . What made the performance all the more remarkable was that Helen was shooting into almost blinding sunlight streaming down through the high Armory windows.[5]

At the camp, Wong caught the attention of famed college basketball player and coach Hank Luisetti. Wong remembers: "I had made about twenty in a row and the camp's coach, basketball great Hank Luisetti, just told me to keep shooting. So, I did. (*She smiles.*)"[6]

Wong honed her skills playing for the Saint Mary's Saints, competing in Catholic school leagues.[7] As a shooting forward, she would regularly sink twenty points in one game. This was impressive given that scores for one game ranged from twenty to forty points for an entire team.[8] With teammates such as Lucille Chong, Lillian Ong, and Jacqueline Yee, the Saints qualified for San Francisco girls' CYO championship playoffs four years in a row, from 1946 to 1949, and brought home titles in 1947 and 1949.[9] In three seasons, the Saints won every game except one.[10] They regularly walloped other teams, outscoring them by over forty points. This was a real feat in games that lasted less than an hour, were governed by restrictive girls' rules, and had no three-point shots (see Figure 5.1).[11]

In addition to league play, Wong and the Chinese Saints participated in exhibition games against high school and amateur women's teams, such as the Hamilton Women's Air Force Service quintet, the Letterman hospital WACs, and the Treasure Island Waves.[12] The exhibition games were held at large venues like Kezar Pavilion as well as in front of crowds ranging anywhere from six hundred to eight hundred people. Beyond competing against white opponents in the CYO league and for exhibition games, Wong and her St. Mary's teammates also played against

Figure 5.1 The championhsip St. Mary's Saints team. Helen Wong Lum is kneeling and in the middle. (*Helen Wong Lum Collection.*)

Japanese American teams, such as the Berkeley Stardusters and the Nisei Rogues.[13]

Wong and her teammates chose to join the Saints because it was one of the few organized teams for Chinese girls and it provided public recognition. Although the Saints represented a Catholic parish, the girls were not as concerned about or interested in the religious affiliation as they were about the opportunity to play basketball.[14] Success provided the young Chinese American women on the team with recognition. At the end of the season, they participated in the formal awards banquet consisting of a dinner, team and individual awards, and entertainment. Local newspapers covered the banquet, making the players visible to the community at large.[15] As captain of the Saints, Wong was called to the stage in front of two hundred people to receive the trophy from the San Francisco archdiocesan youth director.[16] Although more resources were available for Chinese American women basketball players in the 1940s than in the previous decade, basketball opportunities for all women were limited in the late 1940s. Women could compete in industrial leagues, but college and professional basketball opportunities were much scarcer. For that reason, Wong decided to focus on tennis in high school and in college.[17] Despite her basketball achievements, Wong found that sports considered more refined and "ladylike" offered more opportunity.

At the Pacific Coast Chinese Tennis Championship and the National Chinese tennis tournaments, Wong won consecutive tennis titles in singles, doubles, and mixed doubles.[18] San Francisco's Chinese Tennis Club hosted these tournaments, drawing players from all over the United States as well as from countries like Canada and Peru. In mainstream tennis competitions, Wong stood out as much for her skills as for her race.[19] For all four years of high school, she won San Francisco's singles and doubles championships.[20] She also captured the under-sixteen Northern California novice tennis championship.[21] On the tennis court, Wong was famous for her strong combination of mental and physical skills. Described by Chinatown residents as "poetry in motion" and "an outstanding athlete," Wong reflects on her tennis game: "Some of it is God-given talent. I was also very disciplined. But most of it is up here. *(She points to head.)* I wasn't that big or strong; I couldn't play an aggressive power game. I went for shot placement."[22]

As a child of a working-class family, Wong was able to learn and compete in tennis only because many people of different racial backgrounds helped her gain access to the sport. The only public court in Chinatown was opened to her for practice, and the Chinese Playground staff assisted Wong: "Paul Whang, one of the Playground directors, got me started on tennis. He use to practice with me after school. And Lillian Yuen, another director, was nice to me also—she use to hit with me too, found a secondhand racquet for me and bought me a sweater and tennis socks, when I couldn't afford it."[23] Father Forrester, the director of St. Mary's Catholic Mission in Chinatown and coach of the St. Mary's Saints basketball team, provided a great deal of mentorship for Wong.[24] "[Father Forrester] got me professional tennis lessons through Mr. Charles Harney, who was the gentleman who built Candlestick

Park. Mr. Harney paid for my lessons [for about a year]."[25] In addition to equipment, training, and practice space, tennis players also needed money for entry fees, lodging, food, and transportation when they competed. Competing away from home also required taking time off from work. "Father [Forrester] used to drive me to tournaments because I couldn't afford the bus fare. And then once or twice he had to approach them for an entrance fee, which in those days it was only about one dollar to three dollars. But if you don't have it, you don't have it."[26] Wong also remembers receiving help from one of the staff members of the Northern California Tennis Association (NCTA): "Mrs. Grabler, she always made sure I was fed. She was a good woman. . . . [B] ecause of the tournaments, you travel and need lunch money. I didn't have that. So she always made sure I ate."[27]

Wong's success in sports exposed her to towns outside of San Francisco and to more upscale living than her family's cramped apartment in Chinatown. Wong recalls: "One interesting trip was going to Santa Barbara. . . . And, I mean, wholly mackerel. . . . It was gorgeous. And what impressed me (*She chuckles.*) . . . was . . . when I went to the bathroom . . . the Kotex was free! I mean they had it out there for you. I said 'my god!' Boy, was I impressed! (*She laughs.*)"[28]

Wong received extensive coverage in the ethnic-based press, which emphasized her athleticism and did not trivialize her as a woman.[29] Photographs in the ethnic-based newspapers depicted her in positions of strength or authority.[30] For example, in an article on the National Chinese Tennis Championships, Wong looks directly at the camera while dressed in athletic wear and standing side-by-side with male athletes.[31] In addition, several Chinese-language newspapers showed Wong in action shots, either hitting a tennis ball or drawing a diagram as a basketball coach.[32] Interestingly, the other sections of the Chinese community newspaper depicted women in more passive roles, whereas the sports section treated women as athletes. The English- and Chinese-language newspapers from the community simply reported Wong's wins without references to her femininity.[33] For example, in a 1950 English-language community newspaper column, H. K. Wong, the self-described "mayor of Chinatown" and one of the cofounders of the Chinese Tennis Association and the Chinese Historical Society of America, writes:[34]

> Helen Wong of S.F. garnered the National Women's Singles crown. . . . With her family and a galaxy of friends to cheer her on, she defeated Sylvia Gee of S.F. 6–4, 6–1 for her 6th consecutive title. Miss Wong won her 1st title when she was 16. The titlist's all around game proved too much for young (16 years old) Miss Gee. Miss Gee is the first girl to get 5 games from Helen in a National final. Helen hasn't dropped a set in the last 6 years of her championship play.[35]

At the 1948 Chinatown Basketball Festival, the promoters referred to Wong only in relation to her basketball skills.[36] Sponsored by the Catholic Chinese Veterans, the basketball festival was San Francisco's counterpart to the National Oriental American Basketball Tournament held in Seattle. Held at Kezar Stadium, it featured games between Woo Wong's San Francisco Saints and the University of San Francisco Freshman Team and between Helen Wong's Chinese Girl Saints and the Treasure Island Waves. Advertising Helen Wong's team as "Truly the Best Girls' Team in the City" and "display[ing] some of the best girls basketball playing ever seen in this area," the program listed each player with a few details about his or her style of play. The Chinatown program uses gender-neutral language, describing Wong as a "terrific sharpshooter, speedy, and clever, led [team] to the Catholic Girls High School League championship in 1947." Treating the male and female athletes equally, the program emphasized basketball skills describing Helen Wong's teammates and opponents with phrases like "clever defensive player," "smooth ball-handler," and "dependable all-around guard."[37]

Wong was as a role model for other Chinatown youths. At a senior center event, Wong was introduced to a Chinese American woman who had grown up in San Francisco's Chinatown and was a few years younger than Wong. The woman effusively talked about how she looked up to Wong as a child, dutifully tracking Wong's accomplishments and saving newspaper articles about her. A few years ago, Wong met a former Playground youth: "He grew up at the Playground and was younger than me. He was so kind. He said I was his idol, watching me play and reading about me in the newspapers. (*She laughs.*) Now he is an orthopedic surgeon. Needless to say, I was tickled to hearing that from such an accomplished grown man. (*She laughs.*)"[38]

In the late 1940s, when Wong hit her stride, mainstream media coverage of her reflected the postwar reconstruction of women as subordinate to men. During World War II, women entered the blue-collar defense industry in larger numbers to replace male workers who were in military service. Although some women wanted to remain in the workforce, these public wage-earning roles for women generally were considered a temporary wartime necessity, and women were expected to return to their homemaking roles when the soldiers came home and reclaimed their jobs.[39] The 1940s mainstream photographs show Wong in the background, gazing at a man in the forefront.

Reinforcing conventional ideas about women playing only supportive roles after the war, graphics and photos in the mainstream newspapers treated women as adornments to men.[40] For example, in a *San Francisco Examiner* advertisement for the St. Mary's Catholic School fundraising bazaar, Wong looks at famed San Francisco 49er quarterback Frankie Albert, who is the focal point of the image.[41] Albert's placement slightly in front of Wong enhances his larger size, and their interaction seems somewhat flirtatious. Wong's athleticism is stripped away to fabricate a playful, sexual encounter.

In another photo advertising the St. Mary's Catholic School fundraiser, Albert occupies the forefront, while Wong and Constance Gong, another Chinese American basketball player, gaze at him.[42] The positioning of the three subjects exaggerates the size differences by magnifying Albert's physical dominance. Similarly, Albert's football uniform connotes authority and power, whereas the young women's dress clothes erase their athletic identities. This picture also very clearly marks the "proper" expression of race in connection to femininity. Both Wong and Gong are American-born Chinese, yet Wong wears "Western" dress, and Gong sports an exotic cheongsam. They become symbols of "Western" and "Eastern" femininity, respectively. Wong looks at Albert longingly from the background of the photo, but he does not return her attention, making direct eye contact with Gong, who smiles back at him. Thus, this image seems to represent the triumph of the traditional Chinese girl in winning the attention of the white male. Ironically, the heading for the photograph reads "Prize for Bazaar." While the image is supposed to advertise the raffle prize of a football signed by Albert, it also suggests that Albert's attention or Gong herself might be a prize. Either way, the dominant white man returns the gaze of the small "China doll" rather than the Americanized Chinese girl. Here, Chinese or an orientalized femininity trumps Westernized Chinese American femininity. The photo implies that, to be more desirable to white men, Chinese American women need to do more than meet Western standards of femininity; to be the coveted "prize," they need to be "China dolls."

After the Second World War, the sports pages followed, and thereby encouraged, the cultural script for two opposing roles of female athletes: the ladies and the muscle molls. Babe Didrikson, the most visible female athlete of the time, was both lauded for her tremendous athletic talent and criticized as uncouth and unfeminine. In 1911, Didrikson was born into a large working-class family in Texas. From 1930 to 1932, she led her team, the Cyclones, to two Amateur Athletic Union (AAU) basketball championships and received AAU all-American honors in women's basketball. For the next two years, she barnstormed around the country, playing professional basketball with the Babe Didrikson's All-Americans.[43] In the 1932 Olympics, Didrikson broke three world records and won gold medals in the javelin and hurdles and a silver medal in the high jump. In 1943, she won seventeen consecutive golf tournaments, including the British Women's Amateur Championship. Between 1932 and 1954, the Associated Press named her the Female Athlete of the Year six times, and in 1950, the Associated Press voted her "Woman Athlete of the Half Century."

The media coverage of Didrikson's sporting achievements in the 1930s and 1940s provides an important context for the way mainstream media framed Wong's athleticism. Didrikson played up her Texan drawl and brought a flip and wisecracking personality to golf.[44] For example, she shocked the golf community when she started a golf game saying, "Well, I'm just gonna have to loosen my girdle and let 'er fly." The media often portrayed her as mannish and uncouth; an example is a 1932 *Vanity Fair* article labeling Didrikson a"muscle moll."[45] Didrikson seemed to enjoy her clashes with middle-class cultural ideals of femininity, but she paid a price for publicly subverting the conventional views of how women should act. The United States Golf Association barred Didrikson from amateur golf tournaments on a technicality. With her career on the line, Didrikson attempted a very public makeover in the fall of 1935, wearing more dresses, makeup, jewelry, and silk stockings in public appearances. In December 1938, she married George Zaharias, a wealthy wrestling celebrity. Publicity photographs showed her in activities that were deemed appropriately feminine, such as wearing an evening gown, cooking and having tea by the fireplace.[46] Her very public performance of heteronormative and middle-class femininity allowed her to continue her lucrative athletic career and her private lesbian relationships. Because she passed as a feminine role model, the sporting establishment forgave what it perceived as her past indiscretions and disregard for dominant ideas of how women should behave.

The mainstream media portrayed the younger Wong as a gifted athlete who was a lady. Mainstream newspapers referred to her with diminutives, such as "young lady," "young miss," and "young girl," contrasting her with what was "freakish" or somehow outside the dominant standard of heterosexual femininity.[47] One newspaper reporter wrote: "Helen is also tennis champion of the Chinese colony, though she isn't big enough to be rated a muscle moll or Amazon."[48] A sports column from the *San Francisco Chronicle* covering Wong's tennis championship distances Wong from the infamous Babe:

> The ladies' champ is Helen Wong, a sort of Celestial Babe Didrikson and sister of Woo-Woo Wong, the USF basketballer. Helen was so gifted in all forms of athletics that she was deemed a muscle moll. *Actually* [emphasis added], she is a little gal and now is a lady of substance. She was graduated from the College of the Holy Names in Oakland and took teaching credentials at S.F. State.[49]

The columnist noted that others called Wong a "muscle moll," but he assured the reader that Wong's education and teaching career proved her to be appropriately feminine. The columnist depicted Wong as the "good Chinese girl," a gendered version of the model minority. The model minority myth emerged to diffuse civil rights unrest in the 1960s by driving a wedge between groups of color. The media characterized Asian Americans—particularly East Asians—as obedient hard workers and role models for overcoming hardship and "pulling yourself up by your bootstraps."[50] While the columnist praises Wong's accomplishments, he almost pats Wong on the head for symbolizing appropriate female athleticism and well-behaved, nonwhite femininity.

Unable to reconcile the cultural conception of femininity with physically athletic or muscular women, 1940s sports reporters struggled to situate talented female athletes in the mainstream models. Susan Birrell and Nancy Theberge write that "sexual labeling is a potent weapon in the social control of women in sport," where "the representation of women athletes [is] either as highly attractive by heterosexual standards or overly masculine."[51] As did the women's basketball rules discussed in Chapter 3, reporters emphasized two models of the female body and ascribed values to them. Athletic women were either highly refined ladies or freaks. While this duality is a social fabrication, the media always presented the differences between misses and amazons as biological.[52] The phrase "muscle moll" suggests a link between these models and sexuality. As M. A. Hall writes, "in reality femininity was a thinly disguised code word for heterosexuality. The real issue behind so much attention to an athlete's femininity was the fear that she might be a lesbian."[53] Susan Brownmiller notes: "Femininity must constantly reassure . . . that, no matter their accomplishments, women athletes are still 'just girls' underneath. Successful women athletes risk being labeled 'mannish,' with generally unspoken implications of lesbianism close to the surface."[54] The muscle molls might be mistaken for lesbians and ruin their chances of attracting men—or worse, they might be lesbians.[55]

The mainstream media depictions of Helen Wong as a lady echoed the 1940s portrayals of visible Chinese and Chinese American women as middle-class, feminine, and committed to public service. Margaret Chung, the first-known Chinese American woman physician and a prominent public figure during the 1930s and 1940s, stands out as an example. Called "Mom Chung," she created a surrogate family for hundreds of American soldiers fighting in the war, cooking dinners in her San Francisco home every Sunday for seventy-five to a hundred Allied soldiers home from the war. As a result of her home-cooked meals, letters, and care packages, Chung was hailed as the good, patriotic woman who cared for Allied fighting forces. Newspapers, magazines, and even a comic book made her visible to mainstream America because she legitimated and exemplified the caring middle-class female figure.[56]

Similarly, Madame Mayling Soong 's fame during the early 1940s redefined America's ideas of Chinese womanhood as educated, Christian, and dedicated to public good. Soong, wife of wartime China's Nationalist leader Generalissimo Chiang Kai-Shek, helped educate Americans about China and the U.S.-China wartime alliance during the early 1940s. Influenced by Christian parents and missionaries in Shanghai, she came to the United States at the age of nine and later attended Wellesley College. Advocating for "American-style, middle class reforms" in China, Soong promoted hygiene, manners, and education for orphans during the Sino-Japanese War.[57] In speeches and writings published in English-language Chinese newspapers, she argued in favor of Chinese women taking "public roles as moral housekeepers and mothers of the nation" in what historian Karen Leong calls "national housekeeping."[58] To the American public, Soong represented the ideal modern woman who preserved her femininity while at the same time taking a public maternal role in helping others. While Wong's media attention occurred after Chung's and Soong's, her portrayal resembled their depictions in American newspapers and the overall mainstream push for middle-class norms of femininity. All three were framed in ways that highlighted the virtues of middle-class femininity; and all were all cast as nurturers and caretakers.

For Wong, basketball and tennis were avenues toward upward mobility. Because of her success in athletic arenas, recruiters offered her college scholarships and financial aid. The only person in her family to earn a bachelor's degree, she graduated from the

College of the Holy Names as part of the first class to study physical education.[59] Wong worked multiple jobs to pay for college and received financial help from her sisters. She taught tennis at Holy Names in lieu of paying tuition and worked nights at the Chinese Playground to cover the cost of books and transportation. She also lived at home and commuted to save money. Considering the substantial economic and social barriers that working-class Chinese American women faced in the 1940s, Wong's leap into college and a career in teaching was as unusual as the mainstream media coverage of her sporting achievements.[60] Wong taught subjects like physical education and Mandarin in the San Francisco public school district. One of the few Asian teachers at secondary level, she was in the forefront of integrating the faculty and staff in San Francisco public schools. In 1968, Wong became the first Asian American counselor and the second minority staff person in the counseling department at San Francisco City College.[61]

Wong's career in coaching, teaching, and counseling allowed her to mentor youth in the same way Father Forrester and the Chinese Playground staff had mentored her. Wong coached the Blue Stars, a girls' basketball team at the Playground. One of the twenty players on that team, Norma Lee Hom, reflects: "We learned how to work with other people. We learned how to be competitive . . . and how to give and take."[62] In addition, the girls coached by Helen Wong found support as young athletic women.[63] Jennie Chong Jue, a Blue Stars player, explains: "[The Blue Stars and Helen Wong] were pretty well-rounded. Sure, there were some girls that were boy-crazy. *(She laughs.)* We liked boys too but we also liked basketball. It was our outlet. . . . There was camaraderie. We supported each other."[64] Jane Chew Wong describes Helen Wong's impact on her as a young female athlete: "Participating [on the team] enabled many of us to . . . broaden our perspective of the world and enrich our lives . . . helped fight the old stereotypes; [and made us believe] that women can be whatever they want to be with no set parameters. . . . We owe a vote of thanks to . . . Helen Wong for what [she] taught and gave us—caring and strong leadership—and for showing us what women can really do or be."[65]

In addition to coaching, Wong felt pulled toward teaching. While she had an illustrious athletic career, she remembers her teaching experiences most vividly:

> Dorothy Ong Quock . . . was a former student of mine. She teaches at Lowell High School now. I had her about thirty odd years ago. Well, she called me up one day and she said "I'd like to invite you to a dinner." And it turned out that she was getting an award that night for being an outstanding educator. When she went up to receive her award she acknowledged me publicly. And that's why she wanted me there. It . . . was so . . . touching.[66]

Wong utilized the opportunities sports brought her to obtain a career that offered both socioeconomic stability and a chance to nourish her interest in public service:

> I believe that whatever God has given you—you should share your talents. I guess I felt I had something to share with my athletic skills. And that's why I wanted to go into PE. I guess basically to share. And you . . . do that in counseling, because you're sharing your experiences with your kids. . . . I view my role as an educator . . . much more than having won these championships.[67]

In 1992, after Wong retired, she and a group of friends created the Father Donald F. Forrester Sports Fund. Because of Forrester's support of her and other young female Chinese athletes, Wong wanted to create an organization to honor his legacy and also "encourage and help young women athletes engage in competitive sports."[68]

In the 1980s, at an age when most people start thinking about retirement, Wong won many national singles titles. In 1986, when she was fifty-five, she won her first national championship at the National Senior Indoor Tennis Tournament. That same year, she also captured the National Senior Hard Court Championship. She then went on to win a total of seven national singles and doubles titles in senior competition.[69] In 1988, she became one of seven women—and the first Chinese American—inducted into the San Francisco Prep Hall of Fame; and she was one of four women inducted into the Northern California United States Tennis Association (USTA) Hall of Fame.

Although Wong won a roomful of trophies and awards, her parents did not get the opportunity to ever see her play: "They were so busy working. Neither of them saw me play tennis or basketball. They weren't against it, which was good. They were just too busy. . . . I remember the day I won my first trophy. I just left it on the kitchen table. And later, I saw my mother sort of pick it up. And she smiled quietly."[70]

Helen Wong broke many barriers, achieving tremendous success in sports. Her lifetime of athletic accomplishments, however, is only part of the story. The sports media coverage in the United States reinforced a model of "ladylike" femininity, and Wong moved within these confines but ultimately transcended them to attain middle-class status and assist others.

Conclusion: The Chinese Playground and Yao Ming in the Era of Globalized Sports

On a sunny, crisp Saturday afternoon in 2002, hundreds of families streamed into Chinatown for the Chinese Playground's seventy-fifth anniversary celebration at the Chinese Recreational Center.[1] Past participants from the Chinese Playground made the pilgrimage from the suburbs to their old stomping ground. A photo exhibit documenting the decades of play, friendship, and connection snaked around the gym. The din reached a fever pitch as people recognized long-lost friends, past mentors, and bygone crushes. A potent alchemy of giddiness, joy, and melancholy permeated the space. People entering the building stopped to greet Paul Whang, director of the Chinese Playground from the 1940s to the 1970s. A second father to generations of young people, Whang was filled with wonder as he located remnants of the young kids in the adult faces.

More than seventy-five years after opening its gates, the Playground still stirs a sense of connection between the staff members and the adults who played there as children. Since the late 1940s, basketball has retained its role as the social glue in Chinatown. Even now, the annual basketball tournament is a huge multigenerational draw. While elementary school kids learn to dribble at basketball summer camps, middle-aged players live for their weekly Chinese American old-timers pickup games. The same St. Mary's Catholic Center that provided a venue for Helen Wong's basketball talent continued to dominate the girls' Catholic Youth Organization league in the late 1990s.

While the athletes featured in this book can no longer pivot, run, and leap, their bodies and spirits remember their special moves on the court and the sweet spot on the backboard. Although they know their time on the court is over, these Chinatown athletes are now avid fans, tracking their favorite basketball players, such as Yao Ming. With great fanfare, Yao was drafted in the National Basketball Association (NBA) as the Houston Rockets' number-one pick in 2002.[2] A five-time NBA all-star, he recently signed a five-year extension contract with the Rockets for an estimated $12 million.[3] My ninety-three-year-old grandmother, who played forward for the Mei Wahs, ardently follows Yao's career, deftly using the remote to flip between network and cable television to find Yao's games. Like the other Chinatown athletes in this book, she connects to Yao in several ways, seeing Yao's experiences in the NBA as an unprecedented opportunity for Chinese and Chinese Americans in mainstream America and as a contemporary example of racial prejudice in sports.

Born and raised in Shanghai, China, Yao is seen by the NBA and other business ventures as an economic entrée into China. Casting Yao as a bridge between two cultures and two sets of consumers, American businesses salivate over growing markets in China, and Chinese companies eye American businesses. Tapped for his global marketability, Yao signed multiyear endorsement contracts with companies such as Nike, Visa, McDonald's, and Gatorade. In addition to signing a high-profile endorsement deal in Asia for telecom company China Unicom Ltd, Yao partnered with 24-Hour Fitness to open gyms in mainland China.[4] With an estimated 300 million people in China playing basketball, the NBA credits the increasing popularity of basketball in China to Yao. NBA commissioner David Stern comments: "That's why Wal-Mart is in [China]. Best Buy is in, GM is building cars, American Express is investing. It's why Coca-Cola is there, Nike, McDonald's. It's because of what China is, an emerging market with an enormous population and an enormous love for basketball."[5] In a country of 1.3 billion people with a rising Chinese middle class, the NBA projects increasing numbers of Chinese basketball players, fans, and consumers.[6]

The first non-American sports figure to be mass marketed to American audiences by the NBA, Yao is cast as a likable figure for the non-Chinese American public.[7] However, similar to the media treatment of Helen Wong, the mainstream media portray Yao as an exemplary ethnic athlete. In mainstream U.S. media outlets, he is depicted as well-mannered with a sense of social responsibility: living with his parents, supporting the Special Olympics World Games, and donating $2 million in the wake of the devastating 2008 earthquake in China.[8] A global marketing executive from McDonald's explains: "Yao has international appeal and also represents the character of our brand. He's youthful, dynamic and has a sense of humour. He's also very caring."[9] The media's praise of Yao's wholesomeness is not necessarily significant by itself. However, when it frames Yao's morality as a counterpoint to supposedly "spoiled" and "misbehaving" African American players, it evokes the racial divide-and-conquer tactics of the model minority myth.[10]

Chinese communities view Yao as an idol, albeit as a hero to communities in both China and the United States. In 2005, the Chinese government named Yao the "vanguard worker," an award given every five years to an exemplary Chinese worker. Hailed as the largest global audience for NBA games, Chinese in China support Yao by watching games televised on over twenty-four stations including China's national network, China Central Television. In 2007, more than 250 million Chinese television viewers, almost as many as the total population of the United States, watched Yao go head-to-head against Yi Jianlian, a 2007 draft pick for the NBA's Milwaukee Bucks and a Chinese Basketball Association star.[11] For many Chinese, Yao represents their country's ascendance in the international scene as an ambassador for the Chinese people.[12] One Shanghai shipping agent explains: "I am proud that Yao is very talented and can show his skills in the NBA. And I am even more proud that Yao is showing that we Chinese are good, polite people."[13] When the Houston Rockets played the Golden State Warriors in Yao's first season, the Oakland Coliseum in Northern California boasted a season-high crowd of 18,401.[14] Asian and Asian American families enthusiastically posed for photos with a life-size cardboard photo of Yao. With a mixture of signs in English and Chinese bobbing up and down, the boisterous sold-out crowd roared as Yao and his teammates entered the main floor to warm up. Kids and adults alike descended to the floor, hoping for an autograph from Yao.

Although Yao is Chinese from Shanghai, many American-born Chinese feel empowered by him. He defies America's image of emasculated Asian males and provides an alternate version of Asian masculinity to mainstream audiences. One journalist describes Yao's toughness: "With a wave of his long fingers, [Yao] dared 2-m guard Prosper Karangwa to attack the basket during a two-on-one break- whereupon Yao hip-checked Karangwa a good 10 feet, bruising the Canadian's ribs so badly that he required a flak jacket throughout the rest of the [basketball tournament]. Make no mistake, Yao is not a gentle giant."[15] Like Woo Wong and the Hong Wah Kues, Yao means something to Chinese American communities—representing a strong Chinese masculinity in the hypermasculine world of competitive basketball.

Gracing the covers of *Sports Illustrated, ESPN,* and *Slam* magazines, Yao Ming takes the visibility of Chineseness to higher level.[16] At the same time he is splashed across major media outlets as an amiable guy, he has been racialized as foreign. On June 28, 2002, Shaquille O'Neal appeared on FoxSportNet's *Best Damn Sports Show Period.* When asked about playing Yao, O'Neal responded by mocking the Chinese language, making faux kung fu gestures, and saying he would like to take an elbow to Yao's face.[17] In a December 2002 appearance on a national radio show, O'Neal responded to a similar question by saying: "Tell Yao Ming, 'ching-chong-yang-wah-ah-soh.'" Like the cartoon depiction of the Hong Wah Kues speaking broken English, Yao and Chinese culture are portrayed as inscrutably foreign. The radio host continued to rebroadcast O'Neal's audio clip and invited listeners to call in with jokes making fun of Chinese.[18] Although the audience is much larger for Yao than it was for the Chinatown athletes featured in this book, goading radio listeners to use anti-Chinese sentiment as entertainment is not far from the 1930s posters advertising the Hong Wah Kues as the "foreign invaders."

Many in the Chinese American community, including the national Organization of Chinese Americans (OCA) and Chinese for Affirmative Action, called for an apology from O'Neal and the NBA. O'Neal said his comments were merely jokes, but he made overtures to Yao, who accepted the apology. Many Chinese Americans situated O'Neal's remarks against the history of anti-Asian prejudice.[19] In a 2003 an editorial critiquing O'Neal, Irwin Tang explains: "Forgive my bitterness. I grew up in Texas, facing those 'ching-chong' taunts daily while teachers averted their ears."[20] For many, O'Neal's remarks amplified their experiences of marginalization in America as Chinese Americans. Charlene Tsang-Kao, president of the Greater Houston chapter of the OCA, reflects: "We as Asian-Americans were born here and live here and have felt the impact of statements by Shaquille O'Neal. We've heard it on the playgrounds, we've heard it in all walks of life. I don't think he [Yao] should have done anything different. But as Asian-Americans we should speak out."[21]

The O'Neal incidents and subsequent community outcry highlight the multiple pressures Yao faces as a Chinese athlete in the NBA and illustrate how ethnic communities use basketball as a form of empowerment—whether as Chinese Americans fans viewing Yao as a rallying point or as the San Francisco Chinatown athletes featured in this book playing basketball as a creative response to oppressive circumstances. In almost every interview, the players talked about Yao. He has particular meaning for them as people who grew up at a time when Chinese Americans were expected to live and work in only one part of town. They devotedly track his career with a critical eye and with empathy. In some ways, Yao intrigues them because he is a Chinese who broke many barriers; and he reminds them of talented Chinese American players who never had the opportunity to play professionally. Yet, watching Yao connects them to something larger than basketball; he reminds them of obstacles still facing Chinese and Chinese Americans, and he nourishes their hope for change.

Notes

Introduction

1. Michael Lee, Interview by author, tape recording, San Francisco, CA, 31 May 2004.

2. Michael Lee interview, 31 May 2004.

3. Chinese Historical Society of America, *The Third Annual Celebration of Roots: Two Steps Forward—Chinese Americans in Sports* (San Francisco: Author, 1996); Joel S. Franks, *Crossing Sidelines, Crossing Cultures: Sport and Asian Pacific American Cultural Citizenship* (Lanham, MD: University Press of America, 2000);"Sports," *Chinese Digest*, 4 September 1936, 13.

4. Among them were the Chicago Huskies, the San Francisco Filipino Mango Athletic Club, the Denver Yamato, the Los Angeles Korean Christian Association, the Oahu-based Asahis, and the Poston Internment Camp Three all-star women's softball team. Dan Cisco, *Hawaii Sports: History, Facts, and Statistics* (Honolulu: University of Hawaii Press, 1999); "Filipino Rassler Now Favorite," *San Francisco Chronicle*, 27 April 1948, 3H; Kerry Yo Nakagawa, *Diamonds in the Rough: Zeni and the Legacy of Japanese-American Baseball* (Los Angeles: Nissei Baseball Research Project, 2000); Brian Niiya, Azuma Eiichiro, and the Japanese American National Museum, *More Than a Game: Sport in the Japanese American Community* (Los Angeles: Japanese American National Museum, 2000); Samuel O. Regalado, "Incarcerated Sport: Nisei Women's Softball and Athletics during Japanese American Internment," *Journal of Sport*

History 27, no. 3 (Fall 2000): 431–444; Samuel O. Regalado, "Sport and Community in California's Japanese American Yamato Colony, 1930–1945," *Journal of Sport History* 19, no. 2 (Summer 1992): 130–143.

5. Louis Fiset, "Nikkei Life in the Northwest: Photographic Impressions," *Pacific Northwest Quarterly* 91, no.1 (1999–2000): 25–41; Azuma Eiichiro Kikumura, Darcie C. Iki, and Japanese American National Museum, *The Kona Coffee Story: Along the Hawaii Belt Road*, (Los Angeles: Japanese American National Museum, 1995); Rebecca Chiyoko King, "Eligible to Be Japanese American: Counting on Multiraciality in Japanese American Basketball Leagues and Beauty Pageants," in *Contemporary Asian American Communities: Intersections and Divergences*, eds. Linda Trinh Vo and Rick Bonus (Philadelphia: Temple University Press, 2002), 120–133; Huping Ling, *Surviving on the Gold Mountain: A History of Chinese American Women and Their Lives* (Albany, NY: State University of New York Press, 1998), 98; Albert Alvin Lowe, "Reading Asian American Representations: Race and Sport in an International Frame" (Ph.D. diss., University of California San Diego, 2000); Diane Mei Lin Mark and Ginger Chih, *A Place Called Chinese America* (Dubuque, IA: Kendall Hunt Pub. Co., 1982); David Mayeda, "From Model Minority to Economic Threat: Media Portrayals of Major League Baseball Pitchers Hideo Nomo and Hideki Irabu," *Journal of Sport and Social Issues* 23 (May 1999): 203–217; Michael L. Mullan, "Ethnicity and Sport: The Wapato Nippons and Pre-World War II Japanese American Baseball," *Journal of Sport History* 26, no. 1 (1999): 82–114; Michael L. Mullan, "Sport, Ethnicity, and the Reconstruction of the Self: Baseball in America's Internment Camps," *International Journal of the History of Sport* 16, no. 1 (1999): 1–21; Kesa Noda, *Yamato Colony: 1906–1960 Livingston, California* (Livingston, CA: Livingston-Merced JACL Chapter, 1981); Haruo Nogawa, "A Study of a Japanese-American Basketball League and the Assimilation of Its Members into the Mainstream of United States Society" *International Review for the Sociology of Sport*, Vol. 19, No. 3–4, (1984): 259–271;Gail Nomura, "Beyond the Playing Field: The Significance of Pre-World War II Japanese American Baseball in the Yakima Valley," in *Bearing Dreams, Shaping Visions: Asian Pacific American Perspectives*, eds. L. A. Revilla and Association for Asian American Studies (Pullman, WA: Washington State University Press, 1993): 15–31; Franklin Odo, Sinoto Kazuko, and Hawaii Immigrant Heritage Preservation Center, *A Pictorial History of the Japanese in Hawaii, 1885–1924* (Honolulu: Hawaii Immigrant Heritage Preservation Center Dept. of Anthropology Bernice Pauahi Bishop Museum, 1985), 78–79; Michael M. Okihiro and Japanese Cultural Center of Hawaii, *AJA Baseball in Hawaii: Ethnic Pride and Tradition*, (Honolulu: Hawaii Hochi, 1999); Roberta J. Park, "Sport and Recreation among Chinese American Communities of the Pacific Coast from Time of Arrival to the 'Quiet Decade' of the 1950s," *Journal of Sport History* 27, no. 3 (Fall 2000): 445–480; Mia Tuan,

Forever Foreigners or Honorary Whites? The Asian Ethnic Experience Today (New Brunswick, NJ: Rutgers University Press, 1998); Jan Weisman, "The Tiger and His Stripes," in *The Sum of Our Parts: Mixed Heritage Americans*, eds. Teresa Williams-Leon and Cynthia Nakashima (Philadelphia: Temple University Press, 2001), 231–243; Henry Yu, "Tiger Woods at the Center of History: Looking Back at the Twentieth Century through the Lenses of Race, Sports, and Mass Consumption," in *Sports Matters: Race, Recreation, and Culture*, eds. John Bloom and Michael Nevin Willard (New York: New York University Press, 2002), 320–353 Susan G. Zieff, "From Badminton to the Bolero: Sport and Recreation in San Francisco's Chinatown, 1895–1950," *Journal of Sport History* 27, no.1 (Spring 2000): 1–29.

6. Judy Yung, *Unbound Feet: A Social History of Chinese Women in San Francisco* (Berkeley: University of California Press, 1995), 125.

7. In addition, Chinatown residents paid more rent for substandard housing than did residents in other parts of San Francisco in the early 1940s. Limited to low-paying jobs in which they earned anywhere from $5 to $9 a week, some families were forced to spend $11 a month for substandard apartments. Lim P. Lee, "Housing Problem: Property Survey Shows Chinatown Rents Exceed Standard S.F. Median," *Chinese Press*, 12 May 1950, 1–2; "Opposes Play Area Cuts: 'Children Need More Facilities,' Says Report," *Chinese Press*, 12 May 1950, 1–2.

8. *Recreation and Park Department News Bulletin*, (San Francisco: McLaren Lodge, Golden Gate Park, 1951), 4.

9. Norma Lee Hom, Interview by author, telephone recording, 15 June 2000; Jennie Chong Jue, Interview by author, telephone recording, 29 June 2000; James Francis "Smokey Joe" Wong, Interview by author, tape recording, San Francisco, CA, 30 July 1998; Helen Wong Lum, Interview by author, tape recording, San Francisco, CA, 23 October 1998.

10. Lim P. Lee, "Chinatown Civic Victory: Playground Request Approved by Local Board of Education," *California Chinese Press*, 11 April 1941, 1; Lim P. Lee, "Housing Problem," 1–2; "Recreation Study by Group Work Council," *Chinese Press*, 10 March 1950, 7; "TB Still Kills Too Many Chinese: S.F. Chinese Birth, Infant Mortality Rates, Both High," *Chinese Press*, 18 March 1948, 1;Works Project Administration Recreation Project (WPARP), "Survey of San Francisco, California by Districts (Recreation), Prepared for the Executive Coordinating Council, 1936–1937" (San Francisco: Author, 1937), 37; "X-Rays Start Oct. 31," *Chinese Press*, 28 October 1949, 1.

11. Marsha King, "Tribes Confront Painful Legacy of Indian Boarding Schools," *Seattle Times*, 3 February 2008; Leon Litwack, *Trouble in Mind: Black Southerners in the Age of Jim Crow* (New York: Knopf, 1998).

12. Yuji Ichioka, *The Issei* (New York: Free Press, 1988), 91, 226–229, 244; Him Mark Lai and Philip P. Choy, *Outlines: History of the Chinese in America*

(San Francisco: Lai and Choy, 1971), 88–102; Megumi Dick Osumi, "Asians and California's Anti-Miscegenation Laws," in *Asian and Pacific American Experiences: Women's Perspectives* ed. Nobuya Tsuchida (Minneapolis: University of Minnesota Press, 1982), 1–37; John S. Park *Elusive Citizenship: Immigration, Asian Americans, and the Paradox of Civil Rights* (New York: New York University Press, 2004).

13. Sucheng Chan, *Asian Americans: An Interpretive History* (Boston: Twayne, 1991), 145–146; Lai and Choy, *Outlines*, 102

14. Gloria Heyung Chun, *Of Orphans and Warriors: Inventing Chinese American Culture and Identity* (New Brunswick, NJ: Rutgers University Press, 2000), 18–19.

15. Yen Le Espiritu, "Asian American Women and Men: Labor, Laws, and Love," in *The Gender Lens*, eds. Judith A. Howard et al. (Thousand Oaks, CA: Sage Publications, 1997), 86–95; Anthony W. Lee, *Picturing Chinatown: Art and Orientalism in San Francisco* (Berkeley: University of California Press, 2001); Josephine Lee, *Performing Asian America: Race and Ethnicity on the Contemporary Stage* (Philadelphia: Temple University Press, 1997); Robert G. Lee, *Orientals: Asian Americans in Popular Culture* (Philadelphia,: Temple University Press, 1999); Gina Marchetti, *Romance and the "Yellow Peril": Race, Sex, and Discursive Strategies in Hollywood Fiction* (Berkeley: University of California Press, 1993), 6; David Palumbo-Liu, *Asian American: Historical Crossings of a Racial Frontier* (Stanford, CA: Stanford University Press, 1999), 17–18, 35–38; William F. Wu, *The Yellow Peril: Chinese Americans in American Fiction, 1850–1940* (Hamden, CT: Archon Books, 1982).

16. Rose Hum Lee, *The Chinese in the United States of America* (Hong Kong: Hong Kong University Press, 1960), 361.

17. Chun, *Of Orphans and Warriors*, 20–21; Espiritu, "Asian American Women and Men," 91; Wu, *The Yellow Peril*, 60.

18. K. Scott Wong, *Americans First: Chinese Americans and the Second World War* (Cambridge: Harvard University Press, 2005), 70–71; Judy Wu, *Doctor Mom Chung of the Fair-Haired Bastards: The Life of a Wartime Celebrity* (Berkeley: University of California Press, 2005), 119–120, 141, 146.

19. Shirley Lim, *A Feeling of Belonging: Asian American Women's Public Culture in the 1930s and 1940s* (New York: New York University Press, 2006) 63–65.

20. However, after the 1949 communist revolution in China, the public's perception of Chinese changed from ally during World War II to communist threat. The emerging cold war led to intense racial profiling and scrutiny of Chinese and Chinese Americans. Examples include the 1950 Internal Security (McCarran) Act and the Federal Bureau of Investigation confession program (1957 to 1965). Sucheng Chan, *Asian Americans*, 141; Peter Kwong, *Chinatown, New York: Labor and Politics, 1930–1950*. (New York: Monthly Review Press,

1979) 143–146; Estelle T. Lau. *Paper Families: Identity, Immigration Administration, and Chinese Exclusion* (Durham, NC: Duke University Press, 2006), 116–119; Victor G. Nee and Brett de Bary Nee, *Longtime Californ': A Documentary Study of an American Chinatown* (Englewood Cliffs, NJ: Prentice-Hall, 1974); Mai Ngai, *Impossible Subjects: Illegal Aliens and the Making of Modern America* (Princeton, NJ: Princeton University Press, 2005), 202–220; Nancy Tucker, *Patterns in the Dust: Chinese-American Relations and the Recognition Controversy, 1949–1950* (New York: Columbia University Press, 1983), 1–18; Judy Wu, *Doctor Mom Chung of the Fair-Haired Bastards*, 192.

21. Pierre Bourdieu contends that sport is the integration of theory and practice in constructing consent below the level of consciousness: "Sport is . . . one of the sites in which is posed with maximum acuity the problem of the relations between theory and practice, and also between language and the body. . . . The teaching of a bodily practice [encloses] a set of theoretical questions of the greatest importance, inasmuch as the social sciences endeavor to theorize conducts that are produced, for the vast majority of them, beneath the level of consciousness." Bourdieu, "Program for a Sociology of Sport," 153–161; Michel de Certeau, *The Practice of Everyday Life* (Berkeley: University of California Press, 1985), 16–17.

22. Sucheng Chan, *Asian Americans*; and Chun, *Of Orphans and Warriors*, 18–19.

23. Thomas Kim, Interview by author, tape recording, Richmond, CA, 12 December 1987.

24. "Champions Again: Troop 3 Scouts Capture Wah Ying Basketball Title for Third Year," *California Chinese Press*, 14 February 1941, 2; Davisson Lee, "Wah Ying Basketball League," *Chinese Digest*, February 1939, 16.

25. James C. Scott, *Domination and the Arts of Resistance: Hidden Transcripts* (New Haven, CT: Yale University Press, 1992).

26. "Basketball Champs: Chinese Cagers Win Again in Second National Tourney," *Chinese Press*, 31 December 1948, 1–2; "Berkeley, SF Chinese Gain Finals," *San Francisco Examiner*, 29 December 1948, 19; "Champion Casaba Tossers," *Chinese Press*, 7 January 1949, 8; "8 Fives Set for Oriental Meet," *Seattle Post-Intelligencer*, 25 December 1947, 23; "Hawaiians, Saints Reach Oriental Basketball Final," *Seattle Post-Intelligencer*, 28 December 1947, 24; 1947 National Oriental Basketball Tournament Program, in William Woo Wong, Scrapbook; "Oriental Meet on Tonight: 8 Teams Set to Play," *Seattle Post-Intelligencer*, 23 December 1948, 15; "These Are Best Chinese-American Basketballers in the Country . . . ," *Chinese Press*, 7 January 1949, 8.

27. Teams such as the San Franciscan Filipino Mangoes, the San Francisco Saints, the San Jose Zebras, and the Berkeley Nisei provided strong representation for the San Francisco Bay Area. "Berkeley Nisei Register Upset," *San Francisco Examiner*, 25 December 1948, 13; "Oriental Tourney: Eight

Casaba Teams Battle for National Title Now," *Chinese Press,* 24 December 1949, 7; "S.F. Saints to Play Berkeley," *San Francisco Chronicle,* 26 December 1948, 1H; "S.F. Saints Win Opener: Oriental-American Cage Defenders Whip San Jose," *San Francisco Chronicle,* 25 December 1948, 3H; William Woo Wong, Interview by author, tape recording, Newark, CA, 14 July 1999.

28. "Cosmopolitan—Above Are Representatives Who Make Up Teams Competing in the Oriental-American Cage Tourney," *Seattle Post-Intelligencer,* 24 December 1948, 15; "8 Fives Set for Oriental Meet," 23; "Hawaiians, Saints Reach Oriental Basketball Final," 24; "Melting Pot: Bay Cagers Vie in Seattle," *San Francisco Chronicle,* 23 December 1948, 3H.

29. Douglas Robert Hartmann, "Rethinking the Relationships between Sport and Race in American Culture: Golden Ghettos and Contested Terrain," *Sociology of Sport Journal* 17 (2000): 232

30. Gerald Early, "Baseball, Boxing, and the Charisma of Sport and Race" (*The Charisma of Sport and Race,* Symposium Proceedings (Berkeley: University of California Press, 1996); Harry Edwards, *Sociology of Sport* (Homewood, IL: Dorsey Press, 1973), 69, 103; D. Stanley Eitzen and George Harvey Sage, *Sociology of American Sport,* 2nd ed. (Dubuque, IA: W. C. Brown Co., 1982); John Hargreaves, *Sport, Power, and Culture: A Social and Historical Analysis of Popular Sports in Britain* (New York: St. Martin's Press, 1986), 8; Peter Levine, *Ellis Island to Ebbets Field: Sport and the American Jewish Experience* (New York: Oxford University Press, 1992), 3; John C. Phillips, *Sociology of Sport* (Boston: Allyn and Bacon, 1993).

31. Susan Birrell and Mary G. McDonald, *Reading Sport: Critical Essays on Power and Representation* (Boston: Northeastern University Press, 2000); Bourdieu, "Program for a Sociology of Sport," 5 (1988): 153–161; Richard S. Gruneau and David Whitson, *Hockey Night in Canada: Sport, Identities, and Cultural Politics* (Toronto: Garamond Press, 1993).

32. Arthur S. Evans, "Differences in the Recruitment of Black and White Football Players at a Big Eight University," *Journal of Sport and Social Issues* 3 (1979): 1–10.

33. George B. Cunningham and Michael Sagas, "Access Discrimination in Intercollegiate Athletics," *Journal of Sport and Social Issues* 29 (2005): 148–163.

34. Andrew C. Billings, Caroline C. Craig, Robert Croce, Kristian M. Cross, Kathryn M. Moore, William Vigodsky, and Victoria G. Watson, " 'Just One of the Guys?' Network Depictions of Annika Sorenstam in the 2003 PGA Colonial Tournament," *Journal of Sport and Social Issues* 30 (2006): 107–114; and Hartmann, "Rethinking the Relationships between Sport and Race," 237.

35. Michael Omi and Howard Winant, *Racial Formation in the United States: From the 1960s to the 1980s* (New York: Routledge, 1986/1989).

36. C. L. Cole and Amy Hribrar, "Celebrity Feminism: Nike Style: Post-Fordism, Transcendence, and Consumer Power," *Sociology of Sport Journal* 12, no. 4 (December 1995): 347–360.

37. Mary G. McDonald, "Queering Whiteness: The Peculiar Case of the Women's National Basketball Association," *Sociological Perspectives* 45, no. 4 (Winter 2002): 379–396.

38. Susan Birrell and Nancy Theberge, "Feminist Resistance and Transformation in Sport," in *Women and Sport: Interdisciplinary Perspectives*, eds. D. M. Costa and S. R. Guthrie (Champaign, IL: Human Kinetics, 1994) 365; Hartmann, "Rethinking the Relationships between Sport and Race," 235, 236; Michael Messner, "Sports and Male Domination: The Female Athlete as Contested Ideological Terrain," *Sociology of Sport Journal* 5 (1988): 197–211.

39. Douglas Hartmann, *Race, Culture, and the Revolt of the Black Athlete: The 1968 Olympic Protests and Their Aftermath* (Chicago: University of Chicago Press, 2003), xii–xiii.

40. Ben Carrington, "Sport, Masculinity, and Black Cultural Resistance," *Journal of Sport and Social Issues* 22, no. 3 (August 1998): 275–298; Lisa Lowe, *Immigrant Acts* (Durham, NC: Duke University Press, 1996) 4, 9, 22, 23.

41. Gerald Early, "Performance and Reality: Race, Sports and the Modern World," *The Nation*, 10–17 August 1998, 12.

42. For example, in the 1930s and 1940s, African American grappled with state-sanctioned marginalization through rigidly enforced segregation in schools, public transportation, parks, restaurants, stores, and social life. Economic segregation manifested in discriminatory hiring practices and sharecropping, while political segregation occurred through the use of literacy tests and poll taxes as barriers to voting. In addition to African Americans, other racial groups in the 1930s encountered racially motivated segregation, removal, and incarceration. For example, from 1879 until the mid-1930s, the United States government took Native American children from their families and placed them in boarding schools for a forced assimilation immersion program. With the philosophy of "kill the Indian and save the man," the schools had military-like conditions and banned Indian language, dress, and beliefs. Punishments ranged from lost privileges to being beaten or locked in a closet. While Indian children were being disciplined in schools, Mexican Americans in the early 1930s were removed or coerced to emigrate to Mexico. An estimated 400,000 people were deported or pressured to leave after facing raids in public places and being denied jobs. Japanese Americans faced racially targeted incarceration when 120,000 persons of Japanese ancestry living in the West Coast were rounded up and imprisoned in desolate, remote areas for up to four years during World War II. Surrounded by barbed wire and armed guards, half of the prisoners were children. Forced to leave their homes, schools, and jobs for years, they were not accused of crimes, and none of the

internees were allowed due process of law. See, for example, David Wallace Adams, *Education for Extinction: American Indians and the Boarding School Experience, 1875–1928* (Lawrence: University Press of Kansas, 1997); Roger Daniels, *Prisoners without Trial* (New York: Hill and Wang, 2004); Abraham Hoffman, *Unwanted Mexican Americans in the Great Depression: Repatriation Pressures, 1929–1939* (Tucson: University of Arizona Press, 1974).

43. Paul Gilroy, *There Ain't No Black in the Union Jack: The Cultural Politics of Race and Nation* (Chicago: University of Chicago Press, 1991), 16–17.

44. Stuart Hall, "Gramsci's Relevance for the Study of Race and Ethnicity," in *Stuart Hall: Critical Dialogues in Cultural Studies,* eds., David Morley and Kuan-Hsing Chen (London: Routledge, 1996), 411–446.

45. Many individuals who research professional basketball were generous with their knowledge and personal archives. In addition to the professional basketball research e-mail list, J. Michael Kenyon's and Kevin Grace's personal research on barnstorming basketball teams, journalist Ben Green's research on the Harlem Globetrotters, the Globetrotter archivist Governor Vaughn, and Terry Bertolino's work on the House of David Bearded Aces were invaluable. Government and university collections include the Library of Congress 1930s Federal Writers Project A29–History of California, University of California at Berkeley Bancroft Library 1975 Combined Asian Oral History Project, the Los Angeles Chinese Historical Society of Southern California Oral History Project, and the San Francisco's Chinese Historical Society Collection at the University of California Berkeley Asian American Studies Library. In addition, I explored oral histories collected in the 1930s and 1940s from various social science studies written during the interwar years such as Eugenia V. Chen, "Survey of Chinese Youth and Student Clubs in New York City, 1945"(Master's thesis, University of Michigan, 1945) and Fisk University, "Orientals and Their Cultural Adjustment; Interviews," *Social Science Source Documents,* No. 4 (Nashville, TN: Social Science Institute, Fisk University, 1946).

46. I use the word *approximately* intentionally because some informal conversations were pseudo-interviews. The context of the community explains why determining what an interview is can be hazy. More often than not, people felt more comfortable in casual discussions and started to recall valuable and vivid memories. However, as soon as I tried to write notes on a napkin or brought up the idea of an interview, they often clammed up.

47. The "contextual" part of my methodology places the athletes' stories within the context of larger historical processes. This research examines the racial, gender, and class politics of basketball at both the structural and individual levels and also looks at the fluid relationship between these two. My purpose is to examine aspects of domination as well as the concomitant human agency. For example, neither in-depth interviews of the daily nuances of

playing basketball in Chinatown in the 1930s nor the statistics of de facto segregation in housing, education, and employment are sufficient on their own to capture and flesh out the dynamics between the micro and the macro. I attempt to use individual stories to examine broader social processes and to explore how these social forces manifest in the daily life.

To this end, I combined oral history with secondary data analysis of text, images, and memorabilia. Because of the potential flaws of relying heavily on oral histories, I combined the interviews with document analysis. The newspaper and government accounts added scope to the interviews, and the interview voices introduced more texture and soul to the written archival sources. By mixing oral histories with analysis of visual and written representations, the book shows the interplay between different types of representations. In other words, how do visual depictions of Chinese American femininity interact with written descriptions in Chinese American newspapers or physical expressions of femininity through basketball? Further, rather than examining either representation or life histories, this work analyzes the depiction and explores the perception of the person being represented.

48. Dennis Tedlock's theory of notating the gestures and dynamics of the speaker is useful for the specific racial, gendered, and generational styles of communication of the athletes in this book. Types of silences, laughter, gestures, shifts in tone, and demeanor of the athletes conveyed certain meanings. For example, some used lengthy pauses at the ends of short, succinct statements to indicate their importance or to show irony in the statements. Because a central part of their narration is strategic silences and pauses, I have included their nonverbal communications (such as pauses, laughter, sounds, and gestures) in parentheses. The transcription of their narratives attempts to represent the cadence and syncopation of their words and storytelling styles. In addition, Cantonese words are written in italics with the English translation following in parentheses. Dennis Tedlock, *The Spoken Word and the Work of Interpretation* (Philadelphia: University of Pennsylvania Press, 1983) 123, 113–115.

49. Bourdieu, "Program for a Sociology of Sport," 153–161.

50. "Cage Tourney Coming Up: Chi-Hi Clubs to Shoot for Basketball Honors in October," *Chinese Press*, 19 September 1941, 4; "College Basketball League Commences," *Chinese Press*, 5 November 1948, 8; Hsien-Ju Shih, "Social and Vocational Adjustment of the Second Generation Chinese High School Students in San Francisco" (E.D. Thesis, University of California, Berkeley, May 1937), 37; "Sports," *Chinese Digest*, 27 March 1936, 13; "Sports," *Chinese Digest*, 3 January 1936, 130.

51. Todd Gould, *Pioneers of the Hardwood: Indiana and the Birth of Professional Basketball* (Bloomington, IN: Indiana University Press, 1998), 22, 24, 30, 79, 88–89, 97–98, 100.

52. Levine, *Ellis Island to Ebbets Field* , 27.

53. Lynne Emery, "From Lowell Mills to the Halls of Fame: Industrial League Sport for Women," in *Women and Sport: Interdisciplinary Perspectives*, eds. D. Margaret Costa and Sharon R. Guthrie (Champaign, IL: Human Kinetics, 1994), 107–122; in same book, see also Joan S. Hult, "The Story of Women's Athletics," in *Women and Sport*, 83–106.

54. Pamela Grundy and Susan Shackelford, *Shattering the Glass: The Remarkable History of Women's Basketball* (New York: New Press, 2005), 53–54; Robert W. Ikard, *Just for Fun: The Story of AAU Women's Basketball* (Fayetteville, AR: University of Arkansas Press, 2003), 14–15, 206–207, 215.

55. Roxanne M. Albertson, "Basketball Texas Style, 1910–1933: School to Industrial League Competition," in *A Century of Women's Basketball*, eds. Joan S. Hult and Marianna Trekell (Reston, VA: American Alliance for Health, Physical Education, Recreation, and Dance, 1991), 158; Elva Bishop and Katherine Fulton, "Shooting Stars: The Hey Dey of Industrial Women's Basketball," *Southern Exposure* 7 (1979): 50–56.

56. Grundy and Shackelford, *Shattering the Glass*, 50–52.

57. Chinese Center Group, *Work Report*, April/May 1929, November 1929; Zieff, "From Badminton to the Bolero," 6, 10, 15; "Chinese Schools: Hoop League Standing Released," *California Chinese Press*, 27 December 1940, 7; Chinn, Thomas W., *Bridging the Pacific* (San Francisco: Chinese Historical Society, 1989), pp. 110, 118, 122, 125–127, 188–191; Conrad Fong and Davisson Lee, "Nam Wah Wins," *Chinese Digest*, May 1938, 17; Joel S. Franks, "Chinese Americans and American Sport, 1880–1940," in *Chinese America: History and Perspectives* (San Francisco: Chinese Historical Society of America, 1996), 142; Franks, *Crossing Sidelines, Crossing Cultures*, 113; Frank Hee, "Basketball in Our Own Backyard," *Chinese Digest*, May–June 1939, 18–19; "Lightweight Cagers Seek Title Tonight," *San Francisco Examiner*, 8 March 1932, S19; Park, "Sport and Recreation Among Chinese American Communities of the Pacific Coast From Time of Arrival to the 'Quiet Decade' of the 1950s," 451, 460; "Y.M.C.A Cage Teams Will Play Wednesday," *San Francisco Examiner*, 17 December 1932, S17.

58. Franks, "Chinese Americans and American Sport," 136; Chinese Historical Society of America, *The Third Annual A Celebration of Roots*, 17.

59. "Berkeley Chinese Athletic Club Eyes Basketball Season with High Optimism," *Chinese Press*, 8 October 1948, 11; "Cage Champs: Salinas Wins 'Four Cities' Crown," *California Chinese Press*, 21 March 1941, 1.; "Chi-Knight Cage Team to Give Stag Part," *California Chinese Press*, 14 April 1941, 4; "Locke Girl Cagers Defeat the Chi-Nettes," *California Chinese Press*, 18 April 1941, 3; "Oakland Casaba Tilt," *Chinese Press*, 4 March 1939, 8; "Oakland 'Y' Loses Title Game," *Chinese Digest*, 20 March 1936, 13; Park, "Sport and Recreation Among Chinese American Communities of the Pacific Coast From Time of Arrival to

the 'Quiet Decade' of the 1950s," 454–460; "Sacramento Chi-Nettes Hold Honor Banquet for Shanghai Guest," *California Chinese Press*, 28 March 1941, 3; "Sacramento Wiah Yen Loses; Franciscans Win in Second Tilt," *California Chinese Press*, 28 February 1941, 4; "Sports," *Chinese Digest*, 15 November 1935; "Sports," *Chinese Digest*, 20 March 1936, 12; "Sports," *Chinese Digest*, 27 March 1936, 13; 13; "Sports," *Chinese Digest*, 6 December 1936, 13; Fred George Woo, "Sports," *Chinese Digest*, 22 November 1935, 13; Fred George Woo, "Sports," *Chinese Digest*, 29 November 1935, 13.

60. "Casaba Teams Entered in Nisei League," *Chinese Press*, 12 November 1948, 7; Chen, "Survey of Chinese Youth"; Lily Chan, Interview #48, Box #12, Southern California Chinese American Oral History Project (Los Angeles: University of California Los Angeles, 1982); Lucie Cheng and Marjorie Lee, *Linking Our Lives: Chinese American Women of Los Angeles* (Los Angeles: University of California Los Angeles Asian American Studies Center and Chinese Historical Society of Southern California, 1984), 93–94, 107–110; Arthur Duffey, "Chinese Girls to Compete: Banner Entry for the E.R.F. for Norfolk Club Meet, *Boston Globe*, 21 February 1935; Arthur Duffey "McDonough Wins 5000 Metre Run: Boston College Athletes Take Point Trophy–Chinese Girls Make Hit in Norfolk Club Meet," *Boston Globe*, 22 February 1935; Conrad Fong and Davisson Lee, "Sports," *Chinese Digest*, April 1938, 18; *California Chinese Press*, 28 February 1941, 28 March 1941, 18 April 1941; "Four Fleet Daughters of China," Denison House Records, 1890–1984, Disassembled Scrapbooks, M-141 Reel 1 Folder 9, Schlesinger Library on the History of Women in America, Radcliffe Institute, Cambridge, MA; Franks, *Crossing Sidelines, Crossing Cultures*, 113, 114, 115, 119; Franks, "Chinese Americans and American Sport," 142; "The Chinese Girls' Basketball Team," Denison House Records, 1890–1984, Disassembled Scrapbooks, Image B27-7-4, Image B27-7-5, Image B27-7-6, Image B27-7-8. M-141 Reel 1 Folder 9 Schlesinger Library on the History of Women in America, Radcliffe Institute, Cambridge, MA; Harvard Library, http://oc hul.harvard.edu/immigration/organizations -Denison.html (accessed 5 June 2007). "Group Portrait of Denison House Chinese Girls' Basketball Team and Their Coach Margaret Stewart, One of the Girls Workers," Photo: B27-7-7, M-141 Reel 1 Folder 7, Schlesinger Library on the History of Women in America, Radcliffe Institute, Cambridge, MA; Billy Lew, Interview #20 Box 12, 7B-09-113, Southern California Chinese American Oral History Project (Los Angeles: University of California Los Angeles, 1982); Museum of Chinese American History in Los Angeles, Summer 1998 Newsletter, http://www.eskimo.com/~camla/newsletter/1998/summer/index.htm (accessed June 23, 2007); Joe McKenney, "South End House Moulds Athletes: Denison 'Back Yard' Incubator of Some Future Sport Stars—Marino Serves as Guiding Hand," *Boston Post*, 13 October 1940; Park, "Sport and Recreation Among Chinese American Communities of the Pacific Coast From Time of

Arrival to the 'Quiet Decade' of the 1950s,"454–456; "Portland Girls Have Basketball Team," *Chinese Digest*, 29 November 1935, 13.

61. "Santa Barbara Has a Chinese Cage Team," *Chinese Press*, 4 March 1949, 8; Seattle Municipal Archives Women in City Government, http://www.seattle.gov/CityArchives/Resources/WomenExhibit/Pearl_Powell.htm (accessed 5 June 2007); Wing Luke Museum Web Site, http://www.wingluke.org/pages/CHC/exhibit1/e10216b.htm (accessed 4 June 2007); "Three Fight for Crown in O.Y.L. Semi-finals," *Chinese Press*, 24 March 1950, 6; Maye Wong, Interview #34, Southern California Chinese American Oral History Project (Los Angeles: University of California Los Angeles, 1982); Elsie Wong, Interview #108, Box #44, Southern California Chinese American Oral History Project (Los Angeles: University of California Los Angeles, 1982); Bill Young, Interview #155, 1B, Southern California Chinese American Oral History Project (Los Angeles: University of California Los Angeles, 1982).

62. Andrew Morris, *Marrow of the Nation: A History of Sport and Physical Culture in Republican China* (Berkeley, CA: University of California Press, 2004) 78–81; Jim Riordan, *Sport and Physical Education in China 1999* (Oxford: Taylor and Francis, 1999).

63. Susan Brownell, *Training the Body for China: Sports in the Moral Order of the People's Republic* (Chicago: University of Chicago Press, 1995), 50; Howard Knuttgen, *Sport in China* (Champaign, IL: Human Kinetics, 1990).

64. U.S. Census Bureau, *Fifteenth Census of the United States–1930–Population Volume I: Number and Distribution of Inhabitants* (Washington, DC: Government Printing Office), 266, 261; U.S. Census Bureau, *Sixteenth Census of the United States–1940–Population, Volume II: Characteristics of the Population—Part 1* (Washington, DC: Government Printing Office) 556.

65. Harry H. L. Kitano and Roger Daniels, *Asian Americans: Emerging Minorities*, 2nd ed. (Englewood Cliffs, NJ: Prentice Hall, 1995), 38.

66. Wong, *Americans First*, 33–34.

67. Kit-King Louis, "A Study of American-Born and American-Reared Chinese in Los Angeles" (Master's thesis, University of Southern California, 1931); Eliot Grinnell Mears, *Resident Orientals on the American Pacific Coast: Their Legal and Economic Status* (Chicago: University of Chicago Press, 1928); Edward K. Strong, *The Second Generation Japanese Problem* (New York: Arno Press, 1970).

68. Sucheng Chan, "Race, Ethnic Cultures, and Gender in the Construction of Identities among Second-Generation Chinese Americans, 1880s–1930s," in *Claiming America: Constructing Chinese American Identities during the Exclusion Era*, eds. Sucheng Chan and Kevin Scott Wong (Philadelphia: Temple University Press, 1998), 147; Lon Kurashige, *Japanese American Celebration and Conflict: A History of Ethnic Identity and Festival, 1934–1990* (Berkeley: University of California Press, 2002); Karen J. Leong, *The China*

Mystique: Pearl S. Buck, Anna May Wong, Mayling Soong, and the Transformation of American Orientalism (Berkeley: University of California Press, 2005); Jerrold Takahashi, *Nisei/Sansei: Shifting Japanese American Identities and Politics* (Philadelphia: Temple University Press, 1998); Wong, *Americans First*; David Yoo, *Growing Up Nisei: Race, Generation, and Culture among Japanese Americans of California, 1924–49* (Chicago: University of Illinois Press, 1999); Xiaojian Zhao, *Remaking Chinese America: Immigration, Family, and Community, 1940–1965* (New Brunswick, NJ: Rutgers University Press, 2002).

Chapter 1. The Chinese Playground

1. Davisson Lee, "Sports—Lightweights," *Chinese Digest*, December 1938, 17.

2. Judy Yung, *Unbound Feet: A Social History of Chinese Women in San Francisco* (Berkeley and Los Angeles: University of California Press, 1995), 296.

3. Rose Hum Lee, *The Chinese in the United States of America* (Hong Kong: Hong Kong University Press, 1960), 39–41; Yung, *Unbound Feet*, 106; Xiaojian Zhao, *Remaking Chinese America: Immigration, Family, and Community, 1940–1965* (New Brunswick, NJ: Rutgers University Press, 2002).

4. Lim P. Lee, "Chinatown Petitions for New Playground to Combat Delinquency. These Are 'Press' Facts and Figures," *California Chinese Press*, 28 February 1941, 1.

5. "Chinatown Needs More Playgrounds," *Chinese Press*, 10 March 1950, 1; Rose Hum Lee, "Community Not Interested in Its Youth, Sociologist Charges," *Chinese Press*, 4 August 1950, 3–4; "Recreational Problems Studied," *California Chinese Press*, 7 February 1941, 6; "A Study of the San Francisco Coordinating Council for Youth Welfare" (San Francisco: Western Office of National Probation and Parole Association California Youth Authority's Delinquency Prevention Section, 1949), 1–15; "Survey of San Francisco, California by Districts (Recreation) Prepared for the Executive Coordinating Council, 1936–1937," (San Francisco: Works Project Administration Recreation Project (WPARP), 1937); Thomas W. S. Wu, "Study Finds Recreation Facilities Inadequate," *Chinese Press*, 10 March 1950, 3, 7.

6. *Recreation and Park Department News Bulletin* (San Francisco: McLaren Lodge, Golden Gate Park, 1951), 4.

7. Gladys Zehnder, "The Chinese Playground," *The Municipal Employee*, July 1927, 44.

8. Dominick Cavallo, *Muscles and Morals: Organized Playgrounds and Urban Reform, 1880–1920* (Philadelphia: University of Pennsylvania Press, 1981), 32–36.

9. Cavallo, *Muscles and Morals*, 36–37.

10. Henry S. Curtis, *The Play Movement and Its Significance* (New York: Macmillan Company, 1917), 119–120.

11. Cavallo, *Muscles and Morals,* 2, 3, 34.

12. Luther Gulick, *A Philosophy of Play* (New York: Charles Scribner's Sons, 1920), 193–194.

13. Organized play advocates had varied opinions on the ideological function of the playground and organized play in relation to ethnic diversity. Some, such as Joseph Lee, felt that young people should be completely Americanized and shed their ethnic pasts. Others, such as Jane Addams, promoted ethnic pluralism in which youth of different ethnic backgrounds could learn to play as a team while maintaining their ethnic identities. Cavallo, *Muscles and Morals,* 37, 44, 109, 161; Louise de Koven Bowen, *Safeguards for City Youth at Work and at Play* (New York: MacMillan Company, 1914); T. F. Chapin, "Play as a Reformative Agency," in *Proceedings of the National Conference of Charities and Correction* (Berkeley: University of California Berkeley, San Francisco Publications, 1914, 437–440; John L. Gillin, *Wholesome Citizens and Spare Time* (Cleveland, OH: Cleveland Foundation Committee, 1918); Luther Gulick, "Play and Democracy," *Charities and the Commons,* 8 (3 August 1907): 481–486; Joseph Lee, "Play as an Antidote to Civilization," *The Playground* (July 1911): 7, 15; Joseph Lee, "Play as a School of the Citizen," *Charities and the Commons,* 18 (3 August 1907): 486–491.

14. Cavallo, *Muscles and Morals,* 44–45.

15. "Chinese Six Companies Wages War on Chinatown Crime," *Chinese Press,* 16 July 1948, 1, 4; Bob Lee, "Blame Them Not: Bob Lee CSCA Secretary on SF Hoodlums," *Chinese Press,* 12 May 1950, 2.

16. "Punk War Hurting Business," *Chinese Press,* 27 January 1950, 1–2.

17. Lim P. Lee, "Letter to the Editor," *Chinese Press,* 12 May 1950, 2.

18. Walter Mails, "Sports Star Deplores Lack of Playfields in Chinatown," *Chinese Press,* 4 February 1949, 12; "Opposes Play Area Cuts: 'Children Need More Facilities,' Says Report," *Chinese Press,* 12 May 1950, 1–2; From the early 1900s until 1946, Officer John Manion was the beat cop in charge of Chinatown and a visible fixture in the neighborhood. Parents encouraged Manion to be tough on the kids. Manion wrote about a wide range of narcotics and crime in Chinatown. Similarly, Officer Jesse Cook, who later rose in the ranks to become chief of police and a police commissioner, was the sergeant who oversaw the officers in Chinatown until the 1930s. In his writings and interviews, Cook also noted the prevalence of drug and sex trafficking related to illicit group activity. Manion and others helped crack down on school truancy and youth criminal activity. Jesse Brown Cook, *Jesse Brown Cook Scrapbooks, 1860–1938* (Berkeley: Bancroft Library, BANC PIC 1996.003—fALB).

19. These organizations included the Chinese Welfare Society, the Chinese Community Center, the Junior Safety League of California, the American Legion, the San Francisco Safety Council, the Women's Safety League of Northern

California, the Chinese American Citizens Alliance, the Chinese Mission, and the Chinese YWCA.

20. Edward W. Chew, "Chinatown Crimewave? 'Kid Glove Bandits' Linked with Six Robberies," *Chinese Press*, 2 December 1949, 1–2; "Chinatown Joins Council; Hopes for Youth Control," *Chinese Press*, 13 January 1950, 1–2; Chinese Center Group, *Work Report*, January 1936. (San Francisco: Chinese Historical Society of America); "Crime, Fights Held Bad Publicity for Chinatown," *Chinese Press*, 27 January 1950, 2; "New Chinese Playground: Site Already Purchased," *Chinese Press*, 16 July 1948, 1; "New Playground: Like Christmas—It Should Be Here Definitely This Year," *Chinese Press*, 8 August 1941, 1; "The Playground Issue: Here's Letter of Recommendation," *Chinese Press*, 13 June 1941, 1; "Playground Seems Certain," *Chinese Press*, 22 August 1941, 1; "Youth Council Meets to Halt Juvenile Delinquency," *Chinese Press*, 6 January 1950, 1; Susan Zieff, "From Badminton to the Bolero: Sport and Recreation in San Francisco's Chinatown, 1895–1950," *Journal of Sport History* 11 (2000): 1–29.

21. The Chinese Playground received $6,970.90 in annual funding and reported twice as much attendance as Michaelangelo Playground, which had 0.43 acres and almost twice as much as funding at $12,651.85. Michaelangelo Playground, however, was located in a wealthier neighborhood on Greenwich Street between Jones and Leavenworth. "Annual Report and Review of Activities,"52, 54–56, 65; "Survey of San Francisco," 30, 31; Thomas W. Chin, *Bridging the Pacific* (San Francisco: Chinese Historical Society, 1989), 134.

22. Bill Simons, "Chinese Playground Fills a San Francisco Need," *San Francisco Chronicle*, 25 September 1939, 10; WPARP, "Survey of San Francisco," 30.

23. "Annual Report and Review of Activities," 36.

24. Zehnder, "The Chinese Playground," 44; Simons, "Chinese Playground Fills a San Francisco Need," 10.

25. Zehnder, "The Chinese Playground," 44.

26. "Survey of San Francisco," 30.

27. Eventually, however, the Playground was not large enough to meet the demands of the community. A Chinese Public Affairs Committee had been advocating for the creation of a "modern recreation center" for many years "to keep youngsters too busy to get into mischief." In 1951, the Chinese Recreation Center on the corner of Washington and Mason streets opened as an annex to the Playground, providing an indoor gymnasium and other services for high school youth. Lim P. Lee, "Chinatown Civic Victory: Playground Request Approved by Local Board of Education," *California Chinese Press*, 11 April 1941, 1; "New Playground," *Chinese Press*, 6 June 1941, 1; "Playground: Board Hearing and Constitution Next Move," *California Chinese Press*, 4 April

1941, 1; "Playground Petition," *California Chinese Press,* 7 March 1941, 1; "The Playground Problem: Plans Developed for Intensive Campaign; Dr. Theodore C. Lee Named Chairman of Civic Group," *California Chinese Press,* 28 March 1941, 1; *Recreation and Park Department News Bulletin,* 4.

28. Richard "Goonie" Tong, Interview by author, tape recording, San Francisco, CA, 16 April 2003.

29. James Francis "Smokey Joe" Wong, Interview by author, tape recording, San Francisco, CA, 29 July 1998.

30. Ruth Whang, Interview by author, tape recording, San Francisco, CA, 12 January 2004.

31. Franche Lee, Interview by author, tape recording, Sunnyvale, CA, 15 August 2007.

32. June Choy Wong, Interview by author, tape recording, San Francisco, CA, 16 June 2000.

33. Tong, Interview by author; Paul Whang, Interview by author, tape recording, 2 December 2003.

34. Franche Lee, Interview by author, tape recording, Sunnyvale, CA, 22 June 2000.

35. Zehnder, "The Chinese Playground," 44; William Woo Wong, Interview by author, tape recording, Newark, CA, 16 June 2000.

36. Felton Suen, Interview by author, tape recording. Daly City, CA, 19 June 2000.

37. Tong interview, 16 April 2003.

38. These generalizations about the Playground apply to the 1930s and 1940s. In the 1960s and 1970s, the spatial layout of the Playground was not in the open. There were allegations that strangers were able to enter and threaten the safety of the children. As Bill Lee documents in his memoir, gang violence was prominent during later decades. Bill Lee, *Chinese Playground: A Memoir* (San Francisco: Rhapsody Press, 1999).

39. Tong interview, 16 April 2003.

40. Ibid.

41. Ibid.; "Sports," *Chinese Digest,* 15 November 1935, 13; "Survey of San Francisco," 30; Paul Whang, Interview by author, telephone recording, San Francisco, CA, 17 December 2003. Other staff included Polly McGuire, Wasso Chan, Fred Mar, Tommy Kim, Gim Yep, Lillian Yuen, Paul Whang, Kenny Kim, Mary Lee, Helen Wong Lum, Lillete Lybelle, Johnny Huang, Richard "Goonie" Tong, Wanda Underhill, and Vera Flowers.

42. "Cage Chatter," *California Chinese Press,* 6 December 1940, 7; "Playground Cagers 130's Win 39–33 over Presidio," *California Chinese Press,* 27 December 1940, 7.

43. "City Cagers: Playground 90s Crush Bernal Quintet," *California Chinese Press,* 22 November 1940, 52–56.

44. Fred George Woo, "Sports," *Chinese Digest*, 7 February 1936, 12.

45. Davisson Lee, "Sports Glimpses," *Chinese Digest*, December 1937, 21.

46. Winston Suen, Interview by author, tape recording, Daly City, CA, 19 June 2000.

47. Whang interview, 2 December 2003.

48. Terry Lee, Interview by author, tape recording, San Francisco, CA, 31 May 2004.

49. Beverly Lee, Interview by author, tape recording, San Francisco, CA, 31 May 2004.

50. Terry Lee interview, 31 May 2004.

51. The recreational league games were not extensively covered in mainstream and ethnic community newspapers beyond scores and league standings. Therefore, it is challenging to gauge today whether the Playground method of playing was localized or widespread. Former Playground team members, however, do not recall any other teams using this style of play. From anecdotal evidence, it seemed that most Chinatown teams played with the style.

52. Mihaly Csikszentmihalyi, *Flow=The Psychology of Optimal Experience* (New York: Harper and Row, 1990); Orlando Espin, *The Faith of the People: Theological Reflections on Popular Catholicism* (Maryknoll, NY: Orbis Press, 1997).

53. William Woo Wong, Interview by author, tape recording, Newark, CA, 14 July 1999.

54. "Sport Short," *California Chinese Press,* 27 December 1940, 7.

55. Franche Lee interview, 22 June 2000.

56. "Annual Report and Review of Activities, 1928–1929,"35.

57. "City Cagers: Chinese Playgrounds Win 4 Opening Tilts," *California Chinese Press,* 13 December 1940, 7.

58. Tong interview, 16 April 2003; Paul Whang interview, 2 December 2003; Paul Whang interview, 17 December 2003.

59. Michael Lee, Interview by author, tape recording, San Francisco, CA, 31 May 2004.

60. Paul Whang interview, 17 December 2003.

61. Norma Lee Hom, Interview by author, telephone recording, 15 June 2000.

62. Jennie Chong Jue, Interview by author, telephone recording, 29 June 2000.

63. "Beauty for a Benefit Show," *California Chinese Press,* 11 April 1941, 1; "Dance to Raise 'Y' Camp Funds," *California Chinese Press,* 28 March 1941, 1; "Mrs. Alice Yu Entertains Square and Circle," *California Chinese Press,* 4 April 1941, 1; Victoria Wong, "Square and Circle Club: Women in the Public Sphere," in *Chinese America: History and Perspectives* (San Francisco, Chinese Historical

Society of America, 1994), 127–154; Judy Tzu-Chun Wu, "Loveliest Daughter of Our Ancient Cathay! Representations of Ethnic and Gender Identity in the Miss Chinatown U.S.A. Beauty Pageant," *Journal of Social History* 31 (Fall 1997): 5–31; Chiou-Ling Yeh, "Celebrating Freedom and Ethnicity," *American Quarterly* 57, no. 1 (March 2005): 279–288.

64. Ruth Whang, interview by author, tape recording, San Francisco, CA, 17 December 2003.

65. Hom interview, 15 June 2000.

66. Mary Jo Festle, *Playing Nice: Politics and Apologies in Women's Sports* (New York: Columbia University Press, 1996), 30, 32; Joan S. Hult, "The Story of Women's Athletics: Manipulating a Dream 1890–1985," in *Women and Sport: Interdisciplinary Perspectives* (Champaign, IL: Human Kinetics, 1994), 89.

67. Angela McRobbie, "Shut Up and Dance: Youth Culture and Changing Modes of Femininity," in *Postmodernism and Popular Culture* (London: Routledge, 1994), 162.

68. Jane Chew Wong, Interview by author, telephone recording, 16 June 2000.

69. Paul Whang interview, 17 December 2003.

70. Franche Lee, Interview by author, tape recording, Sunnyvale, CA, 14 December 2003.

71. Tong interview, 16 April 2003.

72. "Berkeley Services for Oliver Chang," *San Francisco Chronicle,* 8 November 1973, 47.

Chapter 2. The Hong Wah Kues Discover America

1. Dara Akiko Tom, "Basketball's Great Chinese Warriors," *San Francisco Examiner,* 9 (September 1996): A-5.

2. Fred Gok, Scrapbook; George Lee, Scrapbook. Tom, "Basketball's Great Chinese Warriors," A-5.

3. Linda Ford, *Lady Hoopsters: A History of Women's Basketball in America* (Northampton, MA: Half Moon Books, 1999). Todd Gould, *Pioneers of the Hardwood: Indiana and the Birth of Professional Basketball* (Bloomington: Indiana University Press, 1998), 22, 24, 30, 79, 88–89, 97–98, 100; Joanne Lannin, *A History of Basketball for Girls and Women: From Bloomers to Big Leagues* (Minneapolis: Lerner Sports, 2000); Sandra Steen and Susan Steen, *Take It to the Hoop: 100 Years of Women's Basketball* (Brookfield, CT: Twenty-First Century Books, 2003), 44, 47.

4. Carl Nolte, "Slam-Dunk Memories 60 Years Ago, Chinatown Had Its Own Pro Basketball Team," *San Francisco Chronicle,* 28 May 1999, A19; Rick Quan, *Hong Wah Kues,* television program (San Francisco: KPIX, March

1998); *Heroic Warriors: Chinese Hoopsters of the Past,* exhibit (San Francisco: Kearny Street Workshop, Chinatown Community Arts Program, Telegraph Hill Neighborhood Center, 2002); Al Young, "Hoop Dreams," *A. Magazine,* February–March 1996, 88.

5. Albert Sonny Lee, Interview by author, telephone recording, 28 July 2000.

6. "First Wah Ying League Games," *Chinese Digest,* January 1938, 16; Conrad Fong and Davisson Lee, "Nam Wah Wins," *Chinese Digest,* May 1938, 17.

7. Gok interview, 13 July 1999; Albert Sonny Lee interview, 28 July, 2000.

8. Quan, *Hong Wah Kues.*

9. Tom, "Basketball's Great Chinese Warriors," A-5.

10. Stanley Frank, "Crossroads Champs," *Collier's,* 8 February 1941, 23, 49–50; Gould, *Pioneers of the Hardwood,* 22, 24, 30, 79, 80, 88–89, 97–98, 100.

11. Nolte, "Slam-Dunk Memories," A19.

12. Albert Sonny Lee, Interview by author, tape recording, San Francisco, CA, 28 July 1998.

13. Young, "Hoop Dreams," 88; Quan, *Hong Wah Kues*; Gok interview, 13 July 1999.

14. Albert Sonny Lee interview, 28 July 1998.

15. Gok interview, 13 July 1999.

16. "St. Mary's Play Chinese Quintet Tomorrow Night," *Ironwood Daily Globe,* 4 December 1939, 8.

17. George Lee, Scrapbook.

18. Gould, *Pioneers of the Hardwood,* 22, 24, 30, 79, 88–89, 97–98, 100.

19. George Lee, Scrapbook.

20. Gok interview, 13 July 1999; George Lee, Scrapbook.

21. Gok interview, 13 July 1999; and George Lee, Scrapbook.

22. Gok interview, 13 July 1999; Gould, *Pioneers of the Hardwood,* 22, 24, 30, 79, 88–89, 97–98, 100; George Lee, Scrapbook; Alexander Saxton, *The Indispensable Enemy: Labor and the Anti-Chinese Movement in California* (Berkeley: University of California Press, 1971), 114, 129, 201–213.

23. Fred Gok, interview by author, telephone recording, 6 October 2000; Tom, "Basketball's Great Chinese Warriors," A-5.

24. Gok interview, 2000.

25. Gok interview, 13 July 1999.

26. Ibid.

27. Ibid.

28. Quan, *Hong Wah Kues*; *Heroic Warriors.*

29. Gok interview, 2000.

30. "Cage Star Is Native of Canton, China—Here Next Sunday," *Cincinnati Enquirer,* 16 February 1941, 34; "Chinese Cager," *Watsonville Register*

Pajorian, 12 February 1940, 2; "Chinese Hoop Club to Play Local Outfit," *Bremerton Daily News Searchlight*, 9 January 1940, 12; "Chinese Hoopsters to Play Here," *Vacaville Reporter*, 2 February 1940, 10; "Sports," *Kellogg Evening News*, 3 January 1940, 4.

31. Gok interview, 2000.

32. George Lee, Scrapbook.

33. Ibid.

34. During this time, newspapers commonly carried cartoon drawings that were not part of the comic section or the editorial page. For example, Robert Le Roy's comic feature "Ripley's Believe It or Not," which consisted of ink drawings and text, was a popular syndicated newspaper feature. The *San Francisco Chronicle* also incorporated graphic articles into its Sporting Green section, which included sports trivia and tips on how to play.

Lyle Brown, "Sports Quiz," *San Francisco Chronicle*, 21 December 1949, 2H; Robert Le Roy Ripley, *Believe It or Not!* (New York: Pocket Books, 1941); "Ripley's Believe It Or Not," *San Francisco Examiner*, 24 January 1948, 15; "Take a Tip From Morie: Meet the Pass," *San Francisco Chronicle*, 23 December 1949, 1H.

35. Dorothy Ko, "The Body as Attire: The Shifting Meanings of Footbinding in Seventeenth-Century China," *Journal of Women's History*, 8, no. 4 (Winter 1997): 10–26.

36. Weikun Cheng, "Politics of the Queue: Agitation and Resistance in the Beginning and End of Qing China," in *Hair: Its Power and Meaning in Asian Culture*, eds. Alf Hiltebeital and Barbara D. Miller (Albany: State University of New York Press, 1998), 123–142.

37. The character of Charlie Chan exemplified the stereotype of the inscrutable and emasculated Chinese man. Chan played the counterpoint of the disciplined Asian to the evil Fu Manchu. Playing a detective, Chan was known for pithy phrases that sounded like fortune cookies. The depiction played on his inability to communicate and his focus on intellect and the mind. Gloria Heyung Chun, *Of Orphans and Warriors: Inventing Chinese American Culture and Identity* (New Brunswick, NJ: Rutgers University Press), 18–19.

38. Sucheng Chan, *Asian Americans: An Interpretive History* (Boston: Twayne, 1991). 32.

39. Tom, "Basketball's Great Chinese Warriors," A-5.

40. George Lee, Scrapbook.

41. Ibid.

42. Quan, *Hong Wah Kues.*

43. "Chinese Squad Plays Tonight; Teds Traveling," *Port Angeles Evening News*, 11 January 1940, 4.

44. Tom, "Basketball's Great Chinese Warriors," A-5.

45. Gok interview, 2000.

46. Albert Sonny Lee interview, 28 July 2000.

47. "Dominoes Beat Chinese," *Victoria* (Canada) *Daily Times*, 13 January 1940, 14.

48. Quan, *Hong Wah Kues*; Young, "Hoop Dreams," 88.

49. Young, "Hoop Dreams," 88.

50. George Lee, Scrapbook; "St. Mary's Play Chinese Quintet Tomorrow Night," *Ironwood Daily Globe*.

51. A discussion of the connection between racial formation in sport and nation building deserves more space than this chapter will allow. See Gail Bederman, *Manliness and Civilization* (Chicago: University of Chicago Press, 1996); Mike Cronin and David Mayall, *Sporting Nationalisms: Identity, Ethnicity, Immigration, and Assimilation* (London: Frank Cass Publishers, 1998); John M. Hoberman, *Sport and Political Ideology*, (Austin: University of Texas Press, 1984); Anne McClintock, *Imperial Leather: Race, Gender, and Sexuality in the Colonial Context* (New York: Routledge, 1995); Martin Barry Vonokur, *More Than a Game: Sports and Politics* (New York: Greenwood Press, 1988).

52. Christopher Jesperson, *American Images of China, 1931–1949* (Palo Alto: CA: Stanford University Press, 1996); Karen J. Leong, *The China Mystique: Pearl S. Buck, Anna May Wong, Mayling Song, and the Transformation of American Orientalism* (Berkeley: University of California Press, 2005).

53. Don Gitersonke, *Baseball's Bearded Boys* (Las Vegas: Don Gitersonke, 1996), 2–3, 5–6, 46; Milton M. Gordon, *Assimilation in American Life: The Role of Race, Religion and National Origin* (New York: Oxford University Press, 1964).

54. Nolte, "Slam-Dunk Memories," A19.

55. Gok interview, 13 July 1999.

56. Ibid.

57. Gok interview, 13 July 1999; Albert Sonny Lee interview, 28 July 1998.

58. Gok interview, 13 July 1999.

59. Saxton, *The Indispensable Enemy*, 114, 129, 201–213.

60. Ibid., 104–109.

61. Frank, "Crossroads Champs," 23, 49–50.

62. "Globe Trotters' Cop World Pro Cage Crown," *Chicago Defender*, 30 March 1940, 22.

63. "Globe Trotters '5' in National Pro Cage Tournament," *Chicago Defender*, 9 March 1940, 24; "Globe Trotters Win 2," *Chicago Defender*, 6 January 1940, 23; "1940 World Professional Basket Champions," *Chicago Defender*, 30 March 1940, 22.

64. "Globe Trotters Win 2," 23; Gould, *Pioneers of the Hardwood*, 22, 24, 30, 79, 88–89, 97–98, 100.

65. "Globe Trotters Win 2," 23.

66. Grace Elizabeth Hale, *Making Whiteness: The Culture of Segregation in the South, 1890–1940* (New York: Pantheon Books, 1998).

67. Frank, "Crossroads Champs," 23, 49–50.

68. Ibid., 23, 49–50.

69. "American Chinese at Alberni Tonight" in George Lee, Scrapbook; "Trotter Five Handles Ball with Finesse," *Cincinnati Post*, 22 February 1941, 10.

70. Joseph Boskin, *Sambo: The Rise and Demise of an American Jester* (Oxford: Oxford University Press, 1988); Joel Taxel, "Charles Waddell Chestnutt's Sambo: Myth and Reality," *Negro American Literature Forum*, 9 (Winter 1975): 105–108.

71. John Blassingame, *The Slave Community: Plantation Life in the Antebellum South* (New York: Oxford University Press, 1979), 225.

72. Ibid., 225, 230.

73. John Bloom, *To Show What an Indian Can Do: Sports at Native American Boarding Schools* (Minneapolis: University of Minnesota Press, 2000); Joseph B. Oxendine, *American Indian Sports Heritage* (Lincoln: University of Nebraska Press, 1995).

74. "Eight Boys Teams in Tri-State Indian School Basketball Tournament," NRE-75-RC(PHO)-31, National Archives and Records Administration, Central Plains Region, Kansas City, MO.

75. Margaret L. Archuleta, Brenda J. Child, and K. Tsianina Lomawaima, eds., *Away from Home: American Indian Boarding School Experiences, 1879–2000* (Phoenix, AZ: Heard Museum, 2000); Brenda J. Child, *Boarding School Seasons: American Indian Families, 1900–1940* (Lincoln: University of Nebraska Press, 1993); Michael C. Coleman, *American Indian Children at School, 1850–1930* (Jackson: University Press of Mississippi, 1993); David Wallace Adams, *Education for Extinction: American Indians and the Boarding School Experience, 1875–1928* (Lawrence: University Press of Kansas, 1995).

76. Kevin Grace, Personal Research Collection on Professional Basketball.

77. Ibid.

78. George Lee, Scrapbook.

79. Philip J. Deloria, *Indians in Unexpected Places* (Lawrence: University Press of Kansas, 2004); Philip J. Deloria, *Playing Indian* (New Haven, CT: Yale University Press, 1998), 6–8, 117; Shari M. Huhndorf, *Going Native: Indians in the American Cultural Imagination* (Ithaca, NY: Cornell University Press, 2001); Alan Trachtenberg, *Shades of Hiawatha: Staging Indians, Making Americans, 1880–1930* (New York: Hill and Wang, 2004).

80. Scholars such as Vine Deloria, Jr., Randy Hanson, John Bloom, John O'Connor, Philip Deloria, and Jacquelyn Kilpatrick have all problematized the motif of the noble savage in popular culture. Confusing history and myth, the image of the fighting Indian male warrior was supposedly romantic because he was already doomed to death yet continued to fight. In this scenario, his noble spirit made him fight the good fight even when he knew he was going to lose to the powerful forces of the West. See, for example, Jacquelyn Kilpatrick,

Celluloid Indians: Native Americans and Film. (Lincoln: University of Nebraska Press, 1999).

81. Gould, *Pioneers of the Hardwood,* 22, 24, 30, 79, 88–89, 97–98, 100.

82. Ibid., 88–89; "Clever Chinese Quintet to Play Bearded Cagers," *Watsonville-Register Pajorian,* 5 February 1940, 2; Joel Hawkins and Terry Bertolino, *House of David Baseball Team* (Chicago: Arcadia Publishing, 2000), 7, 11, 145, 91.

83. Hawkins and Bertolino, *House of David Baseball Team,* 8–9, 50.

84. Poster, courtesy of Kevin Grace, Personal Research Collection on Professional Basketball.

85. Gok interview, 13 July 1999.

86. Rachel Lee, Interview by author, San Francisco, CA, 26 July, 1999.

87. Albert Sonny Lee interview, 28 July 1998.

88. Ibid.

89. Ibid.

90. Ibid.

91. Ibid.

92. Gok interview, 13 July 1999.

93. Nolte, "Slam-Dunk Memories," A19; Lee interview, 28 July 2000.

94. *"Heroic Warriors: Chinese Hoopsters of the Past."*

95. Albert Sonny Lee interview, 28 July 1998.

96. Ibid.

97. Albert Sonny Lee interview, 28 July 1998; Quan, *Hong Wah Kues;* Tom, "Basketball's Great Chinese Warriors," A-5.

98. Albert Sonny Lee interview, 28 July 1998.

99. George Lee, Scrapbook; Albert Sonny Lee interview, 28 July 2000.

100. Fred Gok, Scrapbook; George Lee, Scrapbook; Robert Lum, Scrapbook.

101. Gok interview, 13 July 1999.

102. George Lee, Scrapbook.

103. Gok interview, 13 July 1999.

104. Gok, Scrapbook, and Albert Sonny Lee interview, 28 July 2000.

105. Gok, Scrapbook; Gok interview, 13 July 1999.

106. George Lee, Scrapbook; Steen and Steen, *Take It to the Hoop,* 44, 47.

107. Gok interview, 13 July 1999.

108. Gok, Scrapbook.

109. Ryan Yip, Interview by author, telephone recording, 17 June 1999.

110. Albert Sonny Lee interview, 28 July 2000.

111. Gok, Scrapbook; Lee, Scrapbook; Lee, 28 July 1998, 28 July 2000.

112. Gok interview, 13 July 1999.

113. Ibid.

114. J. Michael Kenyon, Personal Research Collection on Professional Basketball; George Lee, Scrapbook.

115. In the 1990s, Chauncey Yip's nephew began promoting the Kues and started a film project. In May 2000, the Kearny Street Workshop created an exhibit on the Kues and the Chinese Saints.

Chapter 3. The Mei Wahs Knew How to Use Their Elbows and Push

1. Franche Lee, interview by author, Sunnyvale, CA, June 22, 2000.

2. Ibid.

3. Chris Shilling, "Physical Capital and Situated Action: A New Direction for Corporeal Sociology," *British Journal of Sociology of Education,* 25, no. 4 (September 2004): 473–484; Ann Swidler, "Culture in Action: Symbols and Strategies," *American Sociological Review,* 51, no. 2 (April 1986): 273–286.

4. Peter Levine, *Ellis Island to Ebbets Field: Sport and the American Jewish Experience (*New York: Oxford University Press, 1992), 8.

5. Evelyn Nakano Glenn, "The Social Construction and Institutionalization of Gender and Race: An Integrative Framework," in *Revisioning Gender,* eds. Myra Marx Ferree, Judith Lorber, and Beth B. Hess (Thousand Oaks, CA: Sage Publications, 1999), 3–43.

6. In addition, most of them had to work after school to help support their families and could not participate on their school teams. Franche Lee, interview, 22 June 2000.

7. Ibid.

8. Alice Chin Leung, Interview by author, tape recording, San Jose, CA, 3 July 1997.

9. Franche Lee, Interview by author, tape recording, Sunnyvale, CA, 12 February 1995; Rachel Lee, Interview by author, tape recording, San Francisco, CA, 7 July 1998; "Cover," *Chinese Digest,* 18 September 1936, 1.

10. Rachel Lee, Interview by author, telephone recording, 27 March 1997; James Francis "Smokey Joe" Wong, Interview by author, tape recording, San Francisco, CA, 30, July 1998; John Henry Wong, Interview by author, tape recording, Livermore, CA, 5 August 1998; "Sports," *Chinese Digest,* December 1938, 21.

11. "Sports," *Chinese Digest,* 16 January 1938, 16; "Sports," *Chinese Digest,* 4 September 1936, 13.

12. Rachel Lee interview, 7 July 1998.

13. Franche Lee interview, 12 February 1995.

14. Rachel Lee interview, 7 July 1998; "Cover," 1; "Chinese Girls Play Tonight," *San Francisco Examiner,* 6 February 1934, 19; "Girl Cagers in 3 Games Tonight," *San Francisco Examiner,* 12 February 1934, 22.

15. Josephine Chan, Interview by author, tape recording, San Francisco, CA, 4 October 1996; Lily Leong, Interview by author, tape recording, San Francisco, CA, 21 July 1998.

16. "Sports," *Chinese Digest*, December 1937, 21; and "Sports," *Chinese Digest*, February 1938, 21.

17. "Catholic Girls' Loop," *San Francisco Examiner*, 7 March 1935, S24; and "16 teams enter Girls' Cage League," *San Francisco Examiner*, 27 November 1932, S16.

18. "Girls' Club Meets Emporium Tonight," *San Francisco Examiner*, 31 March 1932, 21; "Telephone Girls Defeat Loyalty Six," *San Francisco News*, 12 March 1935, 18; "P.A. Girl Cagers to Play Wednesday," *San Francisco News*, 12 March 1935, 17; "Catholic Girls Play Tonight," *San Francisco News*, 12 March 1935, 17; "I.A.A. Girl Cagers Tangle Tonight," *San Francisco News*, 11 March 1935, 15; Linda D. Williams, "An Analysis of American Sportswomen in Two Negro Newspapers: The *Pittsburgh Courier*, 1924–1948, and the *Chicago Defender*, 1932–1948" (Ph.D. diss., Ohio State University, 1987); Mary Jo Festle, *Playing Nice: Politics and Apologies in Women's Sports* (New York: Columbia University Press, 1996), 38; "Women in Athletics," the *Chicago Defender*, 1 February 1930, 8 February 1930, 15 February 1930, 22 February 1930, 8–9; Marianna W. Davis, *Contributions of Black Women to America* (Columbia, SC: Kenday Press, 1982), 559; Arthur Ashe, *A Hard Road to Glory: A History of the African-American Athlete* (New York: Warner Books, 1988); Pamela Grundy and Susan Shackelford, *Shattering the Glass: The Remarkable History of Women's Basketball* (New York: New Press), 28–29, 53, 61–65, 71–79; Sandra Steen and Susan Steen, *Take It to the Hoop: 100 Years of Women's Basketball* (Brookfield, CT: Twenty-First Century Books, 2003), 44, 47; Joanne Lannin, *A History of Basketball for Girls and Women: From Bloomers to Big Leagues* (Minneapolis, MN: Lerner Sports, 2000); Elva E. Bishop, *Women's Basketball: The Road to Respect*, Documentary; John A. Molina, All American Redheads, 1936–1986: http://www.allamericanredheads.com/index.html (accessed 1 July 2007); Susan E. Cayleff, "The 'Texas Tomboy': The Life and Legend of Babe Didrikson Zaharias," OAH *Magazine of History* 7, no. 1 (Summer 1992): 28–33; http://www.oah.org/pubs/magazine/index.html (accessed 22 October 2008); Linda Ford, *Lady Hoopsters: A History of Women's Basketball in America* (Northampton, MA: Half Moon Books, 1999); Joan S. Hult, "The Story of Women's Athletics: Manipulating a Dream 1890–1985," in *Women and Sport: Interdisciplinary Perspectives*, eds. D. Margaret Costa and Sharon R. Guthrie (Champaign, IL: Human Kinetics, 1994), 89; Ronald A. Smith, "The Rise of Basketball for Women in Colleges," in *The American Sporting Experience: a Historical Anthology of Sport in America* ed. Steven A. Riess (New York: Leisure Press, 1984), 239–254; Janice A. Beran, "Iowa, the Longtime 'Hot Bed' of Girls Basketball," in *A Century of Women's Basketball*, eds. Joan S. Hult and Marianna Trekell (Reston, VA: American Alliance for Health, Physical Education, Recreation, and Dance, 1991), 185–186.

19. Agnes Cora Ruth Stillman, "Senda Berenson Abbott: Her Life and Contributions to Smith College and to the Physical Education Profession"(M.S. thesis, Smith College, 1971); Hult, "The Story of Women's Athletics," 83–106.

20. Alice W. Frymir and Marjorie Hillas, *Team Sports for Women* (New York: A. S. Barnes, 1935), 34–35.

21. Carroll Smith-Rosenberg and Charles Rosenberg, "The Female Animal: Medical and Biological Views of Women and Their Role in Nineteenth-Century America," in *From "Fair Sex" to Feminism: Sport and the Socialization of Women in the Industrial and Post-Industrial Eras*, eds. J. A. Mangan and Roberta J. Park (Totowa, NJ: F. Cass, 1987), 13–37.

22. Festle, *Playing Nice,* 30–32.

23. Frymir and Hillas, *Team Sports for Women,* 53.

24. Ibid., 36, 62–63.

25. Frymir and Hillas, *Team Sports for Women,* 59.

26. Ibid., 58–59.

27. Ibid., 59.

28. Ibid., 65.

29. Festle, *Playing Nice,* 30.

30. Susan Cahn, *Coming on Strong: Gender and Sexuality in Twentieth-Century Women's Sports* (New York: Free Press), 99.

31. Toril Moi, "Appropriating Bourdieu: Feminist Theory and Pierre Bourdieu's Sociology of Culture," *New Literary History,* Vol. 22, No. 4 (1991): 1017–1049.

32. Nathan Miller, *New World Coming: The 1920s and the Making of Modern America* (Cambridge, MA: Da Capo Press, 2004), 46–47. 253–272; Michael E. Parrish*: America in Prosperity and Depression, 1920–1941* (New York: W.W. Norton, 1992), 135–157; Stanley Coben, *Revolt against Victorianism: The Impetus for Cultural Change in 1920s America* (New York: Oxford University Press, 1991).

33. Festle, *Playing Nice,* 4.

34. Smith-Rosenberg and Rosenberg, "The Female Animal," 14, 17.

35. Helen Lenskyj, "A Kind of Precipitate Waddle: Early Opposition to Women Running," in *Sport and the Sociological Imagination: Refereed Proceedings of the 3rd Annual Conference of the North American Society for the Sociology of Sport, Toronto, Ontario, Canada, November 1982,* ed. Ontario North American Society for the Sociology of Sport (Toronto: Nancy Theberge and Peter Donnelly, 1982), 155.

36. Stanley D. Eitzen and George Harvey Sage, *Sociology of American Sport.* 2nd ed. (Dubuque, IA: W. C. Brown, 1982), 272; John C. Phillips, *Sociology of Sport* (Boston: Allyn and Bacon, 1993), 213–214.

37. Susan Brownell, *Training the Body for China: Sports in the Moral Order of the People's Republic* (Chicago: University of Chicago Press, 1995), 225–228.

38. James C. Scott, *Weapons of the Weak: Everyday Forms of Peasant Resistance* (New Haven, CT: Yale University Press, 1985), xvi; James C. Scott, *Domination and the Arts of Resistance: Hidden Transcripts* (New Haven, CT: Yale University Press, 1992), 118, 137; Robin D. G. Kelley, *Race Rebels: Culture, Politics, and the Black Working Class* (New York: Free Press, 1994).

39. Franche Lee interview, 12 February, 1995.

40. Ibid.

41. Leong interview, 21 July 1998. .

42. Rachel Lee interview, 7 July 1998.

43. Chan interview, 4 October 1996.

44. Ibid.

45. Franche Lee interview, 31 October 1996.

46. Josephine Chan, interview by author, tape recording, Richmond CA, 12 December 1987.

47. Franche Lee interview, 4 October 1996.

48. Sucheng Chan, *Asian Americans: An Interpretive History,* (Boston: Twayne, 1991), 103, 111.

49. Yen Le Espiritu, "Asian American Women and Men: Labor, Laws, and Love," in *The Gender Lens,* eds. Judith A. Howard et al. (Thousand Oaks, CA: Sage Publications, 1997), 16–21.

50. Yung, *Unbound Feet: A Social History of Chinese Women in San Francisco.* (Berkeley: University of California Press, 1995), 106–107, 198.

51. Wong, *Fifth Chinese Daughter,* 127–154; Shirley Lim, *A Feeling of Belonging: Asian Americans Women's Public Culture in the 1930s and 1940s.* (New York: New York University Press, 2006), 11–46; Yung, *Unbound Feet,* 153.

52. Examples include the first Chinese American San Francisco public school teacher, Alice Fong Yu, who worked with Christian organizations, and Dr. Margaret Jessie Chung and her "adopted" family of servicemen. Judy Tzu-Chun Wu, *Doctor Mom Chung of the Fair-Haired Bastards: The Life of a Wartime Celebrity* (Berkeley: University of California Press, 2005), 49, 120–121; Yung, *Unbound Feet,* 1995, 207–208.

53. Yung, *Unbound Feet,* 207, 231–232, 241–243; and K. Scott Wong, *Americans First: Chinese Americans and the Second World War* (Cambridge: Harvard University Press, 2005), 39–42.

54. Yung, *Unbound Feet,* 201–204; Lorraine Dong, "The Forbidden City Legacy and Its Chinese American Women," *Chinese America: History and Perspectives* 6 (1992): 125–48; and Karen J. Leong, *The China Mystique: Pearl S. Buck, Anna May Wong, Mayling Soong, and the Transformation of American Orientalism.* (Berkeley: University of California Press, 2005), 57.

55. Stacey G. H. Yap, "Gather Your Strength, Sisters: The Emerging Role of Chinese Women Community Workers" (Ph.D. diss., Boston University, 1983); Yung, *Unbound Feet,* 209–222.

56. Franche Lee interview, 4 October 1996.

57. Gor Yun Leong, *Chinatown Inside Out* (New York: B. Mussey, 1936); Jade Snow Wong, *Fifth Chinese Daughter* (Seattle, WA: University of Washington Press, 1989); Huping Ling, *Surviving on the Gold Mountain: A History of Chinese American Women and Their Lives* (Albany: State University of New York Press, 1998); Victoria Wong, "Square and Circle Club: Women in the Public Sphere," *Chinese America: History and Perspectives* (San Francisco: Chinese Historical Society of America, 1994), 127–154.

58. Loic J. D. Wacquant, "The Pugilistic Point of View—How Boxers Think and Feel about Their Trade," *Theory and Society,* 24, no. 4 (1995): 501.

59. Franche Lee interview, 31 October 1996.

60. Kit-Kit Louis, "A Study of American-Born and American-Reared Chinese in Los Angeles," (Master's thesis, University of Southern California, 1931), 3–5, 29, 50, 91.

61. Franche Lee interview, 22 June 2000.

62. Franche Lee interview, 12 February 1995.

63. Franche Lee, interview, 12 February 1995, 22 June 2000.

64. Chan, *Asian Americans,* 145–146; Him Mark Lai and Philip P. Choy. *Outlines: History of the Chinese in America* (San Francisco: Lai & Choy, 1971), 102; Rose Hum Lee, *The Chinese in the United States of America* (Hong Kong: Hong Kong University Press, 1960).

65. Franche Lee interview, 12 February 1995.

66. Alice Chin Leung, Interview by author, tape recording, San Jose, CA, 3 July 1997; and Rachel Lee interview, 7 July 1998.

67. Eitzen and Sage, *Sociology of American Sport,* 333.

68. Rachel Lee interview, 7 July 1998; Albert Sonny Lee, Interview by author, tape recording, San Francisco, CA, 28 July 1998.

69. Cindy Himes Gissendanner, "African-American Women and Competitive Sport, 1920–1960," in *Women, Sport, and Culture,* eds. Susan Birrell and Cheryl L. Cole (Champaign, IL: Human Kinetics, 1994), 81–92.

70. Leith Mullings, "Images, Ideology, and Women of Color," in *Women of Color in U.S. Society,* eds. Bonnie Thornton Dill and Maxine Baca Zinn (Philadelphia: Temple University Press, 1994), 265–290.

71. Patricia Hill Collins, *Black Feminist Thought: Knowledge, Consciousness, and the Politics of Empowerment* (London: Harper Collins Academic, 1990); Glenn, "The Social Construction and Institutionalization of Gender and Race," 3–43.

72. Yung, *Unbound Feet,* 206.

73. "Cover," *Chinese Digest,* 4 September 1936, 1.

74. Fred George Woo, "Sporting News," *Chinese Digest,* 18 September 1936, 23.

75. James Francis, ibid.

76. Smokey Joe Wong interview, 30 July 1998.

77. Alfred Lee, Interview by author, tape recording, San Francisco, CA, 9 July 1999.

78. John Henry Wong interview, 5 August 1998.

79. Kelley, *Race Rebels,* 169.

Chapter 4. "Mr. Chinese Cager" Plays Madison Square Garden

1. "Willie Woo Woo Wong, Chinese Cage Ace Chooses USF over Fordham, Seton Hall," in William Woo Wong, Scrapbook.

2. John Giosso, Interview by author, telephone recording, 3 July 2005.

3. William Woo Wong, Interview by author, tape recording, Newark, CA, 14 July 1999.

4. William Woo Wong, Interview by author, tape recording, Newark, CA, 16 June 2000.

5. Ibid.

6. Ibid.

7. Ibid.

8. Ibid.

9. Ibid.

10. Ibid.

11. "27 out of 48," in W. Wong, Scrapbook

12. Percy Chu, Interview by author, telephone recording, 3 July 2005.

13. "1947 National Oriental Basketball Tournament Program," in W. Wong, Scrapbook ; "These Are Best Chinese American Basketballers in the Country . . . ," *Chinese Press,* 7 January 1949, 8.

14. W. Wong, Scrapbook

15. "Heroic Warriors: Chinese Hoopsters of the Past," Exhibit (San Francisco: Kearny Street Workshop, Chinatown Community Arts Program, Telegraph Hill Neighborhood Center), 2002.

16. Bruce Jenkins, *A Good Man: The Pete Newell Story* (Berkeley: Frog, Ltd., 1999).

17. Wong interview, 24 July 1999.

18. "Column," 9 February 1949, in W. Wong, Scrapbook.

19. Wong interview, 24 July 1999.

20. "Sport Briefs," *Chinese Press,* 31 December 1948, 7; W. Wong, Scrapbook; "'Woo Woo' Wong Is Outstanding Casaba Tosser for USF Frosh," *Chinese Press,* 21 January 1949, 15; "'Woo Woo' Wong Stars for USF in PAA Tilt," *Chinese Press* 25 February 1949, 8; "USF Frosh Tips S.F. Chinese Cagers," *Chinese Press,* 18 February 1949, 7.

21. Woo's full name was William Woo Wong. His family and friends called him Woo, and mainstream newspapers often referred him to as Willie. "Woo Woo's Clutch Shots Saves Frosh," in W. Wong, Scrapbook.

22. Bill Leiser, "USF's Big Chance March 19," *San Francisco Chronicle,* 19 March 1949, 1H; Jack McDonald, "USF Has Come a Long Way Along Nat'l Cage Pike," *San Francisco Call Bulletin Sports,* 1 March 1949, 17; I. R. McVay," Dons Fight Way to Cage Final," *San Francisco Chronicle,* 18 March 1949, 1H; Stan Opotowsky, "USF 4- Point NY Underdog," *San Francisco Chronicle,* 17 March 1949, 1H.

23. In the late 1940s, the National Collegiate Athletic Association (NCAA) tournament was considered the lesser tournament. Wong interview, 24 July 1999.

24. Stan Opotowsky, "USF Dons Capture Cage Crown," *San Francisco Chronicle,* 20 March 1949, 1H.

25. Bob Brachman, "USF Cagers Off for East—Still Gunning for National Tourney," *San Francisco Examiner,* 30 January 1950, 22.

26. Bob Brachman, "USF Off for US Title Bid," *San Francisco, Examiner,* 9 March 1950, 29.

27. Curley Grieve, "Dons' Inspired Drive Garners N.Y. Bid—USF-and-Brachman-Win Cage," *San Francisco Examiner,* 5 March 1950, 23.

28. Franklin Lewis Column, 2 March 1950, in W. Wong, Scrapbook.

29. "Don Spurt Trounces Gaels; Cards Stave off Bronc Bid," *San Francisco Examiner,* 22 January 1950, 20; *University of San Francisco Yearbook, 1949–1950,* 53–59; "USF Roars Past Stanford, 54–39," *San Francisco Examiner,* 21 January 1950, 15.

30. Bob Brachman, "Dons Face N.Y.'s Best in Garden Tonight," *San Francisco Examiner,* 22 December 1949, 20; Bob Brachman, "USF Cagers Open Title Defense Today," *San Francisco Examiner,* 11 March 1950, 18; "Sad Night for Coast: St. John's Surges over Dons, 60–44; CCNY Ruins Bears," *San Francisco Chronicle Sporting Green,* 23 December 1949, 1H; "St. John's Five Routs San Francisco 60–44; C.C.N.Y. Crushes California 76–46," *New York Herald Tribune,* 23 December 1949, 18.

31. Wong interview, 16 June 2000.

32. Cap Lavin, Interview by author, telephone recording, 30 July 2005.

33. " 'Woo Woo' Willie's an Old SF Favorite," in W. Wong, Scrapbook.

34. "Cager Champs," " 'Woo Woo' Willie's an Old SF Favorite," and "Woo Woo Wong Is Outstanding Casaba Tosser for USF Frosh," in W. Wong, Scrapbook ; "Sports," *The Monitor,* 23 December 1949, 16; "Woo Woo in PA Bow," *San Francisco Examiner,* 17 February 1948, 22.

35. "Woo-Woo Will Do," in W. Wong, Scrapbook.

36. Pete Newell, Interview by author, telephone recording, 1 August 2005.

37. "'Woo Woo' Wong Is Outstanding Casaba Tosser for USF Frosh," 15.

38. Lavin interview, 30 July 2005.

39. Ibid.

40. Dwight Chapin, "All of 5–5, USF's Wong Stood Tall With the Best in College Game," *San Francisco Chronicle*, 13 April 2005, D1, D6.

41. Wong interview, 16 June 2000.

42. Gail Bederman, *Manliness and Civilization: A Cultural History of Gender and Race in the United States, 1880–1917* (Chicago: University of Chicago Press, 1996).

43. Grieve, "Dons' Inspired Drive Garners N.Y. Bid," 23; "Obituaries: Bob Brachman, Examiner Sports Reporter," *San Francisco Examiner*, 5 January 1993, A-13.

44. Bob Brachman, "USF Star Tanks 45 for P.A. Mark!—Wong Racks 29, but Buksar Steals Show," *San Francisco Examiner*, 18 February 1948, 22; Bob Brachman, "Wong, Buksar on Spot as 54 Teams Vie in Examiner-PA Tourney Today," *San Francisco Examiner*, 22 February 1948, 21.

45. Helen Wong Lum, Interview by author, tape recording, San Francisco, CA, 24 November 2002.

46. "San Francisco Plays Xavier at Sportscenter Tuesday," *Owensboro Messenger*, 5 February 1950, 9A; "St. John's Meets San Francisco, C.C.N.Y. Faces California at Garden," *New York Herald Tribune*, 22 December 1949, 26.

47. Wong interview, 24 July 1999.

48. "Don Lofgran . . . USF's All-American Candidate," *News and Observer*, 2 January 1950, 9; "Dons' Coach Explains," *News and Observer*, 3 January 1950, 13; "Three Dons Named on All-Stars," *San Francisco Call Bulletin Sports*, 21 March 1949, 13.

49. Novelty sports photos during this time usually placed children and women in the subordinate position relative to adult men. Visually, only white men were strong, aggressive, and powerful. If adult men were in playful poses, the media depicted all the men in the photo as being equally comical with comparable standing. "Champin' at the Bit," *San Francisco Examiner*, 10 March 1948, 21; Chapin, All of 5–5, USF's Wong Stood Tall," D1, D6; "Dons' 'Mutt and Jeff,'" *Buffalo Courier-Express*, 31 December 1949, 13; "Fair and Warmer!" *San Francisco Examiner*, 19 January 1950, 16; "Pack Meets Dons on Tuesday," *News and Observer*, 1 January 1950, 4 ; "Ready for Test!" *San Francisco Examiner*, 22 December 1949, 20; "Utah's Starting Five against Canisius Tonight," *Buffalo Courier-Express*, 29 December 1949, 19.

50. Originating in the *San Francisco Chronicle's* sports pages, "Mutt and Jeff" eventually became a syndicated favorite on comic pages across the nation. As evidence of the strip's popularity, the characters expanded into comic books, animated cartoon shorts, and weekly single-reel comedy pictures. See obituary of "Mutt and Jeff" Cartoonist Al Smith, *Albany Times*

Union, 26 November 1986, 8C; Jerry Robinson, *The Comics: An Illustrated History of Comic Strip Art* (New York: Putnam, 1974); Matthew P. McAllister, Edward H. Sewell, and Ian Gordon, eds., *Comics and Ideology: Popular Culture and Everyday Life*, vol. 2 (New York: Peter Lang Publishing, 2001); Roger Sabin, *Comics, Comix and Graphic Novels* (London: Phaidon, 1996).

51. "It's a Cinch," in W. Wong, Scrapbook.

52. Newell interview, 1 August 2005.

53. W. Wong, Scrapbook.

54. "Low Man Between," *Chinese Press*, 9 December 1949, 22; "St. John's Meets San Francisco," 26. The caption reads: "Towering Protectors, Wee Willie Wong gets plenty of protection on this shot during a practice session of the University of San Francisco basketball team here yesterday. . . . Wong is the smallest player in major competition to appear in the Garden."

55. "St. John's Meets San Francisco," 26.

56. Ruth Frankenberg, *Displacing Whiteness: Essays in Social and Cultural Criticism* (Durham, NC: Duke University Press, 1997); George Lipsitz, *The Possessive Investment in Whiteness: How White People Profit from Identity Politics* (Philadelphia: Temple University Press, 1998).

57. Chapin, "All of 5–5, USF's Wong Stood Tall," D1, D6.

58. "'Woo Woo' Hits Big Time," *Chinese Press*, 28 December 1949, 6.

59. Lavin interview, 30 July 2005.

60. "Basketball Champs: Chinese Cagers Win Again in Second National Tourney," *Chinese Press*, 31 December 1948, 1–2; "Berkeley, SF Chinese Gain Finals," *San Francisco Examiner*, 29 December 1948, 19; "Champion Casaba Tossers," *Chinese Press*, 7 January 1949, 8; "Hawaiians, Saints Reach Oriental Basketball Final," *Seattle Post-Intelligencer*, 28 December 1947, 24; "Oriental Meet on Tonight: 8 Teams Set to Play," *Seattle Post-Intelligencer*, 23 December 1948, 15; "Saints Down Berkeley Five: Willie Wong Leads S.F. Chinese to U.S. Oriental Title," *San Francisco Chronicle*, 27 December 1948, 2H; "Saints Win Second Title: San Francisco Five Cops Tournament," *Seattle Post-Intelligencer*, 27 December 1948, 13; "S.F. Chinese Grab Title; Wong Star," *San Francisco Examiner*, 27 December 1948, 17; "S.F. Chinese Team Wins Oriental Hoop Tourney," *Seattle Post-Intelligencer*, 27 December 1947, 16; "S.F. Saints Defeat Nisei," *Seattle Post-Intelligencer*, 25 December 1948, 14; "These Are Best Chinese-American Basketballers in the Country," 8; "Wong Stars Again As SF Five Rolls On," *San Francisco Examiner*, 28 December 1947, 14.

61. 1947 National Oriental Basketball Tournament Program, in W. Wong, Scrapbook.

62. W. Wong, Scrapbook.

63. Ibid.

64. Lorraine Dong, "The Forbidden City Legacy and Its Chinese American Women," *Chinese America: History and Perspectives,* 6 (1992): 125–148; Edward Said, *Orientalism* (New York: Vintage Books, 1979).

65. Mai Ngai, *Impossible Subjects: Illegal Aliens and the Making of Modern America.* (Princeton, NJ: Princeton University Press, 2005), 202–224.

66. Joel S. Franks, *Crossing Sidelines, Crossing Cultures: Sport and Asian Pacific American Cultural Citizenship* (Lanham, MD: University Press of America, 2000), iv–xvi, 1–4.

67. "San Jose, Chinese Quints Top Play in Examiner-P.A. Meet," in W. Wong, Scrapbook.

68. "Stockton Five Shades Wong," in W. Wong, Scrapbook.

69. W. Wong, Scrapbook.

70. Richard Bak, *Joe Louis: The Great Black Hope* (Dallas, TX: Taylor Pub., 1996); M. Jill Dupont, "'The Self in the Ring, the Self in Society': Boxing and American Culture from Jack Johnson to Joe Louis" (Ph.D. diss., University of Chicago, Chicago, 2000); Andrew Miles Kaye, "'A Tiger in the Ring and a Pussycat Outside': American Attitudes towards Black Prizefighters, 1810–1938" (MA thesis, Emory University, Atlanta, 1997).

71. C. L R. James, *Beyond a Boundary* (New York: Pantheon Books, 1983).

72. Wong interview, 24 July 1999.

73. "Heroic Warriors" Exhibit, 2002; "'Woo-Woo' Most Valuable Player," *Chinese Press,* 8 December 1950, 8; W. Wong, Scrapbook.

74. This was an amateur league that broke through many of the color lines before the civil rights movement gained momentum. For example, John B. McLendon was the first black coach in the league in 1959 and led his team to the league championship.

75. The AAU tournament has existed since 1897.

76. Becky Bowman, "San Francisco Playground Renamed for Basketball Hero," *San Francisco Chronicle,* 20 January 2006, B-3; "USF to Induct Four into the Athletic Hall of Fame," http://usfdons.cstv.com/genrel/012307aab.html (accessed June 8, 2007).

77. Wong interview, 24 July 1999.

78. Lavin interview, 30 July 2005.

Chapter 5. Helen Wong and the "Muscle Molls"

1. Helen Wong Lum, Interview by author, tape recording, San Francisco, CA, 23 October 1998.

2. Ibid.

3. Ibid.

4. William Woo Wong, Interview by author, tape recording, Newark, CA.,14 July, 1999. Hank Wong, Interview by author, telephone recording, 30 June 1999.

5. Brachman, "Hey, Fellows," 23.

6. Credited with making the one-handed set shot a staple, Hank Luisetti led his Stanford team to the NCAA championships; experts described him as "probably the greatest basketball player who ever lived." A two-time all-American, Luisetti scored fifty points in one game and averaged a stellar twenty-two points a game in an era when teams usually combined to score fifty points total. Bob Brachman, "800 Kids Swarm to Cage School!" *San Francisco Examiner,* 20 December 1949, 22; Bob Brachman, "Examiner Cage School Adds 3 All Americans to Staff," *San Francisco Examiner,* 18 December 1949, 25; Bob Brachman, "Examiner Cage School Comes to Thrilling Close," *San Francisco Examiner,* 1 February 1948, 26; Bob Brachman, "Helen Wong Makes Phenomenal Shots in Basketball School Competition," *San Francisco Examiner,* 31 December 1948, 8; Bob Brachman, "Hey, Fellows," 23; "Hot Shots' in Test Today at Examiner Cage Finale," *San Francisco Examiner,* 27 December 1948, 17; Dan Cisco, *Hawaii Sports: History, Facts, and Statistics* (Honolulu: University of Hawaii Press, 1999), 54; Bill Mulligan, "Hank Luisetti's Markmanship Class Fascinates Examiner Cage Students," *San Francisco Examiner,* 18 January 1948, 24; "Nice Knowing You," *San Francisco Examiner,* 28 December 1948, 19; "3 in Second Places of Cage Shooting Battle," *Chinese Press,* 14 January 1949, 8;"Wong Sister's Top Basket Shooters," in Helen Wong Lum, Scrapbook.

7. "Helen Wong Sets Scoring Record," "Aurora Newsletter," "Helen Wong Stars," "Chinese Girls Quintet Win,s" in Lum, Scrapbook; "Title Game for CYO Girl Cagers," *The Monitor*; 7 December 1946, 6.

8. "Girls' Basketball," *The Monitor,* 31 October 1947, 6; "St. Anne's, St. Cecilia's Cagers Tied for Lead," *The Monitor,* 25 November 1949, 15; "St. Mary's Chinese to Meet Winner of Sunset League," *The Monitor,* 16 December 1949, 22.

9. During the 1946 season, St. Cecilia, St. Anne, St. Brigid, Star of the Sea, St. Monica, and Holy Name usually competed in the Sunset Division of the league. Holy Family, St. Mary's, Dolorians, St. Phillips "B," Epiphany, St. Emydius, St. Peter, St. Paul, and St. Phillips "A" competed in the Mission Division of the League during the 1946 season. "Girls' Basketball," *The Monitor,* 17 October 1947, 6; "Girls' Parish Section Basketball Games," *The Monitor,* 26 October 1946, 6; 2 November 1946, 6; 9 November 1946, 6; 16 November 1946, 6; 23 November 1946, 6; "Holy Family Is the Team to Beat in Girls' Parish League," *The Monitor,* 28 November 1947, 6; "St. Cecilia Five Win Girls' Title," *The Monitor,* 14 December 1946, 6; "St. Mary's Chinese to Meet Winner Of Sunset League," 16 ; "Girls' Basketball," *The Monitor,* 7 November 1947, 6; "Victory Banquet for Girl Saints," *Chinese Press,* 6 January 1950, 7.

10. "CYO Basketball Tonight, Girls Play Title Games" and "Woo Woo's Sis" in Lum, Scrapbook; "Girls Cage League," *The Monitor,* 12 December 1947, 6; "St. Cecilia Five Wins Girls' Title," 6; "Girl Cagers Near End of Tourney," *The Monitor,* 30 November 1946, 6; "Girls' Basketball," *The Monitor,* 14 November 1947, 6; "Holy Family Is the Team to Beat," 6; "Titles Near in Girls' CYO Cage Loops," *The Monitor,* 9 December 1949, 17;

11. "Aurora Newsletter,' '"Chinese Girls Quintet Wins," and "Helen Wong Stars" in Lum, Scrapbook; "Girl Cagers Set Fast Pace in Parish League," *The Monitor,* 21 November 1947, 6; "Girls CYO Loop Opens," *The Monitor,* 4 November 1949, 19; "Holy Family Is The Team to Beat," 6; "Title Game for CYO Girl Cagers," 6.

12. "Basketball Festival at Kezar Sunday," *Chinese Press,* 7 January 1949, 7, "Filipino Olympic All-Stars Clip S.F. Chinese in Basketball Festival," *Chinese Press,* 14 January 1949, 7; "SF Chinese Hoopsters Face Amblers Tonight," *Chinese Press,* 10 December 1948, 7; and "Triple Header: Chinese Girls' Hoop Tourney," *San Francisco Chronicle,* 9 January 1949, 3H.

13. The Nisei Rogues were coached by Kenny Kim, a Korean American, who was a staff member at the Chinese Recreation Center and who profoundly impacted youth through sports in Chinatown. Rachel Gordon, "Kenneth Kim: Educator Specialized in Recreation for Kids," *San Francisco Chronicle,* 23 February 2003, A-28; "Chinese and Nisei Fives Meet Tonight," "Helen Wong Sets Scoring Record," and "Nisei Five Tops Chinese Men, 46–43" in Lum, Scrapbook; K. Scott Wong, *Americans First: Chinese Americans and the Second World War* (Cambridge: Harvard University Press, 2005), 33, 35, 39; "Woo Woo, Sister to Share Spotlight," *San Francisco Examiner,* 13 March 1948, 25.

14. Wong Lum interview, 1998.

15. "Helen Wong Stars," in Lum, Scrapbook; "Outstanding Chinese Girl Cagers," *Chinese Press,* 14 January 1949, 1; "St. Cecilia Five Wins Girls' Title," 6; "Title Game for CYO Girl Cagers," *The Monitor,* 7 December 1946, 6.

16. "Top Honors," *The Monitor,* 26 December 1947, 6; "Victory Banquet for Girl Saints," *Chinese Press,* 6 January 1950, 7.

17. Wong Lum Interview, 1998.

18. "Chopsticks" and H. K. Wong, "Sports," in Lum, Scrapbook.

19. "First Chinese: Helen Wong Home from Jr. Davis Cup Matches," *Chinese Press,* 25 November 1949, 7.

20. In addition to competing in California state junior tennis championships, she won the under-sixteen Northern California novice tennis championship. In the recreational league, she was the Girls Class III winner of the inter-playground tournament in 1946 and 1947 as well as the first Chinese winner. Chinese Historical Society of America, *The Third Annual A Celebration of Roots: Two Steps Forward—Chinese Americans in Sports* (San Francisco: Author, 1996), 26; "Four Chinese-American Net Stars Enter U.S. National Hard

Court Meet," *Chinese Press,* 1 October 1948, 7; "Helen Wong Is CYO Net Champ" and "Helen Wong Retains CYO Net Title," in Lum, Scrapbook; "Tennis-SFCTC Active in Tourneys, H. K. Wong," *Chinese Press,* 21 November 1950, 7.

21. The prestigious Junior Wightman Cup competition was part of the Northern California Tennis Association's (NCTA) competition for some of the best players in the California. "Helen Wong Cops State Fair Titles," *Chinese Press,* 16 September 1949, 7; "Helen Wong to Play Jr. Davis Matches," *Chinese Press,* 11 November 1949, 3.

22. Dayton Lee, Interview by author, tape recording, San Francisco, CA, 12 May 2000; William Woo Wong interview, 2000; Wong Lum Interview, 1998.

23. Ibid.

24. Father Forrester Foundation, *Father Forrester Tournament 1999 Chinese New Year Basketball Jamboree Program—8th Annual* (San Francisco, CA: 1999).

25. Wong Lum Interview, 1998.

26. Ibid.

27. Helen Wong Lum, Interview by author, tape recording, San Francisco, CA, 24 November 2002.

28. Wong Lum Interview, 1998.

29. "Exclusive: Story of How Tennis Champs Fought for '49 Titles," *Chinese Press,* 16 September 1949, 1; "Girls' Casaba Game," *Chinese Press,* 5 November 1949, 7; "Helen Wong Home from Jr. Davis Cup Matches," *Chinese Press,* 25 November 1949, 7; "Helen Wong Makes Phenomenal Shots in Basketball School Competition," *Chinese Press,* 31 December 1948, 8; "Tennis Tourney Underway Tomorrow," *Chinese Press,* 25 August 1950, 8 "Sports," *Chinese Press,* 8 October 1948, 117; "Four Chinese American Net Stars Enter U.S. National Hardcourt Meet," 7; "Helen Wong to Play Jr. Davis Matches," 3.

30. "Exclusive: Story of How Tennis Champs Fought for '49 Titles," 1.

31. "Good Sportsmanship," "1949 Tennis Champions," and "17th Pacific Coast Chinese Championships," in Lum, Scrapbook.

32. Lum, Scrapbook.

33. "Helen Wong Cops State Fair Titles," 7; "Chu, Wong Win Tennis Crowns," "Helen Wong Again Captures Title in Chinese Tennis," and "Helen Wong Net Finalist," in Lum, Scrapbook; "The No. California Tennis Championship," *Chinese Press,* 23 June 1950, 8; "Oakland Father, 45, Wins Net Title: Gene Louie Beats Wing Jue in 4 Sets; Helen Wong Keeps Crown 3rd Time," *Chinese Press,* 16 September 1949, 7; "Tennis Tourney Ends: Peter Gee, Helen Wong Win in Singles Finals," *Chinese Press,* 17 September 1948, 11; H. K. Wong, "Sports," *Chinese Press,* 24 November 1950, 7; "Gene Louie Singles

Champ, Favorites Win in Nationals," *Chinese Press,* 15 September 1950, 7; "Wong-Mock Wing Doubles in Finals of Junior Tennis Tournament," *Chinese Press,* 24 June 1949, 8.

34. Chinese Historical Society of America, *Third Annual A Celebration of Roots.*

35. H. K. Wong, "National Chinese Tennis Tourney," in Lum, Scrapbook.

36. It should be noted that the ethnic-based newspapers also depicted Chinese American women in ways that supported dominant mainstream depictions of middle-class femininity. See, for example, Edward W. Chew, "Are Country Lassies Prettier—Do City Girls Play Second-Fiddle to Suburban Sis?" *Chinese Press,* 6 January 1950, 1, 6; "Gold Rush Starts Tomorrow . . . Official History of This Women's Service Club," *Chinese Press,* 21 October 1949, 3; "Stepping Out with 'Goo-Mah', Square and Circle Club Benefit Show," *Chinese Press,* 1 December 1950, 1.

37. Souvenir Program, 1948 Chinatown Basketball Festival (San Francisco: 1948), Ben Hom Collection, Chinese Historical Society, Box #1, Folder #3, Ethnic Studies Library, University of California Berkeley.

38. Wong Lum Interview, 24 November 2002.

39. Mary Anderson, "The Postwar Role of American Women," *The American Economic Review,* 34, no. 1, part 2, in *Supplement, Papers and Proceedings of the Fifty-Sixth Annual Meeting of the American Economic Association* (March 1944), 237–244; Linda Eisenmann. *Higher Education for Women in Postwar America, 1945–1965.* (Baltimore: Johns Hopkins University Press, 2006); Wu, *Doctor Mom Chung of the Fair-Haired Bastards,* 149.

40. Margaret Carlisle Duncan, "Sports Photographs and Sexual Difference: Images of Men and Women in the 1984 and 1988 Olympic Games," *Sociology of Sport Journal,* 7 (March 1990): 22–43; "Fairway Finalist," *San Francisco Examiner,* 29 January 1950, 25; Michael A. Messner, Margaret Carlisle Duncan, and Faye Linda Wachs, "The Gender of Audience-Building: Televised Coverage of Men's and Women's NCAA Basketball," *Sociological Inquiry,* Vol. 66, No. 4 (Fall 1996): 422–439.

41. Lum, Scrapbook.

42. Ibid.

43. Susan E. Cayleff, "The 'Texas Tomboy': The Life and Legend of Babe Didrikson Zaharias," *OAH Magazine of History,* 7, no. 1 (Summer 1992): 28–33.

44. Susan E. Cayleff, *Babe: The Life and Legend of Babe Didrikson Zaharias* (Champaign: University of Illinois Press, 1996), 122.

45. Ibid., 115.

46. Ibid., 127–133, 190; Mary Jo Festle, *Playing Nice: Politics and Apologies in Women's Sports* (New York: Columbia University Press, 1996), 33–34.

47. "Helen Wong Stars" and "Helen Wong Is Star," in Lum, Scrapbook.

48. "Now It Comes Up Basketball Season," in Lum, Scrapbook.

49. Will Connolly, "Nation's Best Chinese Netters Competing Here," *San Francisco Chronicle*, 29 August 1954, 4H.

50. Robert G. Lee, *Orientals: Asian Americans in Popular Culture, Asian American History and Culture* (Philadelphia: Temple University Press, 1999), 10, 145–160.

51. Susan Birrell and Nancy Theberge. "Ideological Control of Women in Sport," in *Women and Sport: Interdisciplinary Perspectives*, eds. D. M. Costa and S. R. Guthrie (Champaign, IL: Human Kinetics, 1994), 353.

52. Susan K. Cahn, *Coming on Strong: Gender and Sexuality in Twentieth-Century Women's Sport* (New York: Free Press, 1994), 13–16; M. Ann Hall, *Feminism and Sporting Bodies: Essays on Theory and Practice* (Champaign, IL: Human Kinetics Books, 1996), 19.

53. Hall, *Feminism and Sporting Bodies*, 19.

54. Susan Brownmiller, *Femininity*. (New York: Linden Press, Simon & Schuster, 1984), 15.

55. Lois Bryson, "Challenges to Male Hegemony in Sport," in *Sport, Men, and the Gender Order: Critical Feminist Perspectives*, eds. M. A. Messner and D. F. Sabo (Champaign, IL: Human Kinetics Books, 1990), 173–184; Cahn, *Coming on Strong*, 87–98; Festle, *Playing Nice*, 33–34; Jennifer Hargreaves, *Sporting Females: Critical Issues in the History and Sociology of Women's Sports* (London: Routledge, 1994).

56. Wu, *Doctor Mom Chung of the Fair-Haired Bastards*.

57. Karen J. Leong, *The China Mystique: Pearl S. Buck, Anna May Wong, Mayling Soong, and the Transformation of American Orientalism* (Berkeley: University of California Press, 2005), 109, 114, 117–154; K. Scott Wong, *Americans First*, 89–109.

58. Leong, *The China Mystique*, 118–119, 133.

59. Wong Lum Interview, 1998.

60. Ibid.

61. "Aurora Newsletter," in Lum, Scrapbook.

62. Norma Lee Hom, Interview by author, telephone recording, 15 June 2000.

63. Jane Chew Wong, Interview by author, telephone recording, 22 June 2000.

64. Jennie Chong Jue, Interview by author, telephone recording, 29 June 2000.

65. Jane Chew Wong interview, 22 June 2000.

66. Wong Lum Interview, 1998.

67. Ibid.

68. Father Forrester Foundation, *Father Forrester Tournament Program*, 7.

69. Chinese Historical Society of America, *Third Annual A Celebration of Roots,* 26; Lum, Scrapbook.

70. Wong Lum Interview, 1998.

Conclusion: The Chinese Playground and Yao Ming in the Era of Globalized Sports

1. This also included a fiftieth anniversary celebration for the Chinese Recreation Center, or "the Center," on Washington and Mason.

2. Yao Ming, *A Life in Two Worlds* (New York: Hyperion, 2004), 9.

3. Liz Clarke, "McDonald's Goes for Gold with Olympic Sponsorships," *Washington Post,* 17 August, 2004, E01; Edward Cody, "Not Your Average Chinese Worker: NBA Star Yao Ming Wins Labor Award, Rankling Compatriots," *Washington Post,* 29 April 2005, A19; Thomas Oates and Judy Polumbaum, "Agile Big Man: The Flexible Marketing of Yao Ming," *Pacific Affairs: An International Review of Asia and the Pacific,* 77 (2004): 187–210; "Yao Ming Signs $75m Contract with Rockets," *China Daily,* 1 September 2005.

4. Peter Hessler, "Home and Away; Yao Ming's Journey from China to the N.B.A, and Back," *The New Yorker,* 1 December 2003, 65.

5. Jonathan Feigen, "Yikes! Yao vs. Yi Is Huge: Matchup of Rockets, Bucks Players Seen as Touchstone among Chinese," *Houston Chronicle,* 9 November 2007, A1.

6. Liz Robbins, "The N.B.A. and China Hope They've Found the Next Yao," *New York Times,* 25 June 2007, D1.

7. Brook Larmer, "Giant on the Court. He Sends Cards Too," *Time Magazine,* 163, no. 17 (26 April 2004): 129.

8. Ana Ley, "Yao Ming to Give $2 Million to Chinese Earthquake Victims," *AOL News,* http://news.aol.com/story/_a/yao-ming-to-give-2-million-to-chinese/n20080610154909990015 (accessed 17 June 2008); Special Olympics, "Special Olympics Reaches New Horizons by Announcing Yao Ming as Global Ambassador," http://www.specialolympics.org/Special+Olympics+Public+Website/English/Press_Room/Global_News_Archive/2004+Global+News+Archive/Yao+Ming ew+Global+Ambassador.htm (accessed 1 June 2008).

9. "McDonald's Goes Supersize with Yao," *USA Today,* 13 February 2004, 23C.

10. Hannah Beech, "Asian Heroes: Yao Ming," *Time Magazine International* 161, no. 107 (24 April 2003): 34.

11. Feigen, "Yikes! Yao vs. Yi Is Huge," A1.

12. "Yao Ming Measures Up in US and China," *People's Daily Online,* http://english.peopledaily.com.cn/200410/12/eng20041012_159901.html (accessed 1 June 2008).

13. Beech, "Asian Heroes," 34.

14. Jayda Evans, "Yao Ming's NBA Success Sparks Asian American Pride," *Seattle Times*, 29 November 2002, E1; Gwen Knapp, "Yao's Appeal Transcends Basketball," *San Francisco Chronicle*, 28 November 2002, C1.

15. Ian Thomsen, "The New Mr. Big," *Sports Illustrated*, 97, no. 17 (28 October 2002): 66.

16. Andrew Eccles, Front Cover, *ESPN Magazine*, 25 December 2000; Front Cover, *Slam*, May 2003; John W. McDonough, Front Cover, *Sports Illustrated*, 28 October 2002.

17. Raymond Wong, "Letters by OCA National President, Raymond Wong," 80-20 Educational Foundation, http://www.80-20educationalfoundation.org/projects/discrimination_Chu_ONeal.asp (accessed 1 June 2008).

18. Brett Ballantini, "Shaquille O'Neal: The Ugly American," *Basketball Digest* 30, no. 5 (March 2003): 6–7.

19. Emil Guillermo, "Shaq's Apology Not Good Enough," *San Francisco Chronicle*, http://www.sfgate.com/cgi-bin/article.cgi?f=/gate/archive/2003/01/14/eguillermo.DTL (accessed 1 June 2008); C. Richard King, "Defacements/Effacements: Anti-Asian (American) Sentiment in Sport," *Journal of Sport and Social Issues*, 30, no. 4 (2006): 340–352; "Shaq says Yao Comments Were Said in Jest, "*Sports Illustrated*, http://sportsillustrated.cnn.com/basketball/news/2003/01/10/shaq_yao_ap/ (accessed 1 June 2008).

20. Irwin Tang, "APA Community Should Tell Shaquille O'Neal to 'Come-Down to Chinatown,'" *AsianWeek*, 23, no. 19 (January 3–9, 2003): 9.

21. "Shaqlash: Asian Group Protests outside Compaq Center," *Sports Illustrated*, http://sportsillustrated.cnn.com/basketball/news/2003/01/17/shaq_comments_ap/ (accessed 1 June 2008).

Bibliography

Adams, David Wallace. *Education for Extinction: American Indians and the Boarding School Experience, 1875–1928*. Lawrence, KS: University Press of Kansas, 1995.

Albertson, Roxanne M. "Basketball Texas Style, 1910–1933: School to Industrial League Competition," in *A Century of Women's Basketball*, eds. Joan S. Hult and Marianna Trekell. Reston, VA: American Alliance for Health, Physical Education, Recreation, and Dance, 1991.

Anderson, Mary. "The Postwar Role of American Women." *The American Economic Review* 34, no. 1, part 2.

Archuleta, Margaret L., Brenda J. Child, and K. Tsianina Lomawaima, eds. *Away from Home: American Indian Boarding School Experiences, 1879–2000*. Phoenix, AZ: Heard Museum, 2000.

Ashe, Arthur. *A Hard Road to Glory: A History of the African-American Athlete*. New York: Warner Books, 1988.

Bak, Richard. *Joe Louis: The Great Black Hope*. Dallas, TX: Taylor Pub., 1996.

Ballantini, Brett. "Shaquille O'Neal: The Ugly American." *Basketball Digest* 30, no. 5 (March 2003): 6–7.

"Basketball Champs: Chinese Cagers Win Again in Second National Tourney." *Chinese Press*, 31 December 1948, 1–2.

"Basketball Festival at Kezar Sunday." *Chinese Press*, 7 January 1949, 7.

"Beauty for a Benefit Show." *California Chinese Press*, 11 April 1941, 1.

Beauvoir, Simone de. *The Second Sex*. New York: Vintage Books, 1989.

Bederman, Gail. *Manliness and Civilization: A Cultural History of Gender and Race in the United States, 1880–1917.* Chicago: University of Chicago Press, 1996.

Beech, Hannah. "Asian Heroes: Yao Ming." *Time Magazine International* 161, no. 107 (24 April 2003): 34.

Beran, Janice A. "Iowa, the Longtime 'Hot Bed' of Girls Basketball." In *A Century of Women's Basketball,* eds. Joan S. Hult and Marianna Trekell. Reston, VA: American Alliance for Health, Physical Education, Recreation, and Dance, 1991, 185–186.

"Berkeley Chinese Athletic Club Eyes Basketball Season with High Optimism." *Chinese Press,* October 1948, 11.

"Berkeley Nisei Register Upset." *San Francisco Examiner,* 25 December 1948, 13.

"Berkeley Services for Oliver Chang." *San Francisco Chronicle,* 8 November 1973, 47.

"Berkeley, SF Chinese Gain Finals." *San Francisco Examiner,* 29 December 1948, 19.

Billings, Andrew C., Caroline C. Craig, Robert Croce, Kristian M. Cross, Kathryn M. Moore, William Vigodsky, and Victoria G. Watson. "'Just One of the Guys?' Network Depictions of Annika Sorenstam in the 2003 PGA Colonial Tournament." *Journal of Sport and Social Issues* 30 (2006): 107–114.

Birrell, Susan, and Mary G. McDonald. *Reading Sport: Critical Essays on Power and Representation.* Boston: Northeastern University Press, 2000.

Birrell, Susan, and Nancy Theberge. "Feminist Resistance and Transformation in Sport." In *Women and Sport: Interdisciplinary Perspectives,* eds. D. M. Costa and S. R. Guthrie. Champaign, IL: Human Kinetics, 1994, 361–376.

———. "Ideological Control of Women in Sport." In *Women and Sport: Interdisciplinary Perspectives,* eds. D. M. Costa and S. R. Guthrie. Champaign, IL: Human Kinetics, 1994, 341–360.

Bishop, Elva, and Katherine Fulton. "Shooting Stars: The Hey Dey of Industrial Women's Basketball." *Southern Exposure* 7 (1979): 50–56.

Blassingame, John. *The Slave Community: Plantation Life in the Antebellum South.* New York: Oxford University Press, 1979.

Bloom, John. *To Show What an Indian Can Do: Sports at Native American Boarding Schools.* Minneapolis: University of Minnesota Press, 2000.

Bloom, John, and Michael Nevin Willard, eds. *Sports Matters: Race, Recreation, and Culture.* New York: New York University Press, 2002.

Boskin, Joseph. *Sambo: The Rise and Demise of an American Jester.* Oxford: Oxford University Press, 1988.

Bourdieu, Pierre. *Logic of Practice.* Palo Alto, CA: Stanford University Press, 1992.

———. "Program for a Sociology of Sport." *Sociology of Sport Journal* 5 (1988): 153–161.

Bowman, Becky. "San Francisco Playground Renamed for Basketball Hero." *San Francisco Chronicle*, 20 January 2006, B-3.

Bowen, Louise de Koven. *Safeguards for City Youth at Work and at Play.* New York: MacMillan Company, 1914.

Bowman, Becky. "San Francisco Playground Renamed for Basketball Hero." *San Francisco Chronicle*, 20 January 2006, B-3.

Brachman, Bob. "Cal Storms To 56–44 Win over USF!" *San Francisco Examiner*, 29 January 1950, 25.

———. "Dons Face N.Y.'s Best in Garden Tonight." *San Francisco Examiner*, 22 December 1949, 20.

———. "Dons Tackle Cards in Cow Palace Feature." *San Francisco Examiner*, 20 January 1950, 25.

———. "800 Kids Swarm to Cage School!" *San Francisco Examiner*, 20 December 1949, 22.

———. "Examiner Cage School Adds 3 All Americans to Staff." *San Francisco Examiner*, 18 December 1949, 25.

———. "Examiner Cage School Comes to Thrilling Close." *San Francisco Examiner*, 1 February 1948, 26.

———. "Helen Wong Makes Phenomenal Shots in Basketball School Competition." *San Francisco Examiner*, 31 December 1948, 8.

———. "Hey, Fellows, Tie This! Girl Cage Phenom Sinks 49 of 51 Shots at Examiner School!" *San Francisco Examiner*, 23 December 1948, 23.

———. "USF Cagers Off for East—Still Gunning for National Tourney." *San Francisco Examiner*, 30 January 1950, 22.

———. "USF Cagers Open Title Defense Today." *San Francisco Examiner*, 11 March 1950, 18.

———. "USF Dons Capture Cage Crown." *San Francisco Chronicle*, 20 March 1949, 1H.

———. "USF Off for US Title Bid." *San Francisco Examiner*, 9 March 1950, 29.

———. "USF Roars to 53–40 Win over UC." *San Francisco Examiner*, 28 December 1949, 22.

———. "USF Star Tanks 45 For P.A. Mark!—Wong Racks 29, but Buksar Steals Show." *San Francisco Examiner*, 18 February 1948, 22.

———. "Wong, Buksar on Spot as 54 Teams Vie in Examiner-PA Tourney Today." *San Francisco Examiner*, 22 February 1948, 21.

Brown, Lyle. "Sports Quiz." *San Francisco Chronicle*, 21 December 1949, 2H.

Brownell, Susan. *Training the Body for China: Sports in the Moral Order of the People's Republic.* Chicago: University of Chicago Press, 1995.

Brownmiller, Susan. *Femininity.* New York: Linden Press, Simon and Schuster, 1984.

Bryson, Lois. "Challenges to Male Hegemony in Sport." In *Sport, Men, and the Gender Order: Critical Feminist Perspectives,* eds. M. A. Messner and D. F. Sabo. Champaign, IL: Human Kinetics Books, 1990.

"Cage Champs: Salinas Wins 'Four Cities' Crown." *California Chinese Press,* 21 March 1941, 1.

"Cage Chatter." *California Chinese Press,* 6 December 1940, 7.

"Cage Star Is Native of Canton, China—Here Next Sunday." *Cincinnati Enquirer,* 16 February 1941, 34.

"Cage Tourney Coming Up: Chi-Hi Clubs to Shoot for Basketball Honors in October," *Chinese Press,* 19 September 1941, 4.

Cahn, Susan K. *Coming on Strong: Gender and Sexuality in Twentieth-Century Women's Sport.* New York: Free Press, 1994.

Carrington, Ben."Sport, Masculinity, and Black Cultural Resistance." *Journal of Sport and Social Issues* 22, no. 3 (August 1998): 275–298.

"Casaba Teams Entered in Nisei League." *Chinese Press,* 12 November 1948, 7.

"Catholic Girls' Loop." *San Francisco Examiner,* 7 March 1935, S24.

Cavallo, Dominick. *Muscles and Morals: Organized Playgrounds and Urban Reform, 1880–1920.* Philadelphia: University of Pennsylvania Press, 1981.

Cayleff, Susan. *Babe: The Life and Legend of Babe Didrikson Zaharias.* Champaign, IL: University of Illinois Press, 1996.

———."The 'Texas Tomboy': The Life and Legend of Babe Didrikson Zaharias," *Organization of American Historians Magazine of History* 7 (Summer 1992): 28–33.

"Champin' at the Bit." *San Francisco Examiner,* 10 March 1948, 21.

"Champion Casaba Tossers." *Chinese Press,* 7 January 1949, 8.

"Champions Again: Troop 3 Scouts Capture Wah Ying Basketball Title for Third Year." *California Chinese Press,* 14 February 1941, 2.

Chan, Josephine. Interview by author. Tape recording. Richmond CA, 12 December 1987.

———. Interview by author. Tape recording. San Francisco, CA, 4 October 1996.

Chan, Lily. 1982. Interview #48, Box #12, Southern California Chinese American Oral History Project. Los Angeles, CA: University of California, Los Angeles.

Chan, Sucheng. *Asian Americans: An Interpretive History, Twayne's Immigrant Heritage of America Series.* Boston: Twayne, 1991.

———. "Race, Ethnic Cultures, and Gender in the Construction of Identities among Second-Generation Chinese Americans, 1880s–1930s." In *Claiming America: Constructing Chinese American Identities during the Exclusion Era,* eds. Sucheng Chan and Kevin Scott Wong. Philadelphia: Temple University Press, 1998.

Chapin, Dwight. "All of 5-5, USF's Wong Stood Tall with the Best in College Game." *San Francisco Chronicle,* 13 April 2005, D1, D6.

Chapin, T. F. "Play As a Reformative Agency." *Proceedings of the National Conference of Charities and Correction.* Berkeley, CA: University of California Berkeley, San Francisco Publications, 1914, 437–440.

Chen, Eugenia V. "Survey of Chinese Youth and Student Clubs in New York City, 1945." M.A. diss., University of Michigan, 1945.

Cheng, Lucie and Marjorie Lee. *Linking Our Lives: Chinese American Women of Los Angeles.* Los Angeles: University of California Los Angeles Asian American Studies Center and Chinese Historical Society of Southern California.1984.

Cheng, Weikun Cheng. "Politics of the Queue: Agitation and Resistance in the Beginning and End of Qing China." In *Hair: Its Power and Meaning in Asian Culture,* eds. Alf Hiltebeital and Barbara D. Miller. Albany, NY: State University of New York Press, 1998.

Chew, Edward W. "Are Country Lassies Prettier—Do City Girls Play Second-Fiddle to Suburban Sis?" *Chinese Press,* 6 January 1950, 1, 6.

———. "Chinatown Crimewave? 'Kid Glove Bandits' Linked with Six Robberies." *Chinese Press,* 2 December 1949, 1–2.

"Chi-Knight Cage Team T\to Give Stag Part." *California Chinese Press,* 14 April 1941, 4.

Child, Brenda J. *Boarding School Seasons: American Indian Families, 1900–1940.* Lincoln, NE: University of Nebraska Press, 1993.

Chin, Thomas W. *Bridging the Pacific.* San Francisco: Chinese Historical Society, 1989.

Chinatown Basketball Festival: Souvenir Program. (San Francisco: 1948.) Ben Hom Collection, Chinese Historical Society, Box #1, Folder #3, Ethnic Studies Library, University of California Berkeley.

"Chinatown Joins Council; Hopes for Youth Control." *Chinese Press,* 13 January 1950, 1–2.

"Chinatown Needs More Playgrounds." *Chinese Press,* 10 March 1950, 1.

"Chinese Cager." *Watsonville Register Pajorian,* 12 February 1940, 2.

Chinese Center Report. Work Report. April/May 1929. San Francisco: Chinese Historical Society of America.

Chinese Center Report. Work Report. November 1929. San Francisco: Chinese Historical Society of America.

Chinese Center Report. Work Report. January 1936. San Francisco: Chinese Historical Society of America.

"The Chinese Girls' Basketball Team." Denison House Records, 1890–1984, Disassembled Scrapbooks, Image B27-7-4, Image B27-7-5, Image B27-7-6, Image B27-7-8 M-141, Reel 1 Folder 9, Schlesinger Library on the History of Women in America, Radcliffe Institute, Cambridge, MA.

"Chinese Girls Play Tonight." *San Francisco Examiner,* 6 February 1934, 19.

Chinese Historical Society of America. *The Third Annual A Celebration of Roots: Two Steps Forward—Chinese Americans in Sports.* San Francisco: Chinese Historical Society of America, 1996.

"Chinese Hoop to Play Local Outfit." *Bremerton Daily News Searchlight,* 9 January 1940, 12.

"Chinese Hoopsters to Play Here." *Vacaville Reporter,* 2 February 1940, 10.

"Chinese Schools: Hoop League Standing Released." *California Chinese Press,* 27 December 1940, 7.

"Chinese Six Companies Wages War on Chinatown Crime." *Chinese Press,* 16 July 1948, 1, 4.

"Chinese Squad Plays Tonight; Teds Traveling." *Port Angeles Evening News,* 11 January 1940, 4.

Chin Leung, Alice. Interview by author. Tape recording. San Jose, CA, 3 July 1997.

Chu, Percy. Interview by author. Telephone recording. 3 July 2005.

Chun, Gloria Heyung. *Of Orphans and Warriors: Inventing Chinese American Culture and Identity.* New Brunswick, NJ: Rutgers University Press, 2000.

Cisco, Dan. *Hawaii Sports: History, Facts, and Statistics.* Honolulu: University of Hawaii Press, 1999.

"City Cagers: Chinese Playgrounds Win 4 Opening Tilts." *California Chinese Press,* 13 December 1940, 7.

"City Cagers: Playground 90s Crush Bernal Quintet." *California Chinese Press,* 22 November 1940, 52–56.

Clarke, Liz. "McDonald's Goes for Gold with Olympic Sponsorships." *Washington Post,* 17 August 2004, E01.

"Coach Explains." *News and Observer,* 3 January 1950, 13.

Coben, Stanley. *Revolt against Victorianism: The Impetus for Cultural Change in 1920s America.* New York: Oxford University Press, 1991.

Cody, Edward. "Not Your Average Chinese Worker NBA Star: Yao Ming Wins Labor Award, Rankling Compatriots." *Washington Post,* 29 April, 2005, A19.

Cole, C. L. "Bounding American Democracy: Sport, Sex and Race." In *Contesting Empire, Globalizing Dissent: Cultural Studies after 9/11,* eds. N. Denzin and M. Giardina. Boulder, CO: Paradigm Press, 2006.

Cole, C. L., and Amy Hribrar. "Celebrity Feminism: Nike Style: Post-fordism, Transcendence, and Consumer Power." *Sociology of Sport Journal* 12 (1995): 347–360.

Coleman, Michael C. *American Indian Children at School, 1850–1930.* Jackson, MS: University Press of Mississippi, 1993.

"College Basketball League Commences." *Chinese Press,* 5 November 1948, 8.

Collins, Patricia Hill. *Black Feminist Thought: Knowledge, Consciousness, and the Politics of Empowerment.* London: Harper Collins Academic, 1990.

"Column," 9 February 1949, in William Wong, Scrapbook.

Connolly, Will. "Nation's Best Chinese Netters Competing Here." *San Francisco Chronicle*, 29 August 1954, 4H.

Cook, Jesse Brown. Scrapbooks, 1860–1938. Berkeley: Bancroft Library, BANC PIC 1996.003—fALB.

"Cosmopolitan—Above Are Representatives Who Make Up Teams Competing in the Oriental- American Cage Tourney." *Seattle Post-Intelligencer*, 24 December 1948, 15.

"Cover." *Chinese Digest*, 18 September 1936, 1.

"Crime, Fights Held Bad Publicity for Chinatown." *Chinese Press*, 27 January 1950, 2.

Cronin, Mike and David Mayall. *Sporting Nationalisms: Identity, Ethnicity, Immigration, and Assimilation.* London: Frank Cass Publishers, 1998.

Csikszentmihalyi, Mihaly. *Flow=The Psychology of Optimal Experience.* New York: Harper and Row, 1990.

Cunningham, George B., and Michael Sagas. "Access Discrimination in Intercollegiate Athletics." *Journal of Sport and Social Issues* 29 (2005): 148–163.

Curtis, Henry S. *The Play Movement and Its Significance.* New York: Macmillan Company, 1917.

"Dance to Raise 'Y' Camp Funds." *California Chinese Press*, 28 March 1941, 1.

Daniels, Roger. *Prisoners without Trial.* New York: Hill and Wang, 2004.

Davis, Marianna W. *Contributions of Black Women to America.* Columbia, SC: Kenday Press, 1982.

de Certeau, Michel. *The Practice of Everyday Life.* Berkeley, CA: University of California Press, 1985.

Deloria, Philip J. *Indians in Unexpected Places.* Lawrence, KS: University Press of Kansas, 2004.

———. *Playing Indian.* New Haven, CT: Yale University Press, 1998.

"Dominoes Beat Chinese." *Victoria Daily Times*, 13 January 1940, 14.

Dong, Lorraine. "The Forbidden City Legacy and Its Chinese American Women." *Chinese America: History and Perspectives* 6 (1992): 125–148.

"Don Lofgran . . . USF's All-American Candidate." *News and Observer*, 2 January 1950, 9.

"Don Spurt Trounces Gaels; Cards Stave Off Bronc Bid." *San Francisco Examiner*, 22 January 1950, 20.

"Dons' Coach Explains," *News and Observer*, 3 January 1950, 13.

Duffey, Arthur. "Chinese Girls to Compete: Banner Entry for the E.R.F. for Norfolk Club Meet." Boston Globe, 21 February 1935. Denison House Records, 1890–1984, Disassembled Scrapbooks, M-141 Reel 1 Folder 9,

Schlesinger Library on the History of Women in America, Radcliffe Institute, Cambridge, MA.

———. "McDonough Wins 5000 Metre Run: Boston College Athletes Take Point Trophy–Chinese Girls Make Hit in Norfolk Club Meet," *Boston Globe,* 22 February 1935. Denison House Records, 1890–1984, Disassembled Scrapbooks, M- 141 Reel 1 Folder 9, Schlesinger Library on the History of Women in America, Radcliffe Institute, Cambridge, MA.

Duncan, Margaret Carlisle. "Sports Photographs and Sexual Difference: Images of Men and Women in the 1984 and 1988 Olympic Games." *Sociology of Sport Journal* 7 (March 1990): 22–43.

Dupont, Jill. "'The Self in the Ring, the Self in Society': Boxing and American Culture from Jack Johnson to Joe Louis." Ph.D. diss., University of Chicago, Chicago, IL, 2000.

Early, Gerald. "Baseball, Boxing, and the Charisma of Sport and Race." In *The Charisma of Sport and Race,* Symposium Proceedings. Berkeley, CA: University of California Press, 1996.

———. "Performance and Reality: Race, Sports and the Modern World." *The Nation.* (10- 17, August 1998): 12.

Eccles, Andrew. Front Cover. *ESPN Magazine.* 25 December 2000.

Edwards, Harry. *Sociology of Sport.* Homewood, IL: Dorsey Press, 1973.

"8 Fives Set for Oriental Meet." *Seattle Post-Intelligencer,* 25 December 1947, 23.

Eisenmann, Linda. *Higher Education for Women in Postwar America, 1945–1965.* Baltimore, MD: Johns Hopkins University Press, 2006.

Eitzen, D. Stanley, and George Harvey Sage. *Sociology of American Sport.* 2nd ed. Dubuque, IA: W. C. Brown Co., 1982.

Emery, Lynne. "From Lowell Mills to the Halls of Fame: Industrial League Sport for Women." In *Women and Sport: Interdisciplinary Perspectives,* eds. D. Margaret Costa and Sharon R. Guthrie. Champaign, IL: Human Kinetics, 1994.

Espin, Orlando. *The Faith of the People: Theological Reflections on Popular Catholicism.* Maryknoll, NY: Orbis Press, 1997.

Espiritu, Yen Le. "Asian American Women and Men: Labor, Laws, and Love." In *The Gender Lens,* ed. Judith A. Howard et al. Thousand Oaks, CA: Sage Publications, 1997.

Evans, Arthur S. "Differences in the Recruitment of Black and White Football Players at a Big Eight University." *Journal of Sport and Social Issues* 3 (1979): 1–10.

Evans, Jayda. "Yao Ming's NBA Success Sparks Asian American Pride." *Seattle Times,* 29 November 2002, E1.

"Exclusive: Story of How Tennis Champs Fought for '49 Titles." *Chinese Press*, 16 September 1949, 1.

"Fair and Warmer!" *San Francisco Examiner*, 19 January 1950, 16.

Father Forrester Foundation. *Father Forrester Tournament Chinese New Year Basketball Jamboree Program—8th Annual*. San Francisco, CA, 1999.

Feder-Kane, Abigail M. "A Radiant Smile from the Lovely Lady: Overdetermined Femininity in Ladies' Figure Skating." In *Reading Sport: Critical Essays on Power and Representation*, ed. Susan Birrell and Mary G. McDonald. Boston: Northeastern University Press, 2000.

Feigen, Jonathan. "Yikes! Yao vs. Yi Is Huge: Matchup of Rockets, Bucks Players Seen As Touchstone among Chinese." *Houston Chronicle*, 9 November 2007, A1.

Festle, Mary Jo. *Playing Nice: Politics and Apologies in Women's Sports*. New York: Columbia University Press, 1996.

"Filipino Olympic All-Stars Clip S.F. Chinese in Basketball Festival." *Chinese Press*, 14 January 1949, 7.

"Filipino Rassler Now Favorite." *San Francisco Chronicle*, 27 April 1948, 3H.

"First Chinese: Helen Wong Home from Jr. Davis Cup Matches." *Chinese Press*, 25 November 1949, 7.

"First Wah Ying League Games." *Chinese Digest*, January 1938, 16.

Fiset, Louis. "Nikkei Life in the Northwest: Photographic Impressions." *Pacific Northwest Quarterly* 91, no. 1 (1999–2000): 25–41.

Fong, Conrad, and Davisson Lee. "Nam Wah Wins." *Chinese Digest*, May 1938, 17.

———. "Sports." *Chinese Digest*, April 1938, 18.

Ford, Linda. *Lady Hoopsters: A History of Women's Basketball in America*. Northampton, MA: Half Moon Books, 1999.

"Four Chinese-American Net Stars Enter U.S. National Hard Court Meet." *Chinese Press*, 1 October 1948, 7.

"Four Fleet Daughters of China." Denison House Records, 1890–1984, Disassembled Scrapbooks, M- 141 Reel 1 Folder 9, Schlesinger Library on the History of Women in America, Radcliffe Institute, Cambridge, MA.

"Four Teams Enter CYO Tourney for St. Mary's." *California Chinese Press*, 27 Month 1940, 7.

Frank, Stanley. "Crossroads Champs." *Collier's*, 8 February 1941.

Frankenberg, Ruth. *Displacing Whiteness: Essays in Social and Cultural Criticism*. Durham, NC: Duke University Press, 1997.

Franklin Lewis Column, 2 March 1950, in William Wong, Scrapbook.

Franks, Joel S. "Chinese Americans and American Sport, 1880–1940." In *Chinese America: History and Perspectives*. San Francisco: Chinese Historical Society of America, 1996.

———. *Crossing Sidelines, Crossing Cultures: Sport and Asian Pacific American Cultural Citizenship.* Lanham, MD: University Press of America, 2000.
Front Cover. *Slam.* May 2003.
Frymir, Alice W., and Marjorie Hillas. *Team Sports for Women.* New York: A. S. Barnes, 1935.
"Gene Louie Singles Champ, Favorites Win in Nationals." *Chinese Press,* 15 September 1950, 7.
Gillin, John L. *Wholesome Citizens and Spare Time.* Cleveland, OH: The Cleveland Foundation Committee, 1918.
Gilroy, Paul. *There Ain't No Black in the Union Jack: The Cultural Politics of Race and Nation.* Chicago: University of Chicago Press, 1991.
Giosso, John. Interview by author. Telephone recording. 3 July 2005.
"Girl Cagers in 3 Games Tonight." *San Francisco Examiner,* 12 February 1934, 22.
"Girl Cagers Set Fast Pace in Parish League." *The Monitor,* 21 November 1947, 6.
"Girl Cagers Near End of Tourney." *The Monitor,* 30 November 1946, 6.
"Girls' Casaba Game." *Chinese Press,* 5 November 1949, 7.
"Girls' Basketball." *The Monitor,* 17 October 1947, 6.
"Girls' Basketball." *The Monitor,* 31 October 1947, 6.
"Girls' Basketball." *The Monitor,* 7 November 1947, 6.
"Girls Basketball." *The Monitor,* 14 November 1947, 6.
"Girls Cage League." *The Monitor,* 12 December 1947, 6.
"Girls' Club Meets Emporium Tonight." *San Francisco Examiner,* 31 March 1932.
"Girls CYO Loop Opens." *The Monitor,* 4 November 1949, 19.
"Girls' Parish Section Basketball Games." *The Monitor,* 26 October 1946, 6.
"Girls' Parish Section Basketball Games." *The Monitor,* 2 November 1946, 6.
"Girls' Parish Section Basketball Games." *The Monitor,* 9 November 1946, 6.
"Girls' Parish Section Basketball Games." *The Monitor,* 16 November 1946, 6.
"Girls' Parish Section Basketball Games." *The Monitor,* 23 November 1946, 6.
Gissendanner, Cindy Himes. "African-American Women and Competitive Sport, 1920–1960." In *Women, Sport, and Culture,* eds. Susan Birrell and Cheryl L. Cole. Champaign, IL: Human Kinetics, 1994, 81–92.
Gitersonke, Don. *Baseball's Bearded Boys.* Las Vegas: Don Gitersonke, 1996.
Glenn, Evelyn Nakano. "The Social Construction and Institutionalization of Gender and Race: An Integrative Framework." In *Revisioning Gender,* eds. Myra Marx Ferree, Judith Lorber, and Beth B. Hess. Thousand Oaks, CA: Sage Publications, 1999.
———. *Unequal Freedom: How Race and Gender Shaped American Citizenship and Labor.* Cambridge, MA: Harvard University Press, 2003.
"Globe Trotters' Cop World Pro Cage Crown." *Chicago Defender,* 30 March 1940, 22.
"Globe Trotters '5' in National Pro Cage Tournament." *Chicago Defender,* 9 March 1940, 24.

"Globe Trotters Win 2." *Chicago Defender*, 6 January 1940, 23.

Gok, Fred. Interview by author. Tape recording. San Francisco, CA, 13 July 1999.

———. Scrapbook. San Francisco, CA.

"Gold Rush Starts Tomorrow . . . Official History of This Women's Service Club." *Chinese Press*, 21 October 1949, 3.

Gordon, Milton M. *Assimilation in American Life: The Role of Race, Religion and National Origin.* New York: Oxford University Press, 1964.

Gordon, Rachel. "Kenneth Kim: Educator Specialized in Recreation for Kids." *San Francisco Chronicle*, 23 February 2003, A-28.

Gould, Todd. *Pioneers of the Hardwood: Indiana and the Birth of Professional Basketball.* Bloomington, IN: Indiana University Press, 1998.

Grace, Kevin. Personal Research Collection on Professional Basketball.

Grieve, Curley. "Dons' Inspired Drive Garners N.Y. Bid—USF-and-Brachman-Win Cage." *San Francisco Examiner*, 5 March 1950, 23.

"Group Portrait of Denison House Chinese Girls' Basketball Team and Their Coach Margaret Stewart, One of the Girls Workers." Photo: B27-7-7, M-141 Reel 1 Folder 7. Camrbidge: Schlesinger Library on the History of Women in America, Radcliffe Institute.

Grundy, Pamela, and Susan Shackelford. *Shattering the Glass: The Remarkable History of Women's Basketball.* New York: New Press, 2005.

Gruneau, Richard S., and David Whitson. *Hockey Night in Canada: Sport, Identities, and Cultural Politics.* Culture and Communication in Canada Series. Toronto: Garamond Press, 1993.

Guillermo, Emil. "Shaq's Apology Not Good Enough." *San Francisco Chronicle.* http://www.sfgate.com/cgi-bin/article.cgi?f=/gate/archive/2003/01/14/eguillermo.DTL (accessed 1 June 2008).

Gulick, Luther. *A Philosophy of Play.* New York: Charles Scribner's Sons, 1920.

Gulick, Luther. "Play and Democracy." *Charities and the Commons*, 8 (3 August 1907): 481–486.

Hale, Grace Elizabeth. *Making Whiteness: The Culture of Segregation in the South, 1890–1940.* New York: Pantheon Books, 1998.

Hall, M. Ann. *Feminism and Sporting Bodies: Essays on Theory and Practice.* Champaign, IL: Human Kinetics Books, 1996.

Hall, Stuart. "Gramsci's Relevance for the Study of Race and Ethnicity." In *Stuart Hall: Critical Dialogues in Cultural Studies*, eds. David Morley and Kuan-Hsing Chen. London: Routledge, 1996.

Hargreaves, Jennifer. *Sporting Females: Critical Issues in the History and Sociology of Women's Sports.* London: Routledge, 1994.

Hargreaves, John. *Sport, Power, and Culture: A Social and Historical Analysis of Popular Sports in Britain.* New York: St. Martin's Press, 1986.

Hartmann, Douglas Robert. *Race, Culture, and the Revolt of the Black Athlete: The 1968 Olympic Protests and Their Aftermath.* Chicago: University of Chicago Press, 2003.

———. "Rethinking the Relationships between Sport and Race in American Culture: Golden Ghettos and Contested Terrain." *Sociology of Sport Journal* 17 (2000): 232.

Harvard Library. http://ocp.hul.harvard.edu/immigration/organizations-Denison.html (accessed 5 June 2007).

"Hawaiians, Saints Reach Oriental Basketball Final." *Seattle Post-Intelligencer,* 28 December 1947, 24.

Hawkins, Joel, and Terry Bertolino. *House of David Baseball Team.* Chicago: Arcadia Publishing, 2000.

Hee, Frank. "Basketball in Our Own Backyard." *Chinese Digest,* May-June 1939, 19.

"Helen Wong Cops State Fair Titles." *Chinese Press,* 16 September 1949, 7.

"Helen Wong Home from Jr. Davis Cup Matches." *Chinese Press,* 25 November 1949, 7.

"Helen Wong Makes Phenomenal Shots in Basketball School Competition." *Chinese Press,* 31 December 1948, 8.

"Helen Wong to Play Jr. Davis Matches." *Chinese Press,* 11 November 1949, 3.

"Heroic Warriors: Chinese Hoopsters of the Past." Exhibit. San Francisco: Kearny Street Workshop, Chinatown Community Arts Program, Telegraph Hill Neighborhood Center, 2002.

Hessler, Peter. "Home and Away; Yao Ming's Journey from China to the N.B.A, and Back." *New Yorker,* 1 December 2003, 65.

Hoberman, John M. *Sport and Political Ideology.* Austin: University of Texas Press, 1984.

Hoffman, Abraham. *Unwanted Mexican Americans in the Great Depression: Repatriation Pressures, 1929–1939.* Tucson: University of Arizona Press, 1974.

"Holy Family Is the Team to Beat in Girls' Parish League." *The Monitor,* 28 November 1947, 6.

Hom, Norma Lee. Interview by author. Telephone recording. 15 June 2000.

Hoppenstand, Gary, and Ray Broadus Browne. *The Defective Detective in the Pulps.* Bowling Green, OH: Bowling Green State University Popular Press, 1983.

"'Hot Shots' in Test Today at Examiner Cage Finale." *San Francisco Examiner,* 27 December 1948, 17.

Hoy, William. "Through a Chinatown Window." *California Chinese Press,* 1941, 1.

Huhndorf, Shari M. *Going Native: Indians in the American Cultural Imagination.* Ithaca, NY: Cornell University Press, 2001.

Hult, Joan S. "The Story of Women's Athletics: Manipulating a Dream 1890–1985." In *Women and Sport: Interdisciplinary Perspectives,* eds. D. Margaret Costa and Sharon R. Guthrie. Champaign, IL: Human Kinetics, 1994.

"I.A.A. Girl Cagers Tangle Tonight." *San Francisco News,* 11 March 1935, 15.

Ichioka, Yuji. *The Issei.* New York: Free Press, 1988.

Ikard, Robert W. *Just for Fun: The Story of AAU Women's Basketball.* Fayetteville, AR: University of Arkansas Press, 2003.

"It's a Cinch," in William Wong, Scrapbook.

James, C. L. R. *Beyond a Boundary.* New York: Pantheon Books, 1983.

Jenkins, Bruce. *A Good Man: The Pete Newell Story.* Berkeley, CA: Frog, Ltd., 1999.

Jesperson, Christopher. *American Images of China, 1931–1949.* Palo Alto, CA: Stanford University Press, 1996.

Jue, Jennie Chong. Interview by author. Telephone recording. 29 June 2000.

Kaye, Andrew Miles. "'A Tiger in the Ring and a Pussycat Outside': American Attitudes towards Black Prizefighters, 1810–1938." MA thesis, Emory University, Atlanta, 1997.

Kelley, Robin D. G. *Race Rebels: Culture, Politics, and the Black Working Class.* New York: Free Press, 1994.

———. *Yo' Mama's Disfunktional: Fighting the Culture Wars in Urban America.* New York: Beacon Press, 1998.

Kenyon, J. Michael. Personal Research Collection on Professional Basketball.

Kidd, Bruce. "Sports and Masculinity." In *Beyond Patriarchy: Essays by Men on Pleasure, Power, and Change,* ed. Michael Kaufman. Toronto: Oxford University Press, 1987.

Kikumura, Azuma Eiichiro, Darcie C. Iki, and Japanese American National Museum. *The Kona Coffee Story: Along the Hawaii Belt Road.* Los Angeles: Japanese American National Museum, 1995.

Kilpatrick, Jacquelyn. *Celluloid Indians: Native Americans and Film.* Lincoln, NE: University of Nebraska Press, 1999.

Kim, Thomas. Interview by author. Tape recording. Richmond CA, 12 December 1987.

King, C. Richard. "Defacements/Effacements: Anti-Asian (American) Sentiment in Sport." *Journal of Sport and Social Issues,* 30, no. 4 (2006): 340–352.

King, Marsha. "Tribes Confront Painful Legacy of Indian Boarding Schools." *Seattle Times,* 3 February 2008.

King, Rebecca Chiyoko. "Eligible to Be Japanese American: Counting on Multiraciality in Japanese American Basketball Leagues and Beauty Pageants." In *Contemporary Asian American Communities: Intersections and Divergences,* eds. Linda Trinh Vo and Rick Bonus. Philadelphia: Temple University Press, 2002.

Kitano, Harry H. L., and Roger Daniels. *Asian Americans: Emerging Minorities.* 2nd ed. Englewood Cliffs, NJ: Prentice Hall, 1995.

Knapp, Gwen. "Yao's Appeal Transcends Basketball." *San Francisco Chronicle,* 28 November 2002, C1.

Knuttgen, Howard. *Sport in China.* Champaign, IL: Human Kinetics, 1990.

Ko, Dorothy. "The Body As Attire: The Shifting Meanings of Footbinding in Seventeenth-Century China." *Journal of Women's History* 8, no. 4 (Winter 1997): 10–26.

Kotlanger, Michael. Interview by author. Telephone recording. 18 September 2003.

Kurashige, Lon. *Japanese American Celebration and Conflict: A History of Ethnic Identity and Festival, 1934–1990.* Berkeley, CA: University of California Press, 2002.

Kwong, Peter. *Chinatown, New York: Labor and Politics, 1930–1950.* New York: Monthly Review Press, 1979.

Lai, Him Mark, and Philip P. Choy. *Outlines: History of the Chinese in America.* San Francisco: Lai and Choy, 1971.

Larmer, Brook. "Giant on the Court. He Sends Cards Too." *Time Magazine,* 163, no. 17 (26 April 2004): 129.

Lau, Estelle. *Paper Families.* Durham: Duke University Press, 2006.

Lavin, Cap. Interview by author. Telephone recording. 30 July 2005.

Lee, Albert Sonny. Interview by author. Tape recording. San Francisco, CA, 28 July 1998.

———. Interview by author. Telephone recording. 28 July 2000.

———. Scrapbook. San Francisco, CA.

Lee, Alfred. Interview by author. Tape recording. San Francisco, CA, 9 July 1999.

Lee, Anthony W. *Picturing Chinatown: Art and Orientalism in San Francisco.* Berkeley, CA: University of California Press, 2001.

Lee, Bill. *Chinese Playground: A Memoir.* San Francisco: Rhapsody Press, 1999.

Lee, Bob. "Blame Them Not' Bob Lee CSCA Secretary on SF Hoodlums." *Chinese Press,* 12 May 1950, 2.

Lee, Davisson. "Playground Illuminated." *Chinese Digest,* August 1938, 17.

———. "Sports Glimpses." *Chinese Digest,* December 1937, 21.

———. "Sports—Lightweights." *Chinese Digest,* December 1938, 17.

———. "Wah Ying Basketball League." *Chinese Digest,* February 1939, 16.

Lee, Dayton. Interview by author. Tape recording. San Francisco, CA, 12 May 2000.

Lee, Franche. Interview by author. Tape recording. Sunnyvale, CA, 12 February 1995.

———. Interview by author. Tape recording. Sunnyvale, CA, 31 October 1996.
———. Interview by author. Tape recording. Sunnyvale, CA, 22 June 2000.
———. Interview by author. Tape recording. Sunnyvale, CA, 14 December 2003.
———. Interview by author. Tape recording. Sunnyvale, CA, 15 August 2007.
Lee, George. Scrapbook. San Francisco, CA.
Lee, Joseph. "Play As an Antidote to Civilization." *The Playground*, July 1911, 7, 15.
———. "Play As a School of the Citizen." *Charities and the Commons* 18 (3 August 1907): 486–491.
Lee, Josephine. *Performing Asian America: Race and Ethnicity on the Contemporary Stage*. Philadelphia: Temple University Press, 1997.
Lee, Lim P. "Chinatown Civic Victory: Playground Request Approved by Local Board of Education." *California Chinese Press*, 11 April 1941, 1.
———. "Chinatown Petitions for New Playground to Combat Delinquency. These Are 'Press' Facts and Figures." *California Chinese Press*, 28 February 1941, 1.
———. "Housing Problem: Property Survey Shows Chinatown Rents Exceed Standard S.F. Median." *Chinese Press*, 12 May 1950, 1–2.
———. "Letter to the Editor." *Chinese Press*, 12 May 1950, 2.
Lee, M. "The Museum of Chinese American History in Los Angeles, Summer 1998 Newsletter." http://www.eskimo.com/~camla/newsletter/1998/summer/index.html (accessed 23 June 2007).
Lee, Marjorie. *Building a Community, Linking Our Lives*. Los Angeles: Chinese Historical Society of Southern California, 1984.
Lee, Michael. Interview by author. Tape recording. San Francisco, CA, 31 May 2004.
Lee, Rachel. Interview by author. Telephone recording. 27 March 1997.
———. Interview by author. Tape recording. San Francisco, CA, 7 July 1998.
Lee, Ray. Interview by author. Telephone recording. 30 December 2003.
———. Interview by author. Tape recording. San Francisco, CA, 31 May 2004.
Lee, Robert G. *Orientals: Asian Americans in Popular Culture, Asian American History and Culture*. Philadelphia: Temple University Press, 1999.
Lee, Rose Hum. *The Chinese in the United States of America*. Hong Kong: Hong Kong University Press, 1960.
———. "Community Not Interested in Its Youth, Sociologist Charges." *Chinese Press*, 4 August 1950, 3–4.
Lee Tom, Beverly. Interview by author. Tape recording. San Francisco, CA, 31 May 2004.

Lee Yep, Terry. Interview by author. Tape recording. San Francisco, CA, 31 May 2004.

Leiser, Bill. "USF's Big Chance March 19." *San Francisco Chronicle,* 19 March 1949, 1H.

Lenskyj, Helen. "A Kind of Precipitate Waddle: Early Opposition to Women Running." In *Sport and the Sociological Imagination: Refereed Proceedings of the 3rd Annual Conference of the North American Society for the Sociology of Sport, Toronto, Ontario, Canada,* eds. Nancy Theberge and Peter Donnelly. Toronto: North American Society for the Sociology of Sport, 1982.

Leong, Gor Yun. *Chinatown Inside Out.* New York: B. Mussey, 1936.

Leong, Karen J. *The China Mystique: Pearl S. Buck, Anna May Wong, Mayling Soong, and the Transformation of American Orientalism.* Berkeley: University of California Press, 2005.

Leong, Lily. Interview by author. Tape recording. San Francisco, CA, 21 July, 1998.

Levine, Peter. *Ellis Island to Ebbets Field: Sport and the American Jewish Experience, Sports History and Society.* New York: Oxford University Press, 1992.

Lew, Billy. 1982. Interview #20 Box 12, 7B-09-113, Southern California Chinese American Oral History Project. Los Angeles, CA: University of California, Los Angeles.

Ley, Ana. "Yao Ming to Give $2 Million to Chinese Earthquake Victims," AOL News. http://news.aol.com/story/_a/yao-ming-to-give-2-million-to-chinese/n20080610154909990015 (accessed June 17, 2008).

Liang, Hua. "Living between the Worlds: Chinese-American Women and their Experiences in San Francisco and New York City, 1848–1945." Ph.D. diss., University of Connecticut, 1996.

"Lightweight Cagers Seek Title Tonight." *San Francisco Examiner,* 8 March 1932, S19.

Lim, Shirley. *A Feeling of Belonging: Asian Americans Women's Public Culture in the 1930s and 1940s.* New York: New York University Press, 2006.

Ling, Huping. *Surviving on the Gold Mountain: A History of Chinese American Women and Their Lives.* Albany, NY: State University of New York Press, 1998.

Lipsitz, George. *The Possessive Investment in Whiteness: How White People Profit from Identity Politics.* Philadelphia: Temple University Press, 1998.

Litwack, Leon. *Trouble in Mind: Black Southerners in the Age of Jim Crow.* New York: Knopf, 1998.

"Locke Girl Cagers Defeat the Chi-Nettes." *California Chinese Press,* 18 April 1941, 3.

Louis, Kit-King."A Study of American-Born and American-Reared Chinese in Los Angeles." M.A. thesis, University of Southern California, 1931.

Lowe, Albert Alvin. "Reading Asian American Representations: Race and Sport in an International Frame." Ph.D. diss., University of California San Diego, 2000.

Lowe, Lisa. *Immigrant Acts.* Durham, NC: Duke University Press, 1996.

"Low Man Between." *Chinese Press,* 9 December 1949, 22.

Mails, Walter. "Sports Star Deplores Lack of Playfields in Chinatown." *Chinese Press,* 4 February 1949, 12.

Marchetti, Gina. *Romance and the "Yellow Peril": Race, Sex, and Discursive Strategies in Hollywood Fiction.* Berkeley, CA: University of California Press, 1993.

Mark, Diane Mei Lin, and Ginger Chih. *A Place Called Chinese America.* Dubuque, IA: Kendall Hunt Pub. Co., 1982.

Mayeda, David. "From Model Minority to Economic Threat: Media Portrayals of Major League Baseball Pitchers Hideo Nomo and Hideki Irabu." *Journal of Sport and Social Issues* 23, (May 1999): 203–217.

McAllister, Matthew P., Edward H. Sewell, and Ian Gordon, eds. *Comics and Ideology: Popular Culture and Everyday Life,* vol. 2. New York: Peter Lang Publishing, 2001.

McClain, Charles. *In Search of Equality.* Berkeley, CA: University of California Press, 1994.

McDonald, Jack. "USF Has Come a Long Way along Nat'l Cage Pike." *San Francisco Call Bulletin Sports,* 1 March 1949, 17.

McDonough, John W. Front Cover, *Sports Illustrated.* 28 October 2002.

McDonald, Mary G. "Queering Whiteness: The Peculiar Case of the Women's National Basketball Association." *Sociological Perspectives* 45 (4) (Winter 2002): 379- 396.

"McDonald's Goes Supersize with Yao." *USA Today,* 13 February 2004, 23C.

McKenney, Joe. "South End House Moulds Athletes: Denison 'Back Yard' Incubator of Some Future Sport Stars—Marino Serves as Guiding Hand," *Boston Post,* 13 October 1940, Denison House Records, 1890–1984, Disassembled Scrapbooks, M-141 Reel 1 Folder 8, Schlesinger Library on the History of Women in America, Radcliffe Institute, Cambridge, MA.

McRobbie, Angela. "Shut Up and Dance: Youth Culture and Changing Modes of Femininity." In *Postmodernism and Popular Culture.* London/New York: Routledge, 1994.

McVay, I. R. "Dons Fight Way to Cage Final." *San Francisco Chronicle,* 18 March 1949, 1H.

Mears, Eliot Grinnell. *Resident Orientals on the American Pacific Coast: Their Legal and Economic Status.* Chicago: University of Chicago Press, 1928.

"Melting Pot: Bay Cagers Vie in Seattle." *San Francisco Chronicle,* 23 December 1948, 3H.

Messner, Michael A., Margaret Carlisle Duncan, and Faye Linda Wachs. "The Gender of Audience-Building: Televised Coverage of Men's and Women's NCAA Basketball." *Sociological Inquiry* Vol. 66, No. 4 (Fall 1996): 422–39.

———. "Sports and Male Domination: The Female Athlete as Contested Ideological Terrain." *Sociology of Sport Journal* 5 (1988): 197–211.

Miller, Nathan. *New World Coming: The 1920s and the Making of Modern America*. Cambridge, MA: Da Capo Press, 2004, 46–47, 253–272.

Ming, Yao. *A Life in Two Worlds*. New York: Hyperion, 2004.

Moi, Toril. "Appropriating Bourdieu: Feminist Theory and Pierre Bourdieu's Sociology of Culture." *New Literary History* 22 (1991): 1017–1049.

Morris, Andrew. *Marrow of the Nation: A History of Sport and Physical Culture in Republican China*. Berkeley, CA: University of California Press, 2004.

"Mrs. Alice Yu Entertains Square and Circle." *California Chinese Press*, 4 April 1941, 1.

Mullan, Michael L. "Ethnicity and Sport: The Wapato Nippons and Pre-World War II Japanese American Baseball." *Journal of Sport History* 26, no. 1 (1999): 82–114.

———. "Sport, Ethnicity, and the Reconstruction of the Self: Baseball in America's Internment Camps." *International Journal of the History of Sport* 16, no. 1 (1999): 1–21.

Mulligan, Bill. "Hank Luisetti's Markmanship Class Fascinates Examiner Cage Students." *San Francisco Examiner*, 18 January 1948, 24.

Mullings, Leith. "Images, Ideology, and Women of Color." In *Women of Color in U.S. Society*, edited by Bonnie Thornton Dill and Maxine Baca Zinn. Philadelphia, PA: Temple University Press, 1994.

Museum of Chinese American History in Los Angeles, Summer 1998 Newsletter, http://www.eskimo.com/~camla/newsletter/1998/summer/index.htm (accessed June 23 2007).

"Mutt and Jeff." *Buffalo Courier-Express*, 31 December 1949, 13.

Nakagawa, Kerry Yo. *Diamonds in the Rough: Zeni and the Legacy of Japanese-American Baseball*. Los Angeles: Nisei Baseball Research Project, 2000.

Nee, Victor G., and Brett de Bary Nee. *Longtime Californ': A Documentary Study of an American Chinatown*. Englewood Cliffs, NJ: Prentice-Hall, 1974.

"New Chinese Playground: Site Already Purchased." *Chinese Press*, 16 July 1948, 1.

Newell, Pete. Interview by author. Telephone recording. 1 August 2005.

"New Playground." *Chinese Press*, 6 June 1941, 1.

"New Playground: Like Christmas—It Should Be Here Definitely This Year." *Chinese* Press, 8 August 1941, 1.

Ngai, Mai. *Impossible Subjects: Illegal Aliens and the Making of Modern America*. Princeton, NJ: Princeton University Press, 2005.

"Nice Knowing You." *San Francisco Examiner*, 28 December 1948, 19.

Niiya, Brian, Azuma Eiichiro, and the Japanese American National Museum. *More Than a Game: Sport in the Japanese American Community.* Los Angeles: Japanese American National Museum, 2000.

"1940 World Professional Basket Champions." *Chicago Defender,* 30 March 1940, 22.

1947 National Oriental Basketball Tournament Program in William Wong, Scrapbook.

Noda, Kesa. *Yamato Colony: 1906–1960 Livingston, California.* Livingston, CA: Livingston-Merced JACL Chapter, 1981.

Nogawa, Haruo. "A Study of a Japanese-American Basketball League and the Assimilation of Its Members into the Mainstream of United States Society." *International Review for the Sociology of Sport* 19, no. 3–4 (1984): 259–271.

Nolte, Carl. "Slam-Dunk Memories 60 Years Ago, Chinatown Had Its Own Pro Basketball Team." *San Francisco Chronicle,* 28 May 1999, A19.

Nomura, Gail. "Beyond the Playing Field: The Significance of Pre-World War II Japanese American Baseball in the Yakima Valley." In *Bearing Dreams, Shaping Visions: Asian Pacific American Perspectives,* eds. L. A. Revilla and Association for Asian American Studies. Pullman, WA: Washington State University Press, 1993.

"Oakland Casaba Tilt." *Chinese Press,* 4 March 1939, 8.

"Oakland Father, 45, Wins Net Title: Gene Louie Beats Wing Jue in 4 Sets; Helen Wong Keeps Crown 3rd Time," *Chinese Press,* 16 September 1949, 7.

"Oakland 'Y' Loses Title Game." *Chinese Digest,* 20 March 1936, 13.

Oates, Thomas, and Judy Polumbaum. "Agile Big Man: The Flexible Marketing of Yao Ming." *Pacific Affairs: An International Review of Asia and the Pacific* 77 (2004): 187–210.

"Obituary of Bob Brachman, Examiner Sports Reporter." *San Francisco Examiner,* 5 January 1993, A-13.

Odo, Franklin, Sinoto Kazuko, and Hawaii Immigrant Heritage Preservation Center. *A Pictorial History of the Japanese in Hawaii, 1885–1924.* Honolulu: Hawaii Immigrant Heritage Preservation Center Dept. of Anthropology Bernice Pauahi Bishop Museum, 1985.

Okihiro, Gary Y. *Margins and Mainstreams: Asians in American History and Culture.* Seattle: University of Seattle Press, 1994.

Okihiro, Michael M., and Japanese Cultural Center of Hawaii. *AJA Baseball in Hawaii: Ethnic Pride and Tradition.* Honolulu: Hawaii Hochi, 1999.

Omi, Michael, and Howard Winant. *Racial Formation in the United States: From the 1960s to the 1980s.* New York: Routledge, 1986/1989.

Opotowsky, Stan. "USF 4-Point NY Underdog." *San Francisco Chronicle,* 17 March 1949, 1H.

"Opposes Play Area Cuts: 'Children Need More Facilities,' Says Report." *Chinese Press,* 12 May 1950, 1–2.

"Oriental Meet on Tonight: 8 Teams Set to Play." *Seattle Post-Intelligencer*, 23 December 1948, 15.

"Orientals and Their Cultural Adjustment: Interviews,"*Social Science Source Documents*, No. 4. Nashville, TN: Social Science Institute, Fisk University, 1946.

"Oriental Tourney: Eight Casaba Teams Battle for National Title Now." *Chinese Press*, 24 December 1949, 7.

Osumi, Megumi Dick. "Asians and California's Anti-Miscegenation Laws." In *Asian and Pacific American Experiences: Women's Perspectives*, ed. Nobuya Tsuchida. Minneapolis: University of Minnesota Press, 1982.

"Outstanding Chinese Girl Cagers." *Chinese Press*, 14 January 1949, 1.

Oxendine, Joseph B. *American Indian Sports Heritage*. Lincoln, NE: University of Nebraska Press, 1995.

"Pack Meets Dons on Tuesday." *News and Observer*, 1 January 1950, 4.

Palumbo-Liu, David. *Asian American: Historical Crossings of a Racial Frontier*. Stanford, CA: Stanford University Press, 1999.

Park, John S. *Elusive Citizenship: Immigration, Asian Americans, and the Paradox of Civil Rights*. New York: New York University Press, 2004.

Park, Roberta J. "Sport and Recreation among Chinese American Communities of the Pacific Coast from Time of Arrival to the 'Quiet Decade' of the 1950s." *Journal of Sport History* 27, no. 3 (Fall 2000): 445–480.

Parrish, Michael E. *America in Prosperity and Depression, 1920–1941*. New York: W.W. Norton, 1992.

Phillips, John C. *Sociology of Sport*. Boston: Allyn and Bacon, 1993.

"Playground: Board Hearing and Constitution Next Move." *California Chinese Press*, 4 April 1941, 1.

"Playground Cagers 130's Win 39–33 Over Presidio." *California Chinese Press*, 27 December 1940, 7.

"Playground Petition." *California Chinese Press*, 7 March 1941, 1.

"Playground Seems Certain." *Chinese Press*, 22 August 1941, 1.

"Portland Girls Have Basketball Team." *Chinese Digest*, 29 November 1935, 13.

"Punk War Hurting Business." *Chinese Press*, 27 January 1950, 1–2.

Quan, Rick. "Hong Wah Kues." Television program. San Francisco: KPIX, March 1998.

"Ready for Test!" *San Francisco Examiner*, 22 December 1949, 20.

"Recreational Problems Studied." *California Chinese Press*, 7 February 1941, 6.

"Recreation and Park Department News Bulletin." San Francisco: McLaren Lodge, Golden Gate Park, 1951, 4.

"Recreation Study by Group Work Council." *Chinese Press*, 10 March 1950, 7.

Regalado, Samuel O. "Incarcerated Sport: Nisei Women's Softball and Athletics during Japanese American Internment." *Journal of Sport History 27*, no. 3 (Fall 2000): 431–444.

———. "Sport and Community in California's Japanese American Yamato Colony, 1930–1945." *Journal of Sport History* 19, no. 2 (Summer 1992): 130–143.

Riordan, Jim. *Sport and Physical Education in China 1999*. Oxford: Taylor and Francis, 1999.

Ripley, Robert Le Roy. *Believe It or Not!* New York: Pocket Books, 1941.

"Ripley's Believe It or Not." *San Francisco Examiner*, 24 January 1948, 15.

Robbins, Liz. "The N.B.A. and China Hope They've Found the Next Yao." *New York Times*, 25 June 2007, D1.

Robinson, Jerry. *The Comics: An Illustrated History of Comic Strip Art*. New York: Putnam, 1974.

Sabin, Roger. *Comics, Comix and Graphic Novels*. London: Phaidon, 1996.

"Sacramento Chi-Nettes Hold Honor Banquet for Shanghai Guest." *California Chinese Press*, 28 March 1941, 3.

"Sacramento Wiah Yen Loses; Franciscans Win in Second Tilt." *California Chinese Press*, 28 February 1941, 4.

"Sad Night for Coast: St. John's Surges over Dons, 60–44; CCNY Ruins Bears." *San Francisco Chronicle Sporting Green*, 23 December 1949, 1H.

Said, Edward. *Orientalism*. New York: Vintage Books, 1979.

"Saints Down Berkeley Five: Willie Wong Leads S.F. Chinese to U.S. Oriental Title." *San Francisco Chronicle*, 27 December 1948, 2H.

"Saints Win Second Title: San Francisco Five Cops Tournament." *Seattle Post-Intelligencer*, 27 December 1948, 13.

"San Francisco Plays Xavier At Sportscenter Tuesday." *The Owensboro Inquirer*, 5 February 1950, 9A.

San Francisco Playground Commission. *Annual Report and Review of Activities, 1928–1929*. San Francisco: Playground Commission.

"San Jose, Chinese Quints Top Play in Examiner-P.A. Meet." in William Wong, Scrapbook.

"Santa Barbara Has a Chinese Cage Team." *Chinese Press*, 4 March 1949, 8.

Saxton, Alexander. *The Indispensable Enemy: Labor and the Anti-Chinese Movement in California*. Berkeley, CA: University of California Press, 1971.

Scott, James C. *Domination and the Arts of Resistance: Hidden Transcripts*. New Haven, CT: Yale University Press, 1992.

———. *Weapons of the Weak: Everyday Forms of Peasant Resistance*. New Haven, CT: Yale University Press, 1985.

Seattle Municipal Archives. Women in City Government. http://www.seattle.gov/CityArchives/Resources/WomenExhibit/Pearl_Powell.htm (accessed June 5, 2007).

"S.F. Chinese Grab Title; Wong Star." *San Francisco Examiner*, 27 December 1948, 17.

"S.F. Chinese Hoopsters Face Amblers Tonight." *Chinese Press,* 10 December 1948, 7.

"S.F. Chinese Team Wins Oriental Hoop Tourney." *Seattle Post-Intelligencer,* 27 December 1947, 16.

"S.F. Saints Defeat Nisei." *Seattle Post-Intelligencer,* 25 December 1948, 14.

"S.F. Saints to Play Berkeley." *San Francisco Chronicle,* 26 December 1948, 1H.

"S.F. Saints Win Opener: Oriental-American Cage Defenders Whip San Jose." *San Francisco Chronicle,* 25 December 1948, 3H.

"Shaq Says Yao Comments Were Said in Jest. "*Sports Illustrated.* http://sportsillustrated.cnn.com/basketball/news/2003/01/10/shaq_yao_ap/ (accessed June 1, 2008).

"Shaqlash: Asian Group Protests outside Compaq Center." *Sports Illustrated.* http://sportsillustrated.cnn.com/basketball/news/2003/01/17/shaq_comments_ap/ (accessed June 1, 2008).

Shih, Hsien-Ju. "Social and Vocational Adjustment of the Second Generation Chinese High School Students in San Francisco." E.D. thesis, University of California, Berkeley, May 1937.

Shilling, Chris. "Physical Capital and Situated Action: A New Direction for Corporeal Sociology." *British Journal of Sociology of Education* 25, no. 4 (September 2004): 473–484.

Simons, Bill. "Chinese Playground Fills a San Francisco Need." *San Francisco Chronicle,* 25 September 1939, 10.

"16 teams enter Girls' Cage League." *San Francisco Examiner,* 27 November 1932, S16.

Smith, Ronald A. "The Rise of Basketball for Women in Colleges." In *The American Sporting Experience: a Historical Anthology of Sport in America,* ed. Steven A. Riess. New York: Leisure Press, 1984, 239–254.

Smith-Rosenberg, Carroll, and Charles Rosenberg. "The Female Animal: Medical and Biological Views of Women and Their Role in Nineteenth-Century America." In *From "Fair Sex" to Feminism: Sport and the Socialization of Women in the Industrial and Post-Industrial Eras,* ed. J. A. Mangan and Roberta J. Park. Totowa, NJ: F. Cass, 1987.

Souvenir Program, 1948 Chinatown Basketball Festival (San Francisco: 1948), Ben Hom Collection, Chinese Historical Society, Box #1, Folder #3, Ethnic Studies Library, University of California Berkeley.

"Special Olympics Reaches New Horizons by Announcing Yao Ming as Global Ambassador." Special Olympics. http://www.specialolympics.org/Special+Olympics+Public+Website/English/Press_Room/Global_News_Archive/2004+Global+News+Archive/Yao+Ming ew+Global+Ambassador.htm (accessed June 1, 2008).

"Sport Short." *California Chinese Press,* 27 December 1940, 7.

"Sports." *Chinese Digest*, 15 November 1935, 13.
"Sports." *Chinese Digest*, 3 January 1936, 13.
"Sports." *Chinese Digest*, 20 March 1936, 12.
"Sports." *Chinese Digest*, 27 March 1936, 13.
"Sports." *Chinese Digest*, 4 September 1936, 13.
"Sports." *Chinese News*, 6 November 1936, 12.
"Sports." *Chinese Digest*, 6 December 1936, 13.
"Sports." *Chinese Digest*, January 1937, 13.
"Sports," *Chinese Digest*, December 1937, 21.
"Sports." *Chinese Digest*, 16 January 1938, 16.
"Sports," *Chinese Digest*, February 1938, 21.
"Sports." *Chinese Digest*, May 1938, 18.
"Sports." *Chinese Digest*, December 1938, 21.
"Sports." *Chinese Press*, 19 September 1940, 4.
"Sports." *Chinese News*, 1 December 1940, 5.
"Sports." *Kellogg Evening News*, 3 January 1940, 4.
"Sports," *Chinese Press*, 8 October 1948, 117.
"Sport Briefs." *Chinese Press*, 31 December 1948, 7.
"St. Anne's, St. Cecilia's Cagers Tied for Lead." *The Monitor*, 25 November 1949, 15.
"St. Cecilia's Upsets Champs in CYO Girls Prep Basketball Play." *The Monitor*, 11 November 1949, 17.
"St. Cecilia Five Wins Girls' Title." *The Monitor*, 14 December 1946, 6.
Stillman, Agnes Cora Ruth. "Senda Berenson Abbott: Her Life and Contributions to Smith College and to the Physical Education Profession." M.S. thesis, Smith College, 1971.
"St. John's Five Routs San Francisco 60–44; C.C.N.Y. Crushes California 76–46." *New York Herald Tribune*, 23 December1949, 18.
"St. John's Meets San Francisco, C.C.N.Y. Faces California at Garden." *New York Herald Tribune*, 22 December 1949, 26.
"St. Mary's Chinese in One-Point Win." *The Monitor*, 2 December 1949, 20.
"St. Mary's Chinese to Meet Winner of Sunset League." *The Monitor*, 16 December 1949, 22.
"St. Mary's Play Chinese Quintet Tomorrow Night." *Ironwood Daily Globe*, 4 December 1939, 8.
"St. Mary's and St. John's Win Girls Cage Titles." *The Monitor*, 13 December 1949, 17.
"Stepping Out with 'Goo-Mah', Square and Circle Club Benefit Show." *Chinese Press*, 1 December 1950, 1.
"Stockton Five Shades Wong." in William Wong, Scrapbook.
Strong, Edward K. *The Second Generation Japanese Problem*. New York: Arno Press, 1970.

Suen, Felton. Interview by author. Tape recording. Daly City, CA, 19 June 2000.

Suen, Winston. Interview by author. Tape recording. Daly City, CA, 19 June 2000.

Swidler, Ann. "Culture in Action: Symbols and Strategies." *American Sociological Review* 51, no. 2 (April 1986): 273–286.

Takahashi, Jerrold. *Nisei/Sansei: Shifting Japanese American Identities and Politics.* Philadelphia: Temple University Press, 1998.

"Take a Tip from Morie: Meet the Pass." *San Francisco Chronicle,* 23 December 1949, 1H.

Tang, Irwin. "APA Community Should Tell Shaquille O'Neal to 'Come Down to Chinatown." *AsianWeek,* 23, no. 19 (3–9 January 2003): 9.

Taxel, Joel. "Charles Waddell Chestnutt's Sambo: Myth and Reality." *Negro American Literature Forum* 9 (Winter 1975): 105–108.

"TB Still Kills Too Many Chinese: S.F. Chinese Birth, Infant Mortality Rates, Both High." *Chinese Press,* 18 March 1948, 1.

Tedlock, Dennis. *The Spoken Word and the Work of Interpretation.* Philadelphia: University of Pennsylvania Press, 1983.

"Telephone Girls Defeat Loyalty Six." *San Francisco News,* 12 March 1935, 18.

"Tennis-SFCTC Active in Tourneys, H. K. Wong." *Chinese Press,* 21 November 1950, 7.

"Tennis Tourney Ends: Peter Gee, Helen Wong Win in Single Finals." *Chinese Press,* 17 September 1948: 17.

"Tennis Tourney Underway Tomorrow." *Chinese Press,* 25 August 1950, 8.

"The No. California Tennis Championship," *Chinese Press,* 23 June 1950, 8.

"The Playground Issue: Here's Letter of Recommendation." *Chinese Press,* 13 June 1941, 1.

"The Playground Problem: Plans Developed for Intensive Campaign; Dr. Theodore C. Lee Named Chairman of Civic Group." *California Chinese Press,* 28 March 1941, 1.

"There Goes Woo Woo!" *San Francisco Examiner,* 25 February 1948, 24.

"These Are Best Chinese American Basketballers in the Country . . ." *Chinese Press,* 7 January 1949, 8.

Thomsen, Ian. "The New Mr. Big." *Sports Illustrated,* 97, no. 17 (28 October 2002): 66.

"Three Dons Named on All-Stars." *San Francisco Call Bulletin Sports,* 21 March 1949, 13.

"Three Fight for Crown in O.Y.L. Semi-finals." *Chinese Press,* 24 March 1950, 6.

"3 in Second Places of Cage Shooting Battle." *Chinese Press,* 14 January 1949, 8.

"Title Game for CYO Girl Cagers." *The Monitor,* 7 December 1946, 6.

"Titles Near in Girls' CYO Cage Loops." *The Monitor,* 9 December 1949, 17.

Tom, Dara Akiko. "Basketball's Great Chinese Warriors." *San Francisco Examiner,* 9 September 1996, A-5.

Tong, Richard "Goonie." Interview by author. Tape recording. San Francisco, CA, 16 April 2003.

"Top Honors." *The Monitor,* 26 December 1947, 6.

Trachtenberg, Alan. *Shades of Hiawatha: Staging Indians, Making Americans, 1880–1930.* New York: Hill and Wang, 2004.

"Triple Header: Chinese Girls' Hoop Tourney." *San Francisco Chronicle,* 9 January 1949, 3H.

"Trotter Five Handles Ball with Finesse." *Cincinnati Post,* 22 February 1941, 10.

Tuan, Mia. *Forever Foreigners or Honorary Whites? The Asian Ethnic Experience Today.* New Brunswick, NJ: Rutgers University Press, 1998.

Tucker, Nancy. *Patterns in the Dust: Chinese-American Relations and the Recognition Controversy, 1949–1950.* New York: Columbia University Press, 1983.

"27 out of 48." in William Wong, Scrapbook.

United States Census Bureau. *Fifteenth Census of the United States–1930–Population Volume I: Number and Distribution of Inhabitants.* Washington, DC: Government Printing Office.

United States Census Bureau. *Sixteenth Census of the United States–1940–Population, Volume II: Characteristics of the Population—Part 1.* Washington, DC:Government Printing Office.

University of San Francisco Yearbook. 1949–1950.

"USF Frosh Tips S.F. Chinese Cagers." *Chinese Press,* 18 February 1949, 7.

"USF Quintet Bounces Back." *San Francisco Chronicle Sporting Green,* 19 December 1949, 4H.

"USF Roars Past Stanford, 54–39." *San Francisco Examiner,* 21 January 1950, 15.

"USF to Induct Four into the Athletic Hall of Fame." http://usfdons.cstv.com/genrel/012307aab.html (accessed June 8, 2007).

"Utah's Starting Five against Canisius Tonight." *Buffalo Courier-Express,* 29 December 1949, 19.

Vertinsky, Patricia. "Women, Sport, and Exercise in the 19th Century." In *Women and Sport: Interdisciplinary Perspectives,* ed. D. M. Costa and S. R. Guthrie. Champaign, IL: Human Kinetics, 1994.

"Victory Banquet for Girl Saints." *Chinese Press,* 6 January 1950, 7.

Wacquant, Loic J. D. "The Pugilistic Point of View—How Boxers Think and Feel about Their Trade." *Theory and Society* 24, no. 4 (1995): 501.

Weisman, Jan. "The Tiger and His Stripes." In *The Sum of Our Parts: Mixed Heritage Americans,* eds. Teresa Williams-Leon and Cynthia Nakashima. Philadelphia: Temple University Press, 2001.

Western Office of National Probation and Parole Association California Youth Authority's Delinquency Prevention Section. "A Study of the San Francisco Coordinating Council for Youth Welfare." San Francisco, 1949.

Whang, Paul. Interview by author. Tape recording. San Francisco, CA, 2 December 2003.

———. Interview by author. Telephone recording. 17 December 2003.

———. Scrapbook. San Francisco, CA.

Whang, Ruth. Interview by author. Tape recording. San Francisco, CA, 17 December 2003.

———. Interview by author. Tape recording. San Francisco, CA, 12 January 2004.

"Where Are You Going?" *Chinese Press*, 28 April 1950, 7.

Williams, Linda D. "An Analysis of American Sportswomen in Two Negro Newspapers: The *Pittsburgh Courier*, 1924–1948, and the *Chicago Defender*, 1932–1948." Ph.D. diss., Ohio State University, 1987.

"Willie Woo Woo Wong, Chinese Cage Ace Chooses USF over Fordham, Seton Hall" in William Woo Wong, Scrapbook.

Wing Luke Museum Web Site. http://www.wingluke.org/pages/CHC/exhibit1/e10216b.htm (accessed 4 June 2007).

Wong, Elsie. 1982. Interview #108, Box #44, Southern California Chinese American Oral History Project. Los Angeles, CA: University of California, Los Angeles.

Wong, Hank. Interview by author. Telephone recording. 30 June 1999.

Wong, H.K. "Sports," *Chinese Press*, 24 November 1950, 7.

Wong Lum, Helen. Interview by author. Tape recording. San Francisco, CA, 23 October 1998.

———. Interview by author. Telephone recording. 15 June 2000.

———. Interview by author. Tape recording. San Francisco, CA, 24 November 2002.

———. Scrapbook. San Francisco, CA.

Wong, Jade Snow. *Fifth Chinese Daughter*. Seattle, WA: University of Washington Press, 1989.

Wong, James Francis "Smokey Joe." Interview by author. Tape recording. San Francisco, CA, 29 July 1998.

———. Interview by author. Tape recording. San Francisco, CA, 30 July 1998.

Wong, Jane Chew. Interview by author. Telephone recording. 16 June 2000.

Wong, John Henry. Interview by author. Tape recording. Livermore, CA, 5 August 1998.

Wong, June Choy. Interview by author. Tape recording. San Francisco, CA, 16 June 2000.

Wong, K. Scott. *Americans First: Chinese Americans and the Second World War*. Cambridge: Harvard University Press, 2005.

Wong, Maye. 1982. Interview #34, Southern California Chinese American Oral History Project. Los Angeles, CA: University of California, Los Angeles.

"Wong-Mock Wing Doubles in Finals of Junior Tennis Tournament," *Chinese Press*, 24 June 1949, 8.

Wong, Raymond. "Letters by OCA National President, Raymond Wong." 80-20 Educational Foundation, http://www.80-20educationalfoundation.org/projects/discrimination_Chu_ONeal.asp (accessed June 1, 2008).

"Wong Stars Again As SF Five Rolls On." *San Francisco Examiner*, 28 December 1947, 14.

Wong, Victoria. "Square and Circle Club: Women in the Public Sphere." In *Chinese America: History and Perspectives.* San Francisco: Chinese Historical Society of America, 1994.

Wong, William Woo. Interview by author. Tape recording. San Francisco, CA, 23 October 1998.

———. Interview by author. Tape recording. Newark, CA, 14 July 1999.

———. Interview by author. Tape recording. Newark, CA, 16 June 2000.

———. Scrapbook. Fremont, CA.

"Won't Hire Chinese: 75% Discrimination State Survey Says." *Chinese Press*, 13 January 1950, 1–2.

Woo, Fred George. "Sporting News." *Chinese Digest*, 18 September 1936, 23.

———. "Sports." *Chinese Digest*, 22 November 1935, 13.

———. "Sports." *Chinese Digest*, 29 November 1935, 13.

———. "Sports." *Chinese Digest*, 7 February 1936, 12.

"'Woo Woo' Hits Big Time." *Chinese Press*, 28 December 1949, 6.

"'Woo-Woo' Most Valuable Player." *Chinese Press*, 8 December 1950, 8.

"'Woo Woo, Sister to Share Spotlight." *San Francisco Examiner*, 13 March 1948, 25.

"Woo-Woo Will Do." in William Wong, Scrapbook.

"'Woo Woo' Willie's an Old SF Favorite." in William Wong, Scrapbook.

"'Woo Woo' Wong Is Outstanding Casaba Tosser for USF Frosh." *Chinese Press*, 21 January 1949, 15.

"'Woo Woo' Wong Stars for USF in PAA Tilt." *Chinese Press*, 25 February 1949, 8.

"Woo Woo's Clutch Shots Saves Frosh." in William Wong, Scrapbook.

Works Project Administration Recreation Project (WPARP). "Survey of San Francisco, California by Districts (Recreation) Prepared for the Executive Coordinating Council, 1936–1937." San Francisco, 1937.

Wu, Judy Tzu-Chun. *Doctor Mom Chung of the Fair-Haired Bastards: The Life of a Wartime Celebrity.* Berkeley: University of California Press, 2005.

———. "Loveliest Daughter of Our Ancient Cathay!': Representations of Ethnic and Gender Identity in the Miss Chinatown U.S.A. Beauty Pageant." *Journal of Social History* 31 (Fall 1997): 5–31.

Wu, Thomas W. S. "Study Finds Recreation Facilities Inadequate." *Chinese Press*, 10 March 1950, 3, 7.

Wu, William F. *The Yellow Peril: Chinese Americans in American fiction, 1850–1940*. Hamden, CT: Archon Books, 1982.

"X-Rays Start Oct. 31." *Chinese Press*, 28 October 1949, 1.

"Yao Ming Measures Up in US and China." *People's Daily Online*. http://english.peopledaily.com.cn/200410/12/eng20041012_159901.html (accessed 1 June 2008).

"Yao Ming Signs $75m Contract with Rockets." *China Daily*, 1 September 2005.

Yap, Stacey G. H. "Gather Your Strength, Sisters: The Emerging Role of Chinese Women Community Workers." Ph.D. diss., Boston University, 1983.

Yeh, Chiou-Ling. "Celebrating Freedom and Ethnicity." *American Quarterly* 57, no. 1 (March 2005): 279–288.

Yip, Ryan. Interview by author. Telephone recording. 17 June, 1999.

"Y.M.C.A Cage Teams Will Play Wednesday." *San Francisco Examiner*, 17 December 1932, S17.

Yoo, David. *Growing Up Nisei: Race, Generation, and Culture among Japanese Americans of California, 1924–49*. Chicago: University of Illinois Press, 1999.

Young, Al. "Hoop Dreams." *A. Magazine* (February-March 1996): 88.

Young, Bill. 1982. Interview #155, 1B, Southern California Chinese American Oral History Project. Los Angeles, CA: University of California, Los Angeles.

"Youth Council Meets to Halt Juvenile Delinquency." *Chinese Press*, 6 January 1950, 1.

Yu, Henry. "Tiger Woods at the Center of History: Looking Back at the Twentieth Century through the Lenses of Race, Sports, and Mass Consumption." In *Sports Matters: Race, Recreation, and Culture*, eds. John Bloom and Michael Nevin Willard. New York: New York University Press, 2002.

Yung, Judy. *Unbound Feet: A Social History of Chinese Women in San Francisco*. Berkeley and Los Angeles: University of California Press, 1995.

Zehnder, Gladys. "The Chinese Playground." *The Municipal Employee*, July 1927, 44.

Zhao, Xiaojian. *Remaking Chinese America: Immigration, Family, and Community, 1940–1965*. New Brunswick, NJ: Rutgers University Press, 2002.

Zieff, Susan G. "From Badminton to the Bolero: Sport and Recreation in San Francisco's Chinatown, 1895–1950." *Journal of Sport History* 27, no. 1 (Spring 2000): 1–29.

Index

Kathleen S. Yep is Assistant Professor of Asian American Studies and Sociology at Pitzer College of the Claremont Colleges.